Oxford Geography Project

Oxford Geography Project

2 European patterns

John Rolfe
Rosemary Dearden
Ashley Kent
Clive Rowe
Neville Grenyer

Second edition

Oxford University Press

Oxford University Press, Walton Street, Oxford OX2 6DP

Oxford London Glasgow
New York Toronto Melbourne Wellington
Kuala Lumpur Singapore Hong Kong Tokyo
Delhi Bombay Calcutta Madras Karachi
Nairobi Dar es Salaam Cape Town

First published 1974
Reprinted four times
Second edition 1979
Second impression 1980

Filmset in Monophoto Times 11 on 13 pt by
Keyspools Ltd, Golborne, Lancs
and printed in Great Britain by
Cambridge University Press, Cambridge

Preface to first edition

This geography course was developed in response to new geographical thinking and to meet changing educational needs. The three books attempt to give the majority of pupils an overall framework of theory in geography and its application to the modern world. For those who intend to pursue the subject further these books should provide a firm grounding.

We have tried to consider both the necessary changes in the content of secondary school geography and the ways and stages in which pupils acquire skills or gain understanding. We should be content to have provided a rich store of materials and ideas for those many teachers who will wish to move beyond the work in these books. But at the same time we feel convinced that the structure we have provided is a significant advance on anything that has preceded it.

John Rolfe   Clive Rowe   *Elstree, July 1973*
Rosemary Dearden   Neville Grenyer
Ashley Kent

Preface to second edition

The authors have welcomed suggestions and criticism from teachers and pupils who have used the first edition over the past five years. In the light of these comments revisions have been made where it was considered by the authors to be most appropriate, especially with pupils' needs and capabilities in mind. Opportunities have been taken to bring statistics as up to date as possible and to reflect changes in factual information which in some cases had become dated. However, the underlying geographical concepts and generalizations hold good and therefore remain largely unchanged.

John Rolfe   Ashley Kent   *November 1978*
Rosemary Dearden   Neville Grenyer

Contents

Contents

Acknowledgements

We should like to thank the following for permission to reproduce photographs:

Aerofilms, 1.7, 2.7, 4.3d, 5.6, 5.25, 7.1
Aerophoto Nederland, Rotterdam, 2.3d.
Aerophoto Schiphol, 2.3b, 8.15.
J. Allan Cash, 5.8.
Articapress, Haarlem, 6.19.
Austrian National Tourist Office, 6.16, 6.17.
Belgian National Tourist Office, 1.4d.
Bremer Lagerhaus-Gesellschaft, 7.5.
British Tourist Authority, 1.3c.
Camera Press, 6.21.
Combi Press Service, 1.4e.
Compagnie Nationale d'Aménagement du Bas-Rhône Languedoc, 3.10, 3.11.
M. D. C. Cuss, 1.4f.
Danish Agricultural Producers, 3.4a, b, c, d.
Documentation Française, 4.5.
French Government Tourist Office, 1.3b, 3.6, 6.13.
Fotoburo Meyer, The Hague, 5.27.
German Embassy, 1.3d, 5.16.
German National Tourist Office, 6.7.
N. Grenyer, 3.13.
Bart Hofmeester, 2.18, 4.11, 5.22, 7.11.
L'Institut d'Aménagement et d'Urbanisme de la Région Parisienne, 4.9.
Italian State Tourist Office, 1.4b.
KLM Aerocarto, 2.1, 2.17.
Kombiverkehr, 8.9.
Luossavaara Kürunavaara Aktiebolag, 6.3, 6.4, 6.5.
Mansell Collection, 4.3b, 5.2, 8.8.

National Foto Persbureau, 2.3c, 6.18.
Naturfoto, 3.1.
Netherlands National Tourist Office, 1.3f.
Nottingham Public Library, Local History Library, 4.16a.
Popperfoto, 4.4.
Port of London Authority, 8.10.
Radio Times Hulton Picture Library, 4.3a, c.
Renault, 6.9, 6.10.
Shell Photographic Service, 7.4.
Siedlungsverband Ruhrkohlenbezirk, 5.19, 5.21.
Sipahioglu, 9.4.
Suddeutscher Verlag, 8.6, 9.3.
Swiss National Tourist Office, 1.3a, 1.4a.
J. R. Tabberner, 1.4c, 5.3, 5.9, 5.11, 5.12.
I. B. Thompson, 6.15.
Tourist Photo Library, 1.3e.
Ville de Paris, Direction de l'Aménagement Urbain, 5.13, 5.14.

We are grateful to those individuals and other sources whose ideas and data we have drawn upon in the course of writing this book. We should particularly like to acknowledge:
Michael Morrish and John Westaway for their advice during the preparation of the second edition.
The Information and Documentation Centre for the Geography of the Netherlands.
Professor J. H. Bird for the original idea upon which the model port in Chapter 7 is based.

Metric measurements

All measurements (including map scales) have been given only in metric units. The tables below show imperial equivalents of some common S.I. ones.

Weight

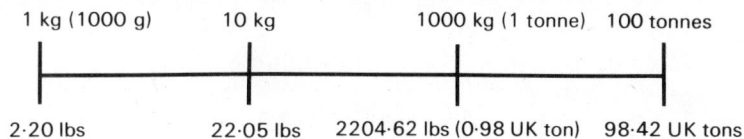

1 kg (1000 g)	10 kg	1000 kg (1 tonne)	100 tonnes
2·20 lbs	22·05 lbs	2204·62 lbs (0·98 UK ton)	98·42 UK tons

Length

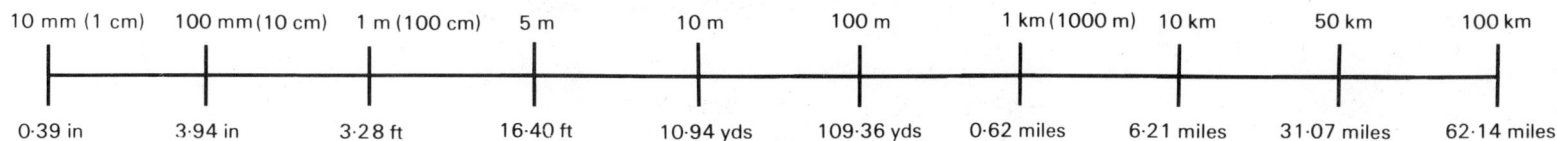

10 mm (1 cm)	100 mm (10 cm)	1 m (100 cm)	5 m	10 m	100 m	1 km (1000 m)	10 km	50 km	100 km
0·39 in	3·94 in	3·28 ft	16·40 ft	10·94 yds	109·36 yds	0·62 miles	6·21 miles	31·07 miles	62·14 miles

Area

1 hectare (ha)	10 ha	1 km^2	10 km^2
2·47 acres	24·71 acres	0·39 sq. miles	3·86 sq. miles

Temperature

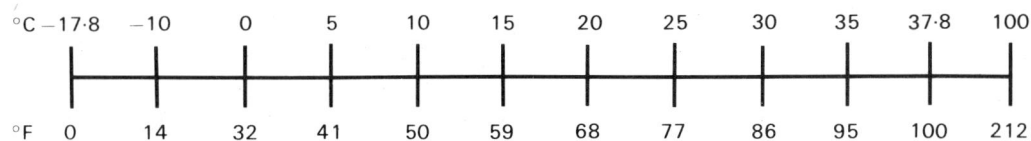

°C	−17·8	−10	0	5	10	15	20	25	30	35	37·8	100
°F	0	14	32	41	50	59	68	77	86	95	100	212

Scale
0   200   400   600   800   1000 km

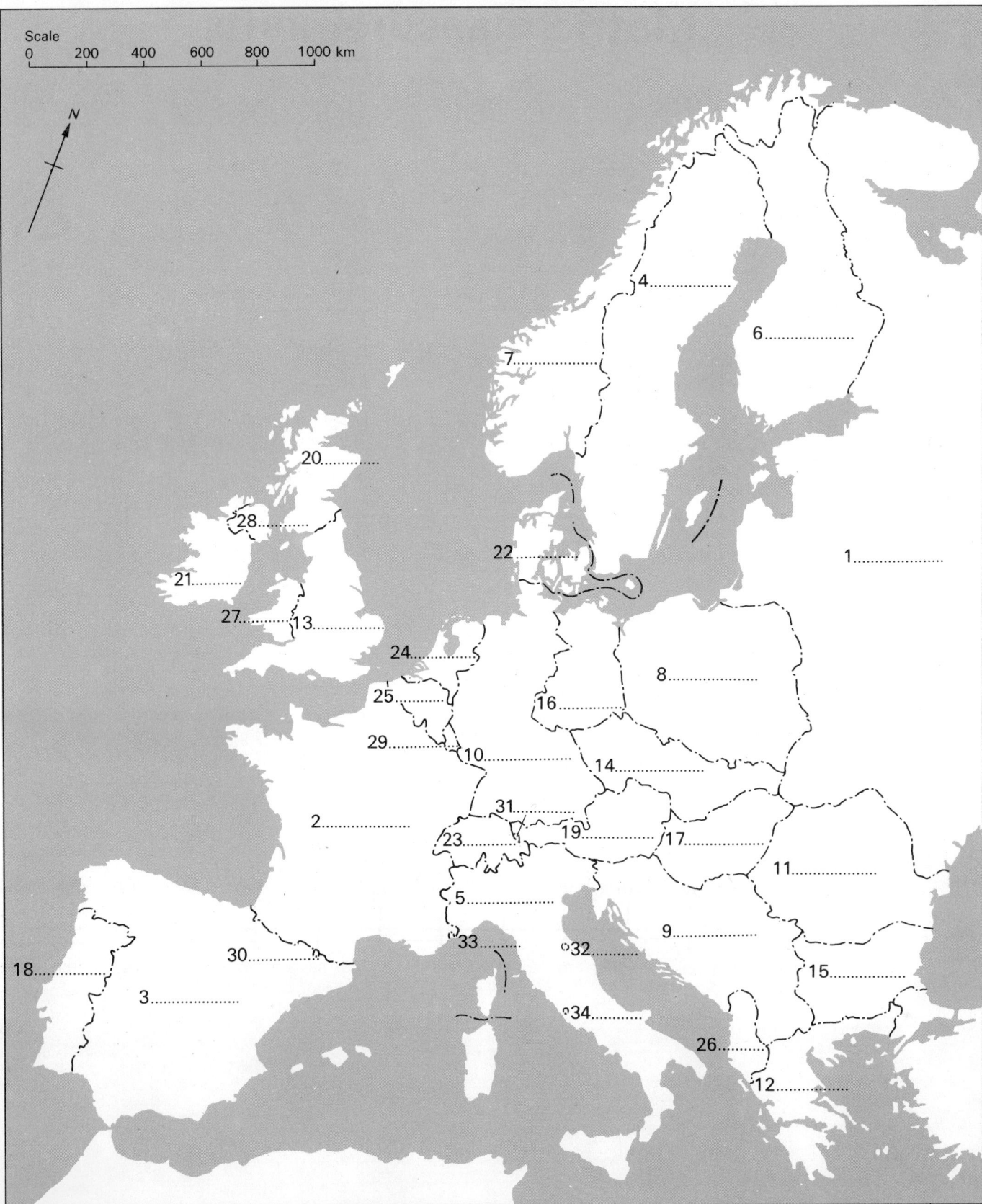

N

20 ....

28 ....

22 ....

1 ....

21 ....

27 ....   13 ....

24 ....

25 ....

29 ....   10 ....

2 ....

23 ....   31 ....
19 ....   17 ....

16 ....

8 ....

14 ....

11 ....

5 ....

9 ....

30 ....

18 ....

3 ....

33 ....   32 ....

34 ....

15 ....

26 ....

12 ....

4 ....

7 ....

6 ....

1 What is Europe?

In Book 1 the region examined was Britain. In this book the subject matter is drawn from a wider area, the continent of Europe, of which Britain is only a small part.

Countries quiz

1 Write down the names of as many European countries as you can think of in five minutes without using a map or atlas.

Britain is part of Europe, yet very few people know all the countries which are in Europe, or where they are. It might be that countries closest to Britain are better known, or that big countries are better known than small ones.

2 Look at the map in Fig. 1.1. How many of the numbered countries can you name? Write them down in pencil on a copy of the map.

3 (a) Working with five other members of your class, check the results by looking at a map of Europe in an atlas. If necessary, correct your copy of Fig. 1.1. Fill in a copy of the table shown in Fig. 1.2 for your group.
(b) Are the biggest countries better known? Do people know the countries closest to Britain best?

Have you any ideas which might explain the results of your group?

How do we come to know the countries of Europe? Is it through tourist brochures and advertisements? Do we learn them from the television news? Perhaps we learn them from sport? It is probable from the results of the survey that everyone has his or her own idea of which countries are in Europe and where they are.

4 Study a copy of a daily newspaper.
(a) How many articles are there about European countries?
(b) Which European country is mentioned most often?

*5 Devise a quiz of ten questions on capital cities, rivers, mountains, and mountain ranges in Europe, using your atlas to help you. For example, your first question might be: What is the name of the river which flows through Paris?

*Indicates an optional exercise.

Name of country	How many people were correct
1. U.S.S.R.	
2. FRANCE	
3.	
4.	
5.	
6.	

Fig. 1.2 Results table for naming European countries

Fig. 1.1 (left) The countries of Europe. They are numbered in order of size beginning with the largest

a

b

c

d

e

f

Fig. 1.3 (left) Photographs for Exercise 6

Fig. 1.4 Photographs for Exercise 7

6 (a) Look at the photographs in Fig. 1.3. They show views of six different European countries:

England   West Germany
Switzerland   The Netherlands
France   Italy

Can you say which country is shown in which photograph?
(b) What reasons can you give for each of your answers?

The six pictures in Fig. 1.3 present a very different idea of Europe from those in Fig. 1.4, which show that in modern Europe places are beginning to look more and more alike.

7 (a) Can you match the photographs in Fig. 1.4 to the following countries?
France   West Germany
Switzerland   Belgium
The Netherlands Italy
(b) Why is it difficult to tell which countries are shown in these photographs?

Not so very long ago many places had their own flavour. Houses in the Netherlands looked very different from Swiss chalets, and neither looked at all like the thatched cottages of England. The national costumes of the people also added to these differences, and the whole landscape, whether in farming areas or in towns, had easily recognizable features. But, as has been seen in Fig. 1.4, the distinctive features of the European landscape which have been built up over the ages are gradually disappearing. Ideas as well as people move easily from country to country and help to make the countries more and more alike.

Fig. 1.5 Land for siting a village or homestead. The letters A B C D E indicate where the resources are found

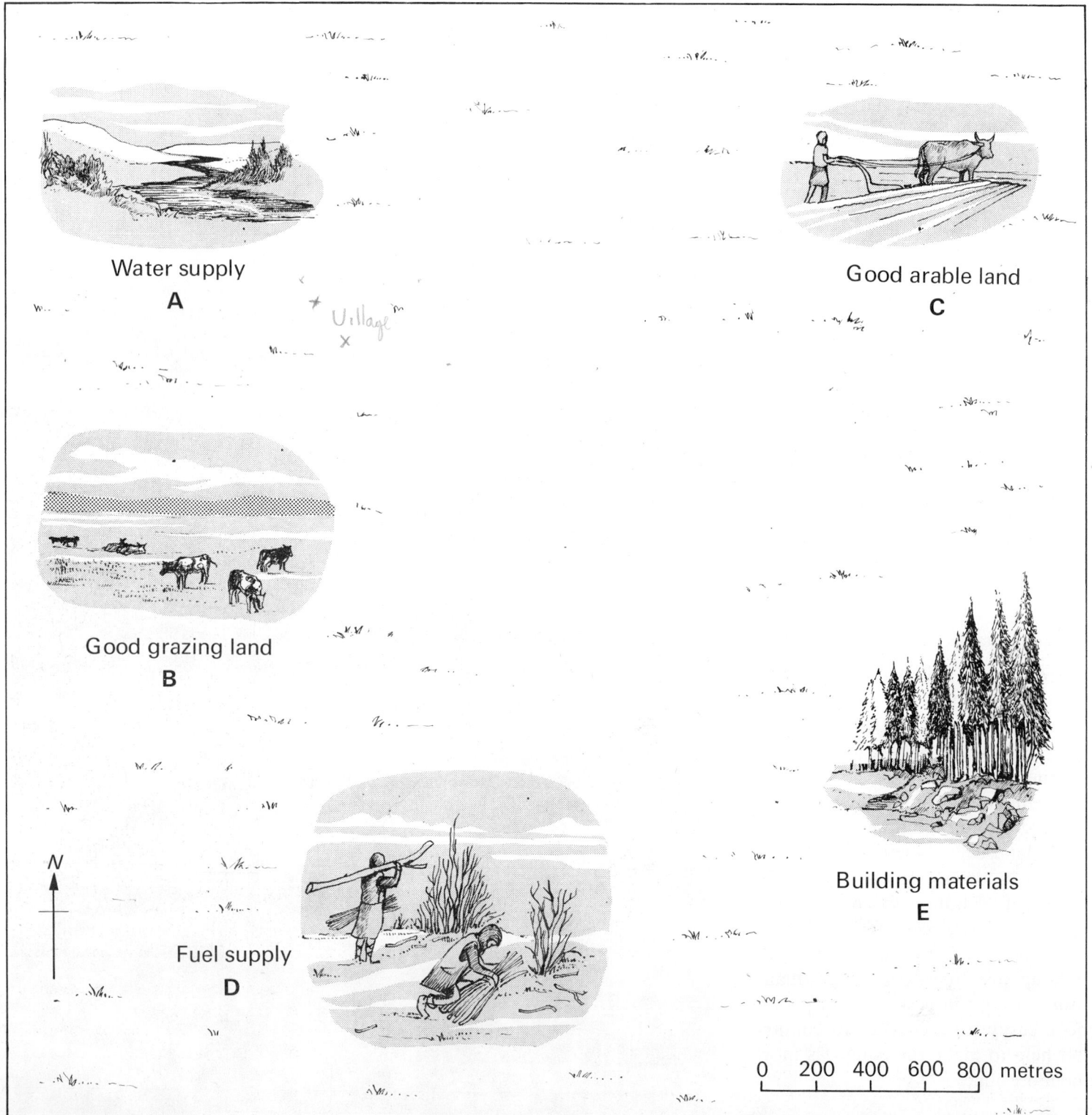

Water supply
A

Good arable land
C

Good grazing land
B

Building materials
E

Fuel supply
D

Village
X

N

0 200 400 600 800 metres

How people spread across Europe

Many of the towns in Britain and Europe have grown up over a long period of time. Over the centuries people have continually moved across Europe to find new places to live in.

Siting an early village

8   Draw a square to represent an area of land 4 km by 4 km on a scale by which 5 cm represents 1 km. On this land a group of early settlers have set up a village or homestead. Mark the positions of the resources as shown by the letters A to E on Fig. 1.   These include water supply for drinking and washing, good arable land to be ploughed and to grow crops, good grazing for pigs and cattle, fuel supply for cooking and for warmth in winter, and finally building materials, including timber and good building stone. The actual spot at which these things are found is marked by a letter in each case.

(a) Choose the best position in your opinion for the settlers to site their village and indicate your choice by a cross on your diagram.

(b) Write a few short sentences explaining why you think it is the best position.

9   Now look at Fig. 1.6; this shows the number of times the villagers would need to visit each resource during the month.

(a) Measure the direct distance from each of the resources to the site you have chosen and enter this information on a copy of Fig. 1.6.

(b) Multiply the distance to each resource by the number of visits made in a month.

(c) Find the total distance travelled by adding the figures in the last column.

(d) Compare your total distance with those of other members of your class; is yours higher or lower than most? The one with the shortest distance will have the best site, when all the villagers' needs are considered together.

(e) Can you now work out the ideal site for the village?

*10   Column A of Fig. 1.6 gives the frequency of visits to each resource. How realistic do you think it is?

Fig. 1.6 Table for calculating suitability of village sites

Resource	Number of visits per month A	Distance from site to resource B	Total distance travelled A × B
Water supply	60		
Grazing land	40		
Arable land	30		
Fuel	20		
Building materials	10		
		Total	

Fig. 1.7 Ashmore in Dorset, an early village site. What resources are visible in the photograph?

The Neolithic game

The first farmers' settlements date from 7000–6000 B.C. in the 'Fertile Crescent' of Asia Minor; this is shown on the south-east corner of Fig. 1.8. Gradually the skills of the New Stone Age (or 'Neolithic') farmers spread westwards across Europe. Archaeologists have carefully studied and dated the remains of their settlements and cultures, their polished stone axes and stone sickles, the contents of their graves or 'long barrows', and especially their pottery. From these studies the archaeologists have worked out the routes they took and how long it took for Neolithic ideas to spread or **diffuse** across Europe to Britain.

11 This game imitates or *simulates* the spread of peoples; the aim is to be the first to reach Britain from the square marked with an X in the south-east corner of the map (Fig. 1.8). You need a die and a copy of Fig. 1.8 or a sheet of tracing paper which can be laid over the map and used for colouring. How to play:
(a) Throw a die. Note the number and find it on the grid below.

6	3	4	5
	2	X	
		1	

If, for example, it is a 4, that number is to be found immediately above the start square X; find X on your base map and shade in the square immediately above it. This square will then become your start square (X) for the next throw.

If the next number you throw is, for example, a 6 find this on the grid and shade in the corresponding square on your base map. This square will then become your start square (X) for the next throw.
(b) So throw again and continue until you reach Britain.

Rules

1. Each throw normally represents a period of 50 years, the time it took for the area to fill up with farming settlements.
2. The mountains are difficult to settle. Each throw should count as 250 years if it lands in mountainous areas so make a separate note of these.
3. No hits should be counted in areas with less than 500 millimetres (mm) of rainfall, which are too dry for successful farming.
4. Sea routes are allowed (Neolithic people did have boats), but no throw should be counted more than two squares away from the coast.
5. If a throw should take you off the map, throw again until you can move. Once again do *not* count wasted throws.

When each person reaches Britain, add up the total number of squares you have shaded in to reach your final settlement. You should count 50 years for each normal square you have settled and 250 years for each square you have settled in the mountains.

Compare your map with those of the other members of the class. Then look at Fig. 1.9 which shows the actual dates of settling each part of
Europe, and Fig. 1.10 which shows the routes that the farmers took over several generations. The western Neolithic farmers (route 1) tended to follow the coastline, except for one route which headed up the valleys of the Rivers Rhône and Saône (route 2); other Neolithic farmers migrated up the fertile Danube Valley (route 3), and another possible route is that of the so called 'Northern Culture' (route 4). Which of these routes is most like your own?

In playing the Neolithic game we have not only simulated the spread of people across Europe but have seen some of the obstacles, such as mountains, that these settlers had to overcome. Not all the settlers finished in Britain (just as in playing perhaps many of you did not), but this exercise shows in part how many of the settlements that we know today came about. The Neolithic peoples were only the first of many groups who have spread across Europe and founded settlements; the Greeks, Romans, Saxons, Vikings, and Normans are some of the others.

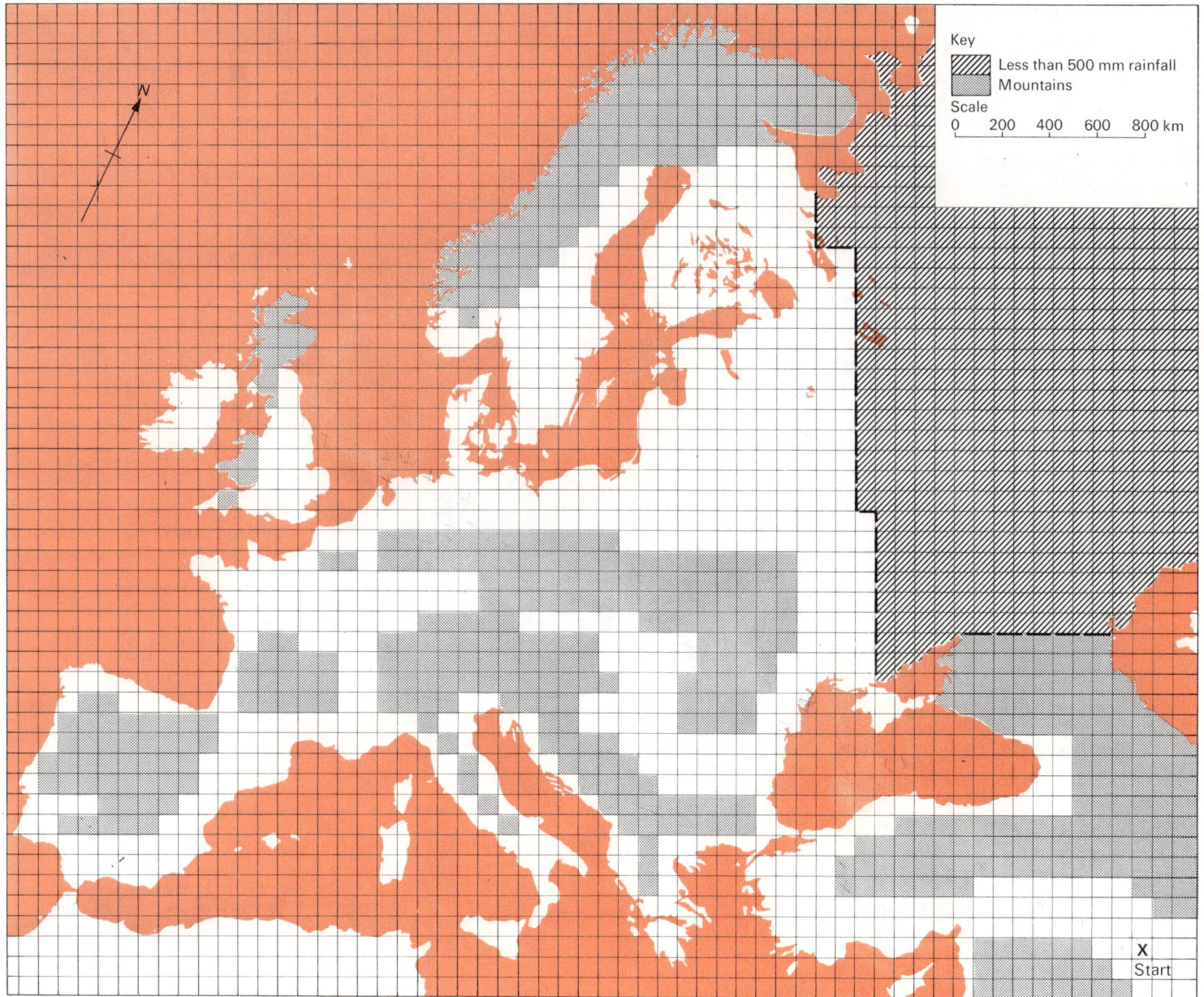

Fig. 1.8 Base map for Neolithic game

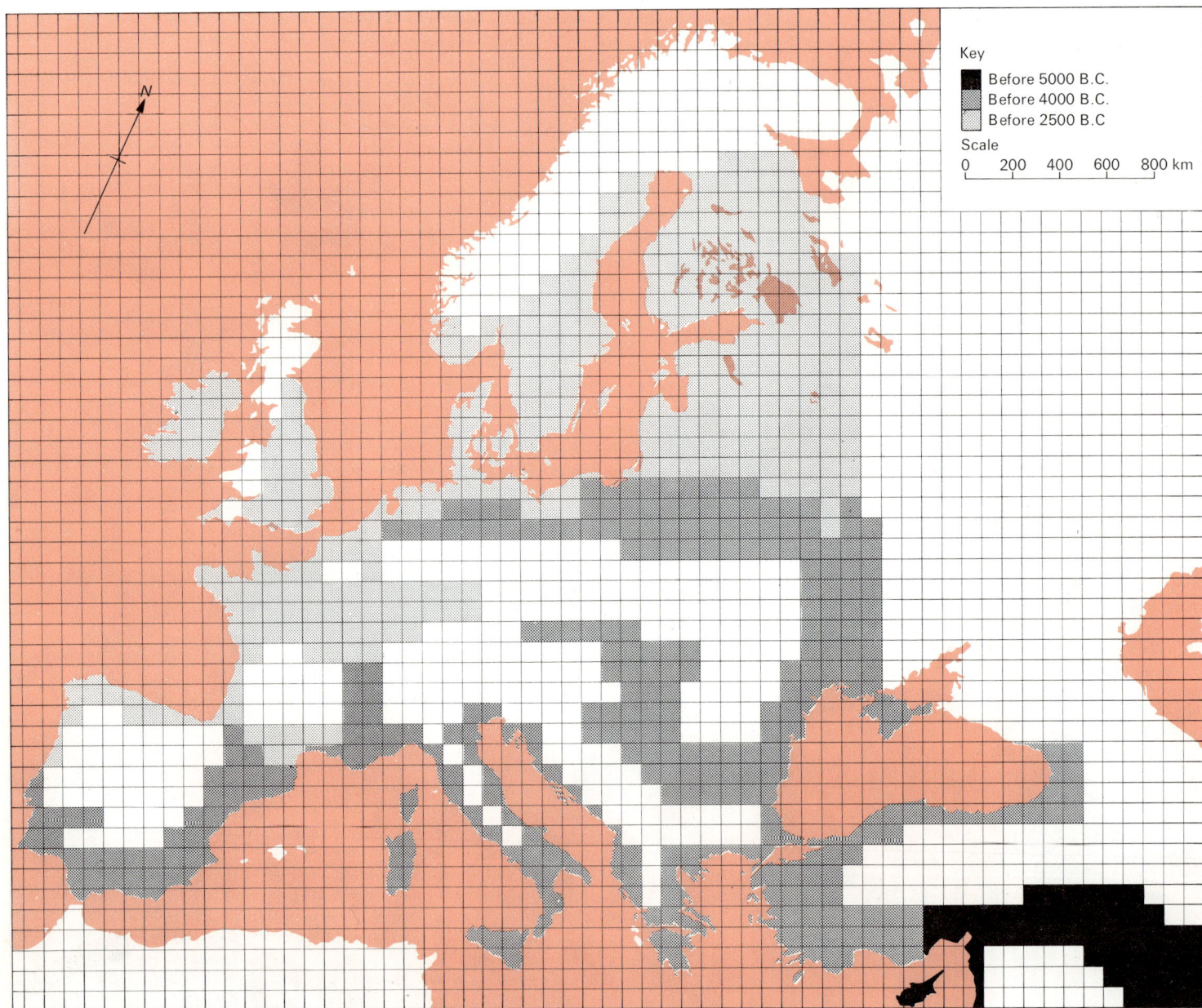

Key

Before 5000 B.C.
Before 4000 B.C.
Before 2500 B.C

Scale

0   200   400   600   800 km

Fig. 1.9 The spread of Neolithic people across Europe

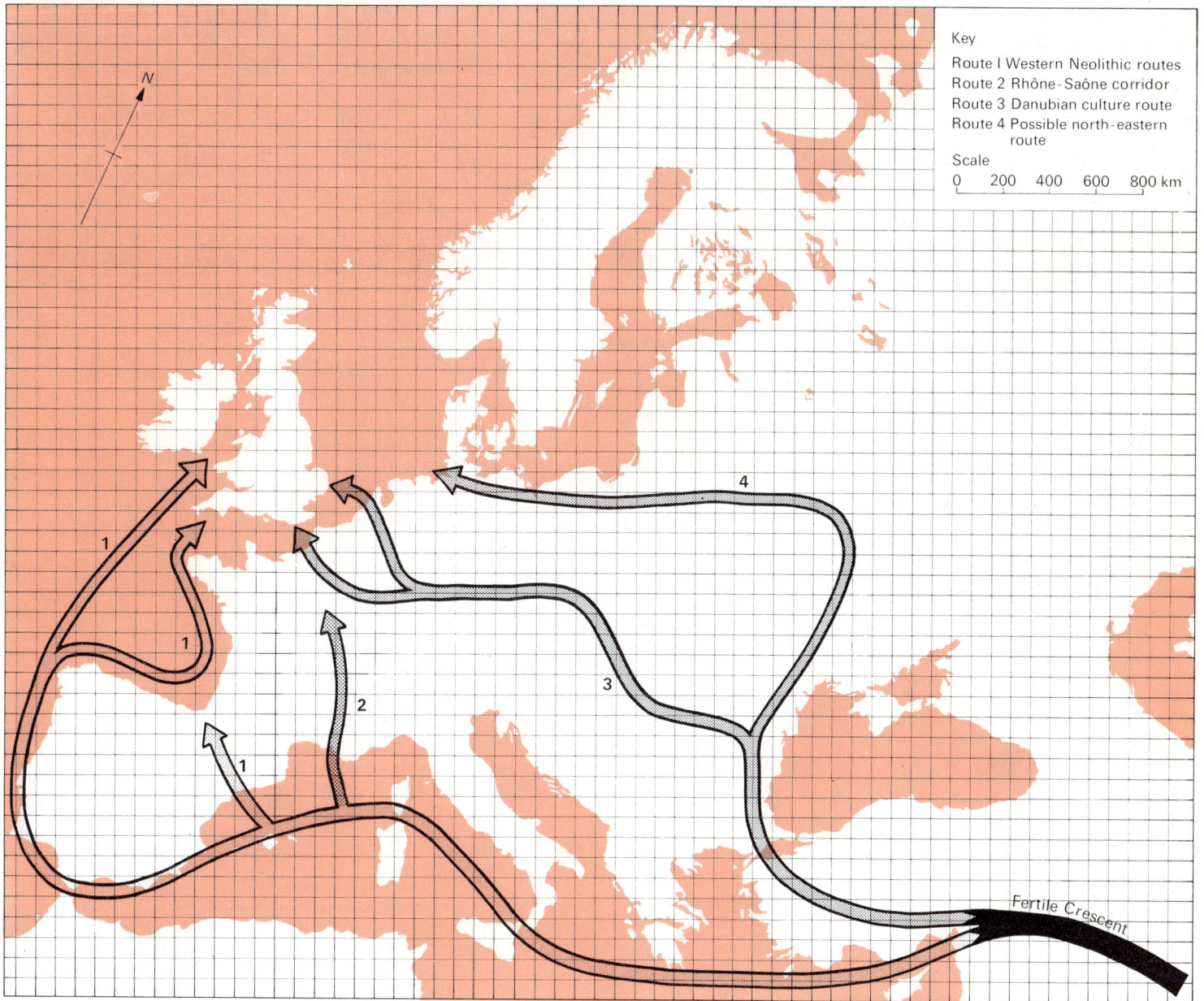

Fig. 1.10 Routes taken by Neolithic peoples

Key

Route 1 Western Neolithic routes
Route 2 Rhône-Saône corridor
Route 3 Danubian culture route
Route 4 Possible north-eastern route

Scale

0 200 400 600 800 km

Fertile Crescent

PARIS
NANTES
BRUSSELS
RHEIMS
AMSTERDAM
LE MANS
COPENHAGEN
OSLO
STOCKHOLM
HAMBURG
MALMO
LYON
INNSBRUCK

Fig. 1.11 Destination cards for Exercise 12

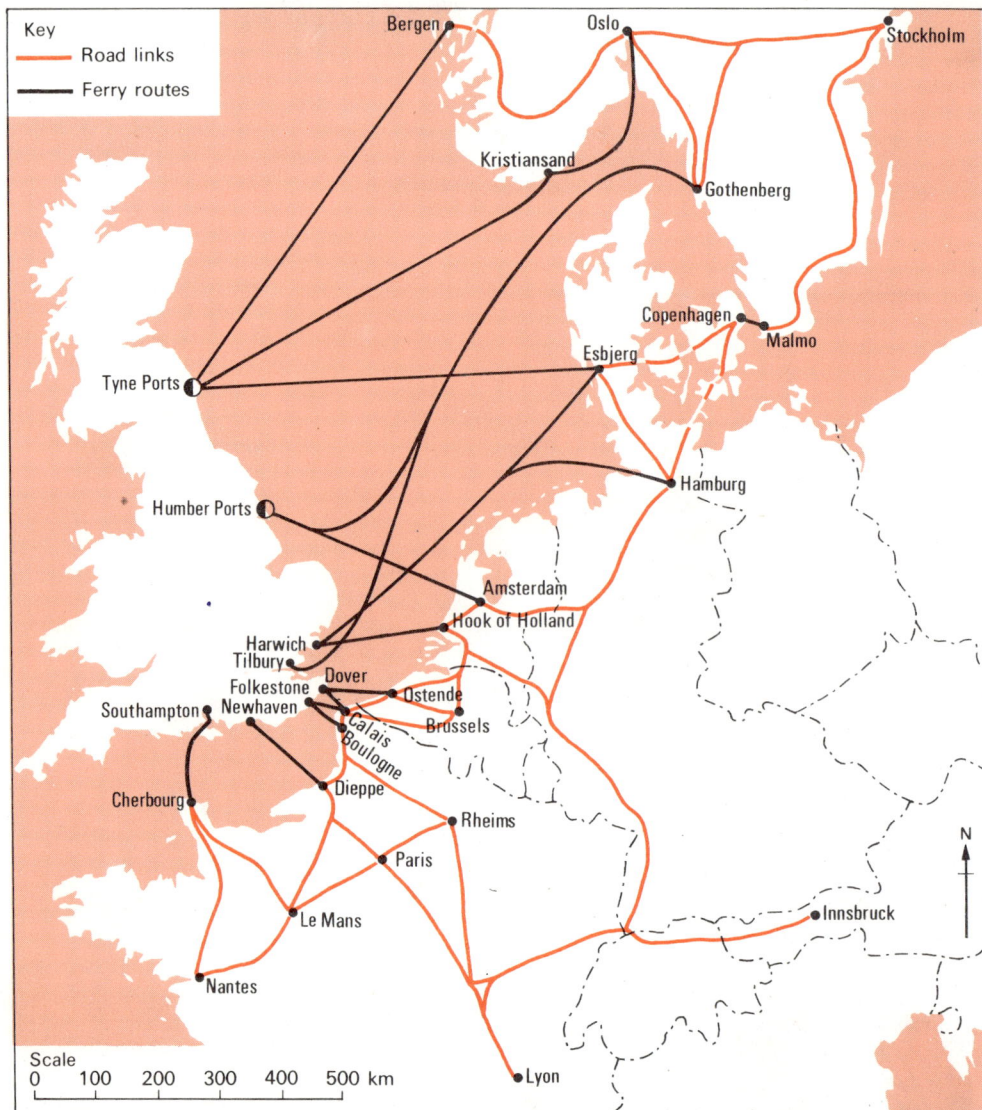

Fig. 1.12 Selected ferry and road links in Europe

Where is Europe?

Travel between the countries of Europe is becoming easier and quicker. The main cities are now less than two hours apart by air, and many are linked by both motorways and railways.

Between Britain and continental Europe travel is complicated by the fact that all routes have to cross either the English Channel or the North Sea. This is no problem to the air passenger, but for goods and people travelling by land the sea crossing causes delays and

adds inconvenience to the journey, as everything and everybody have to board a ferry for the sea crossing. This has had the effect of making the rest of Europe seem to be further away than it really is.

12 Copy the destination cards in Fig. 1.11, and cut them out. Shuffle them, and take the top six cards. Make a note of the names of the six towns you have drawn before returning the cards to the pack. Starting and ending your journey in London, plan the shortest route visiting your six

towns, using the ferries and roads shown in Fig. 1.12.

13 (a) Which ports would you use to take the shortest route from your home town to:
  (i) Paris?
  (ii) Stockholm?
  (iii) Amsterdam?
  (b) Imagine that there is a road tunnel under the English Channel from Dover to Calais. What difference, if any, would this make to your choice of routes or form of travel, and why?

Where Europeans live

What makes some areas crowded, and leaves others nearly empty? Why should some places attract more people to live in them than others?

14 Here are six types of places:
(i) Rugged mountainous country.
(ii) Land with long freezing winters.
(iii) Land near a coal mine.
(iv) A flat fertile plain.
(v) An area with long, hot, dry summers.
(vi) A place close to the sea.
What advantages and disadvantages would each of these places have to live and work in?

The following exercise tries to see if it is possible to predict where most people will live in Europe.

*15 (a) Lay a piece of tracing paper over Fig. 1.13 and according to whether you think the relief of the area is attractive to people or not, write a number between 0 and 10 in each square in which there is some land. If you think it is a very attractive square to live in, give it a high number. If it seems a bad place to live in, give it a low number. Do not be afraid to use 0 or 10. Label this tracing 'Relief'.

Fig. 1.13 Gridded outline of Europe showing major relief features

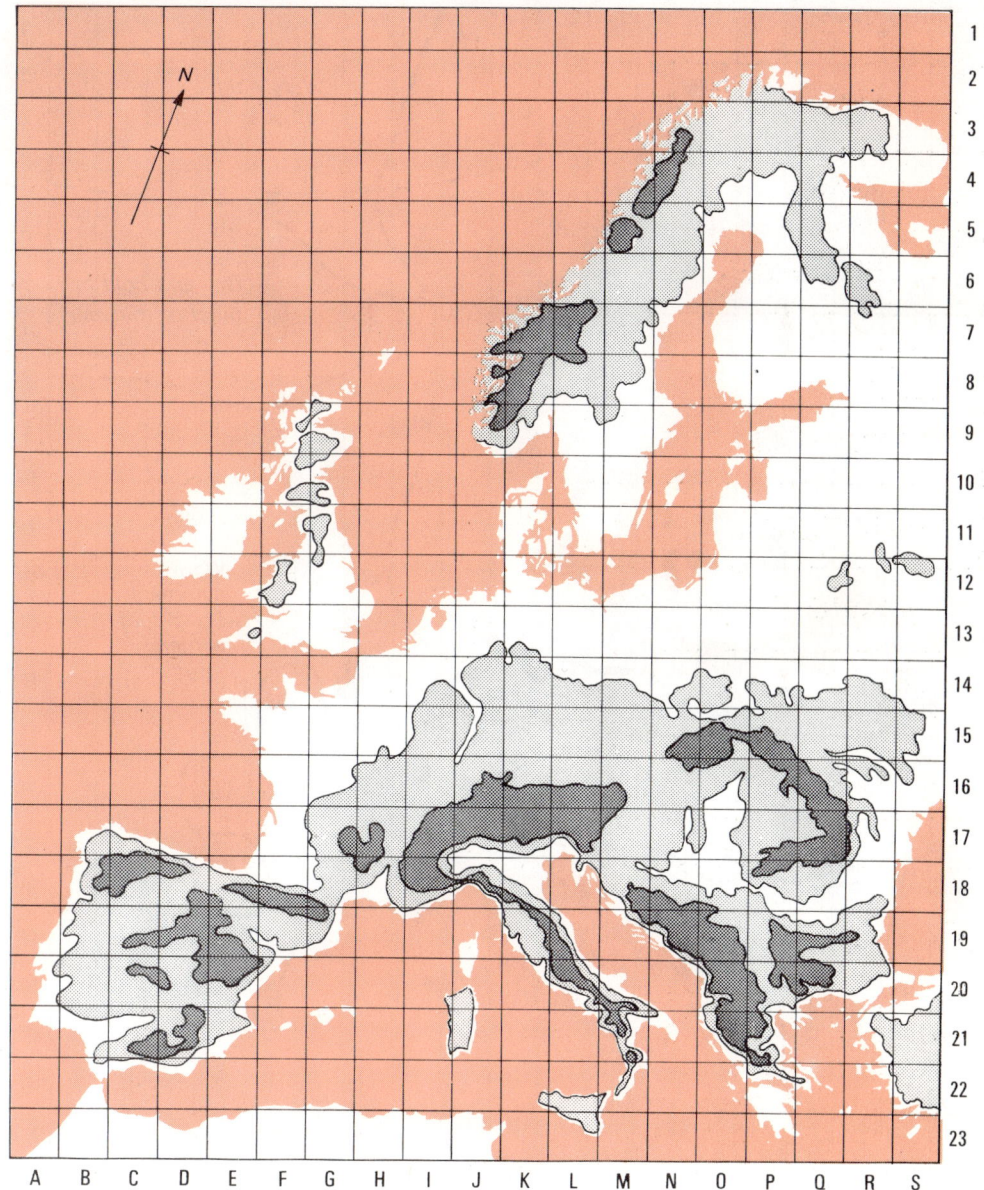

Key
Height above sea level

Under 200 m
200 – 900 m
Over 900 m

Scale
0   500   1000 km

Fig. 1.14 Climate and coalfields of Europe

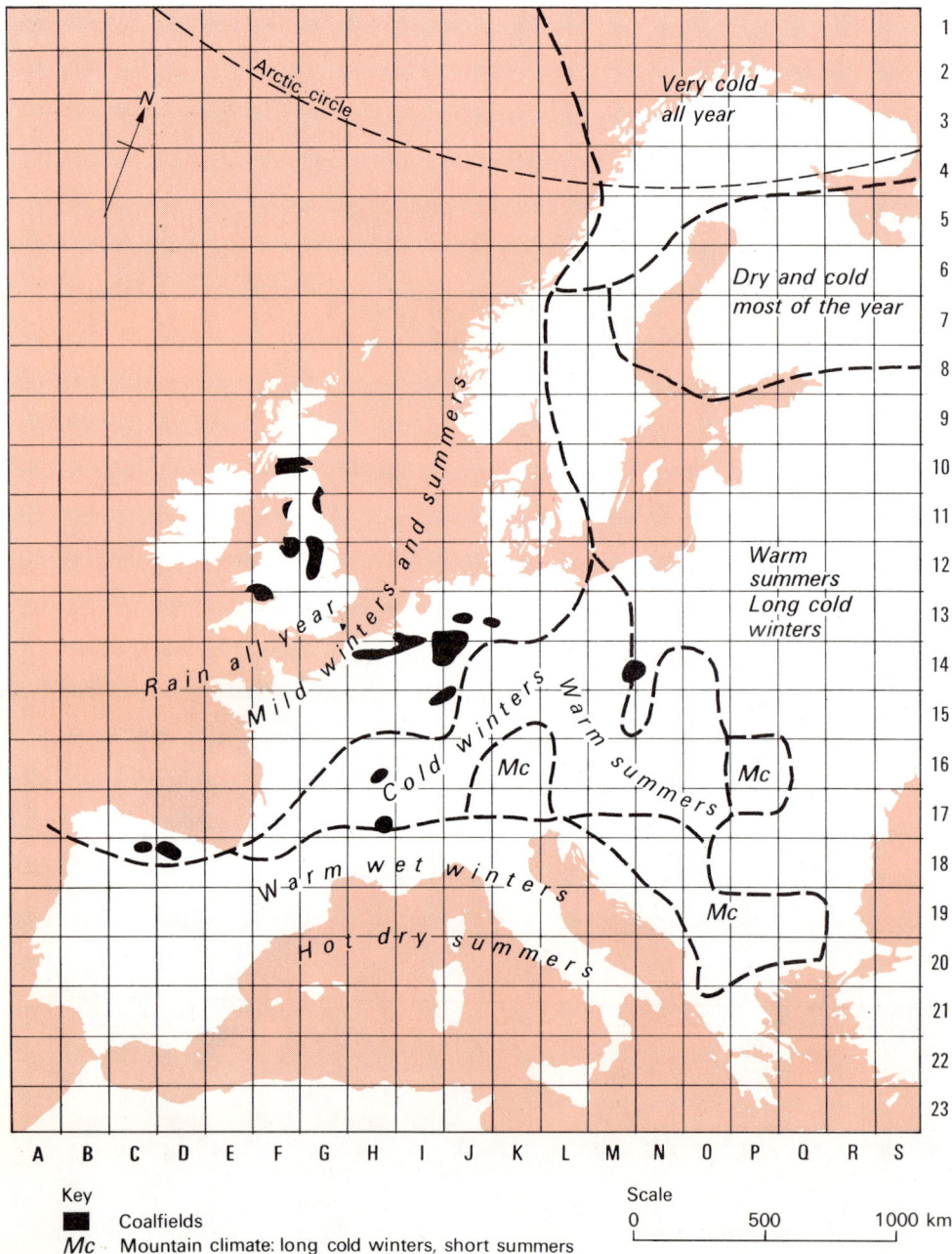

Key

■ Coalfields

Mc Mountain climate: long cold winters, short summers

Scale

0   500   1000 km

(b) Lay another sheet of tracing paper over Fig. 1.14, and using the information about the climate of Europe, give numbers between 0 and 10 to each square according to whether you think its climate is attractive to people or not. Label this tracing 'Climate'.

(c) Add together the two numbers you have given to each square, and put your answers on to a third tracing. Label this tracing 'Relief and climate'.

(d) On this last sheet, add 10 to each square which contains a coalfield or part of a coalfield, as shown in Fig. 1.14. This is because in the nineteenth century many towns were built on coalfields, and have since grown into huge cities. You now have the total score for each square. No square can score more than 30.

(e) On your final tracing or on a gridded outline map of Europe:

    (i) Shade in black all squares which scored 20 or over.

    (ii) Shade in red all squares which scored between 15 and 19.

    (iii) Shade in yellow all squares which scored between 10 and 14.

    (iv) Leave blank all squares which scored less than 10.

Label the finished map 'The predicted density of population in Europe' and add a key.

(f) Are the areas with black shading similar in both your map and Fig. 1.15 which shows the actual density of population in Europe?

(g) Are the areas which are blank on your map also blank on Fig. 1.15?

(h) How well does your map agree with Fig. 1.15?

16 Use your atlas to find the following big cities in the crowded areas of Europe: Liverpool, London, Rotterdam, Dusseldorf, Hanover, Paris,

Fig. 1.15 Distribution of population in Europe

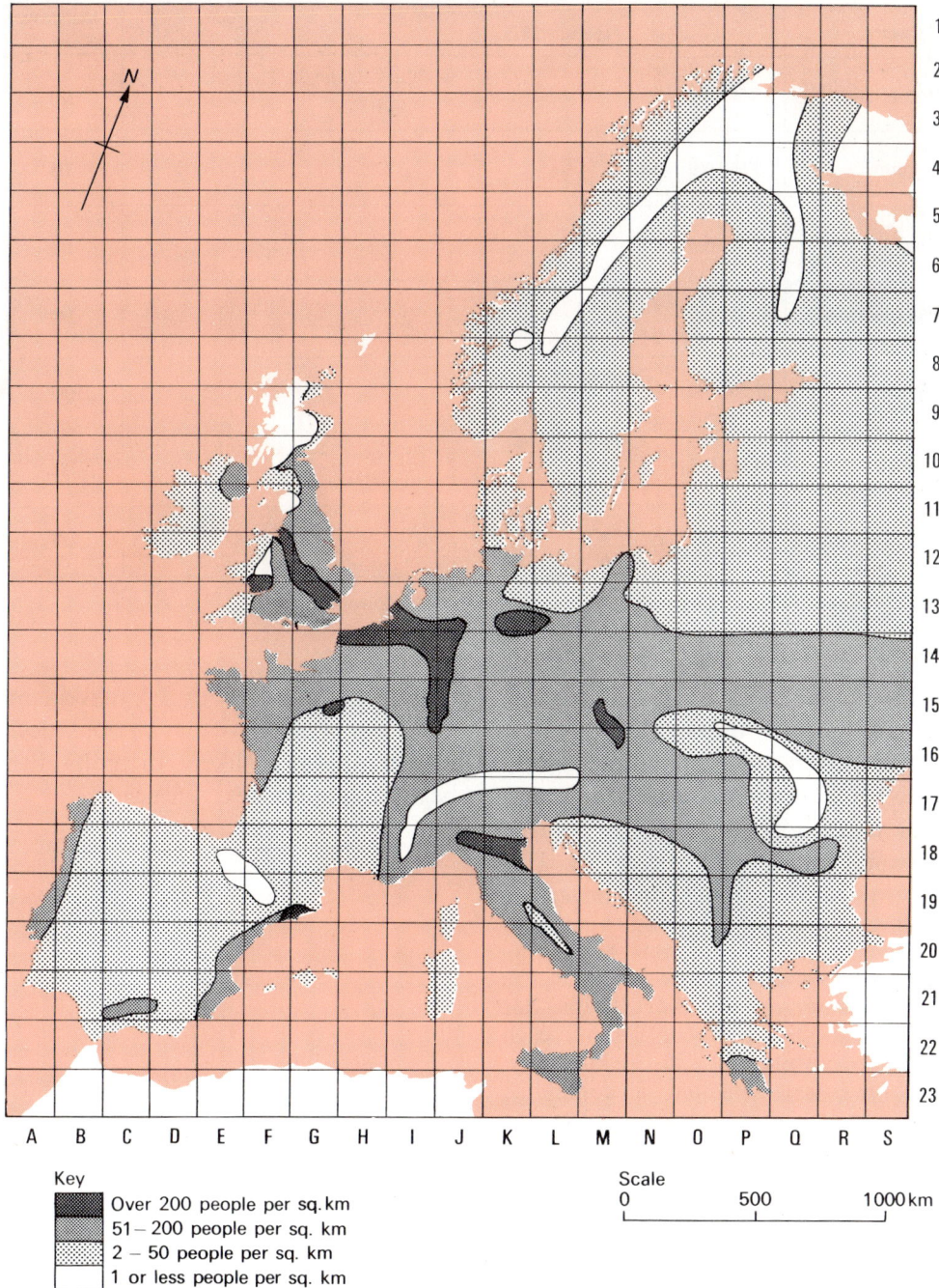

Milan. Mark these on either your own map of predicted density of population or on a copy of Fig. 1.15.

17 Using the maps of relief, climate, and coalfields (Figs. 1.13 and 1.14) to help you, can you suggest any reasons why:

(a) The areas coloured black on Fig. 1.15 should have so many people?

(b) So few people live in the blank areas on Fig. 1.15?

Key

■ Over 200 people per sq. km
▓ 51 – 200 people per sq. km
░ 2 – 50 people per sq. km
□ 1 or less people per sq. km

Scale
0   500   1000 km

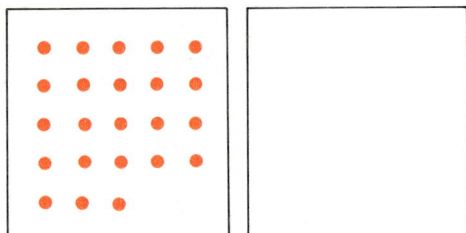

United Kingdom   Netherlands

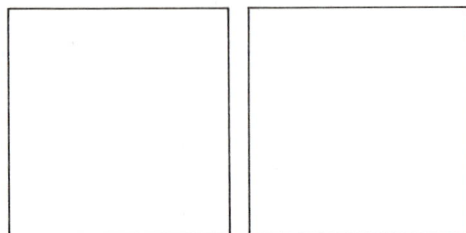

West Germany   France

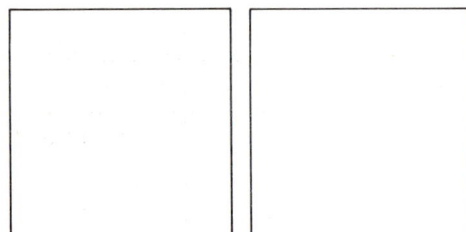

Belgium   Luxembourg

Italy

1 dot represents
10 people per sq.km

Fig. 1.16 Squares for use in Exercise 18

Country	Population 1975			Inhabitants per sq. km
Netherlands	13 599 000			333
Belgium	9 651 000			316
Luxembourg	357 000			138
West Germany	61 992 000			249
France	52 590 000			96
Italy	54 683 000			182
United Kingdom	55 981 000			229

Fig. 1.17 Population densities in some countries of north-west Europe

The countries of north-west Europe contain one of the world's greatest concentrations of population and a problem facing many European countries is a shortage of land. Bearing in mind that the countries in Fig. 1.17 vary in size you can see how uneven the density of population is.

18 Draw seven squares of equal size as shown in Fig. 1.16. If one dot represents ten people, and each square represents a square kilometre, the United Kingdom will contain 23 dots in its square. Complete the remaining squares to represent the population densities shown in Fig. 1.17.

The Netherlands is clearly the most densely populated country. The present population is approximately 13·5 million compared with 3·5 million in 1870. Experts believe that a population of 15 million is likely there by the beginning of the next century.

Tourists' Europe

So far we have been concerned with the density of population in Europe, and how crowded some parts are compared with others. Apart from people who live and work permanently in Europe, many others go there just for a short time on holiday. The distribution pattern of these tourists may very well be different from the pattern of population we have seen so far.

19. On a gridded outline map of Europe and using Figs. 1.13 and 1.14 to help you:
(a) Colour the squares which you would expect to be popular for winter sports holidays.
(b) Colour in a different colour the squares where you would expect sun and seaside holidays to be important.
(c) Mark on the following ten towns and cities where historic monuments and buildings are an attraction: Florence, Venice, Rome, Paris, London, York, Bruges, Salzburg, Amsterdam, and Avignon. Use an atlas to help you. Title your map 'Tourist attractions of Europe'.

20. (a) Which three of the European countries in Fig. 1.18 would you most like to live in?
(b) Which three of the countries in Fig. 1.18 would you choose to go to for a holiday?
(c) Fill in a copy of Fig. 1.18 with the results for the whole of your class. Which is the most popular country to go to for a holiday?

21. Fig. 1.19 shows the percentage of holiday-makers in thirteen European countries in 1975, who came from Britain.
(a) On an outline map of Europe,

Fig. 1.18 Table for Exercise 20

Country	Countries to live in	Countries to go to on holiday
Scandinavia		
West Germany		
Netherlands		
Belgium and Luxembourg		
France		
Irish Republic		
Switzerland		
Austria		
Italy		
Spain and Portugal		
Greece		

shade in the countries using the following colour scheme:
light colour—less then 5 per cent
medium colour—5–15 per cent
dark colour—over 15 per cent.
(b) Look again at your own map of the predicted population density for Europe. Which does it match best, the pattern of population density, or the pattern of holiday preferences?

When you did your prediction of population density it is quite possible that you were too influenced by those things which would make a place suitable for a holiday rather than as a place to live and work.

Fig. 1.19 Percentage of holiday-makers in thirteen European countries who came from Britain

Country	Percentage	
	1951	1975
Scandinavia	2	1
West Germany	3	5
Netherlands	4	2
Belgium & Luxembourg	15	2
France	39	14
Irish Republic	26	4
Switzerland	14	3
Austria	5	3
Italy	14	7
Spain & Portugal	5	34
Greece	1	4

Workback

22 Look again at the maps you drew in answer to Exercises 19 and 21, and at all the information you have on conditions in Europe.
(a) What kinds of things do you think the British holiday-makers in Europe in 1975 were looking for?
(b) Fig. 1.19 shows the percentage of tourists in Europe who came from Britain for 1951 as well as 1975. What is the biggest change since 1951? Can you suggest any reasons for it?

23 Fig. 1.20 shows four routes for a European car rally finishing in Monte Carlo. Imagine you have entered and have to choose which route to follow. First you need to trace the map.
(a) Using a piece of string or the edge of a blank sheet of paper, work out the length of each route. Which route would you choose on this basis?
(b) Name the check points shown on the map by their initial letter and write them in full on your tracing; for example, 'V' in Spain is Valencia.

(c) Name on your map, and show by shading, the main mountains and seas that each route has to cross.
(d) Each of the features shown on your map in answer to (c) will increase the difficulty of the routes. Bearing this in mind would you still choose the route you decided on in (a)?

*24 How well did the pattern of the Neolithic game work out?
(a) What effect would it have to change the pattern of the grid to those shown below?

(b) Does it make any difference if you start from the bottom right-hand square instead of the start square X?
(c) Did the time-scale work out correctly? If not, could you change the rules to make it work?
(d) Can you suggest any other improvements to the game?
(e) What other types of diffusion could you simulate using this method?

Summary

In this opening chapter you have found out where the major cities and countries of Europe are on the map. You have seen how people originally came into Europe and settled, and how they are distributed over the continent today. You have also seen briefly its tourist attractions.

Fig. 1.20 Routes for car rally

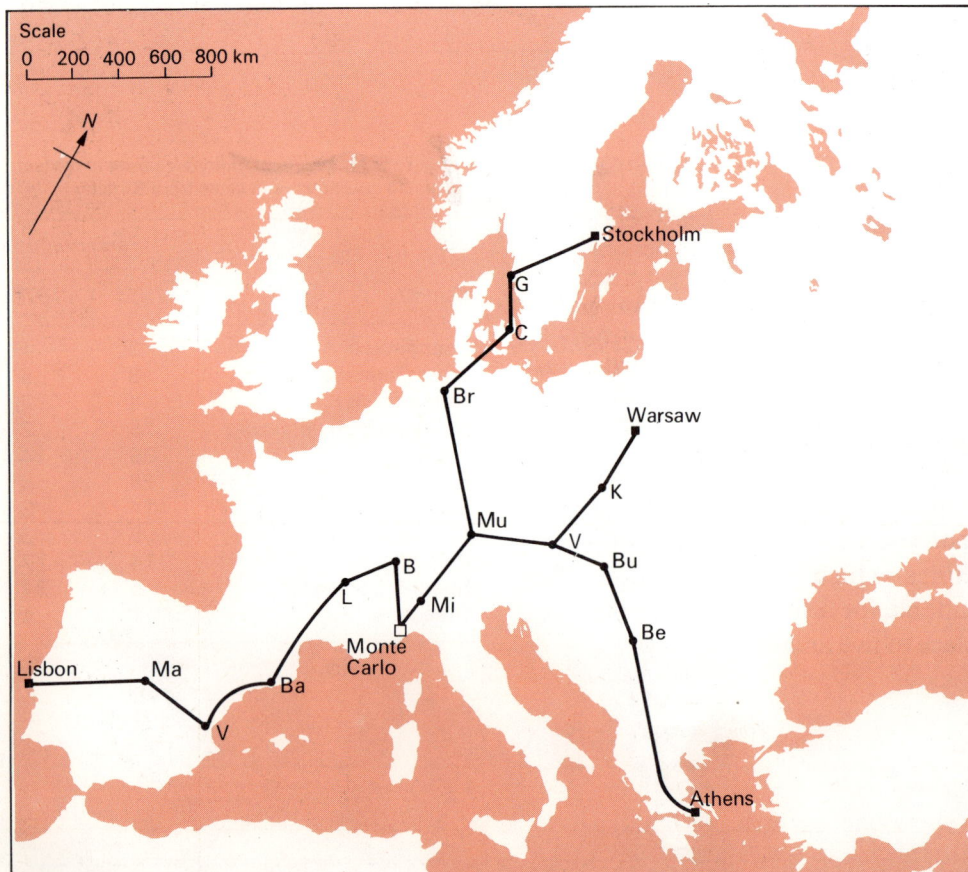

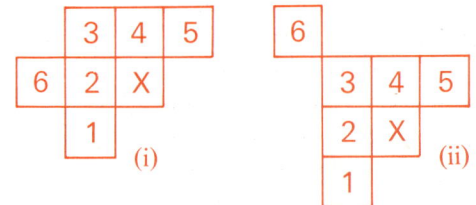

2 Rural land use

This chapter looks at rural areas, where many people live either on farms or in villages and small towns, usually making their living from farming.

Building a polder

The Netherlands is the most densely populated country in Europe. Look again at your answer to Exercise 18 in Chapter 1. This crowding means that it is important to use all the land as carefully as possible. In fact, over the centuries Dutch engineers have become experts at draining marshlands and the shallow waters of their coasts to create completely new land, or polders, suitable for occupation and farming.

The biggest polder project so far has been the damming of parts of the shallow bay, once called the Zuider Zee, to make the IJssel Lake (Fig. 2.1). Parts of this lake were then drained to create four polders (Fig. 2.2). The drawings and photographs in Fig. 2.3 show in more detail how a polder is made.

1   (a) Make a simple sketch of the photo of the completed polder in Fig. 2.3d.
    (b) Label your drawing with as many features of a polder as you can, using the rest of Fig. 2.3 to help you.

The massive engineering works for a polder cost a great deal of money and take a long time to build, so the new land must be very carefully laid out and efficiently farmed to make all the work worthwhile.

Fig. 2.1 Closing the dam of the former Zuider Zee

Fig. 2.2 (right) Dutch polderlands

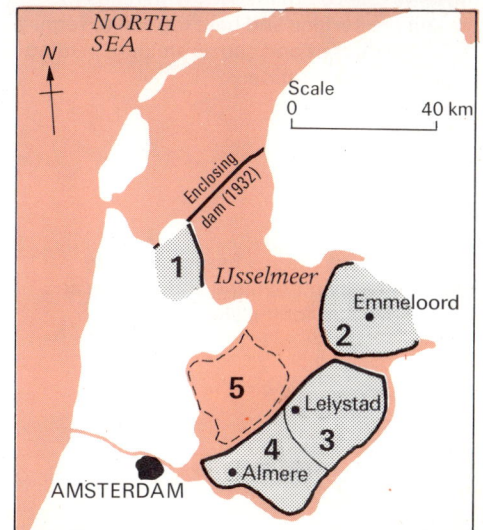

Key
Polders in order of construction
1 Wieringermeer (1930)
2 North-East Polder (1942)
3 Eastern Flevoland (1957)
4 Southern Flevoland (1968)
5 Markerwaard (projected)
— Polder dykes

27

Fig. 2.3b (right) The dam enclosing the IJsselmeer
c Soil testing on a newly drained polder
d A completed and settled polder

Fig. 2.3a Building a polder

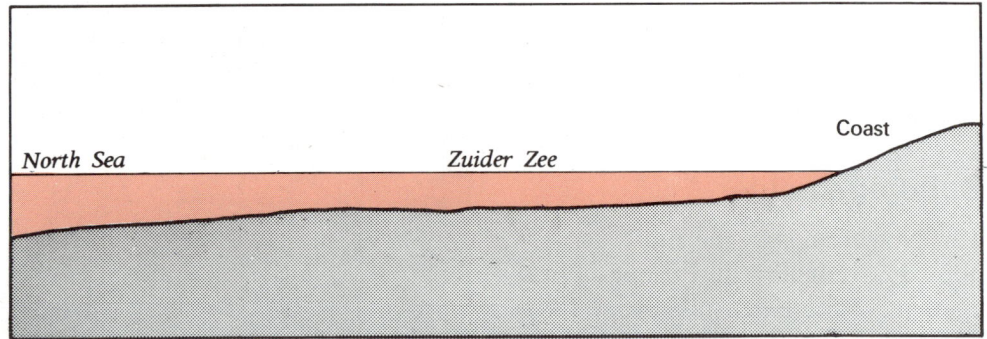

Stage 1
The Zuider Zee is a shallow bay open to the
North Sea and its tides.

North Sea — Zuider Zee — Coast

Stage 2
The enclosing dam shuts off the bay from the
sea to form a lake of fresh water. Gates in the
dam let water out into the sea at low tide but
do not let sea water in.

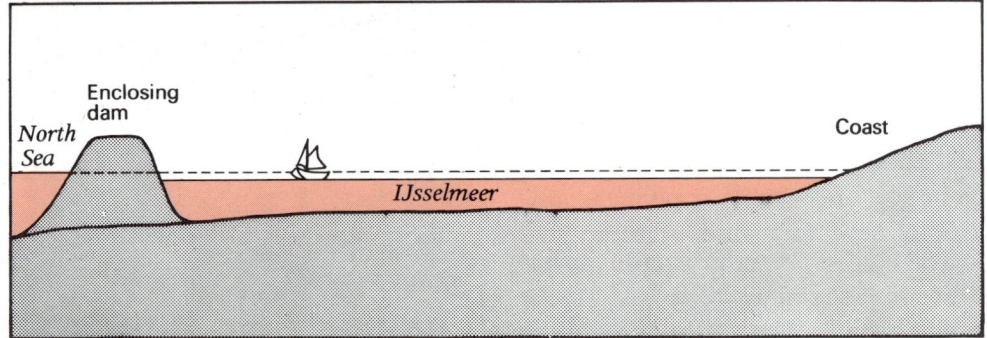

North Sea — Enclosing dam — IJsselmeer — Coast

Stage 3
Part of the lake is separated from the rest by a
dyke. The water is pumped out of this part
into the IJsselmeer. As the lake floor behind
the dyke dries out it is sown with reeds to
protect the surface and help the soil to form.
Drainage ditches and canals are dug, leading
to the pumping station.

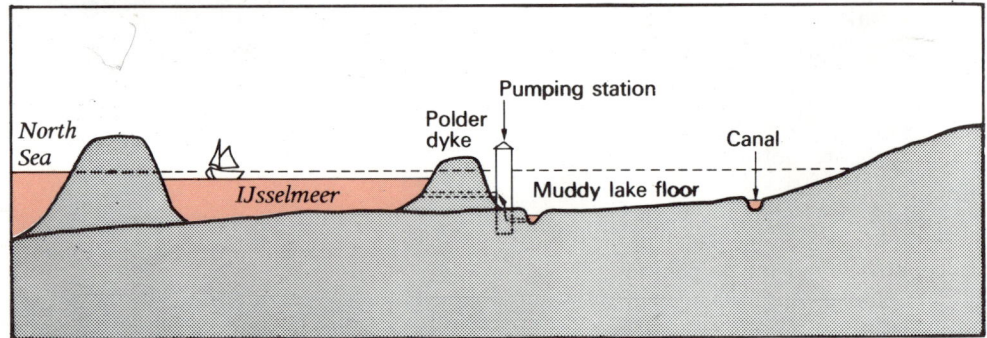

North Sea — IJsselmeer — Polder dyke — Pumping station — Muddy lake floor — Canal

Stage 4
After five years the soil has formed. The
polder is ready for farming and settling and
forms new land for the Netherlands.

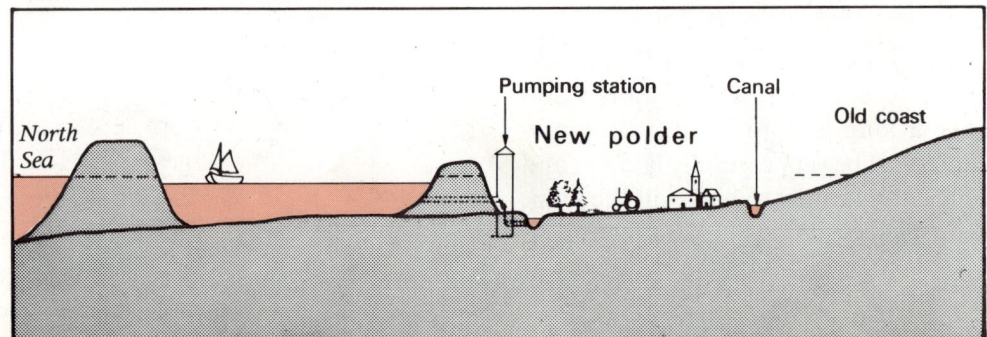

North Sea — Pumping station — New polder — Canal — Old coast

28

d

29

Fig. 2.4 Plans for dividing up Scroogeland

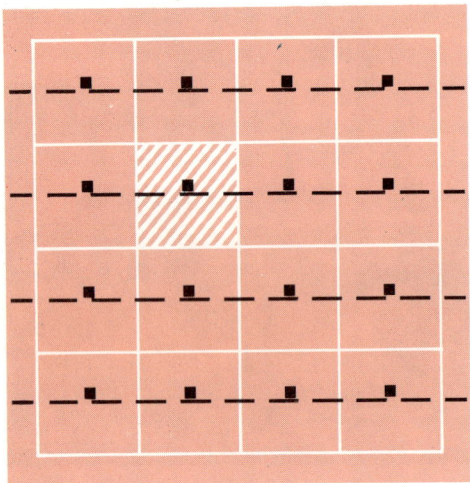

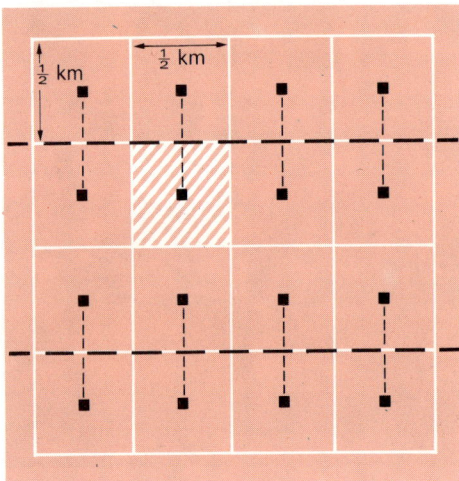

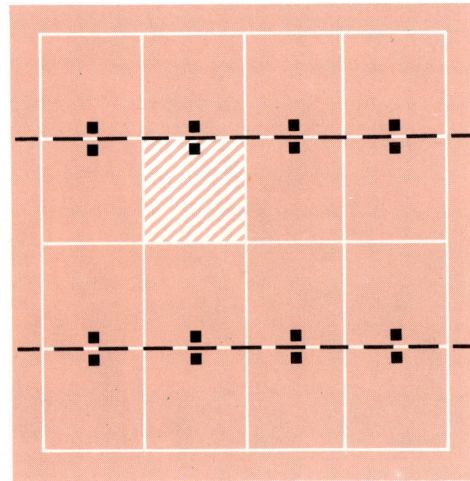

Plan A
(i) Farms are square.
(ii) Farmhouses are in the middle of the farm.
(iii) Four main roads cross the area.
(iv) Roads pass through the middle of the farms.

Plan B
(i) Farms are square.
(ii) Farmhouses are in the middle of the farm.
(iii) Two main roads cross the area.
(iv) Roads pass along the edge of the farm so farmers have to build their own farm tracks to reach them.

Plan C
(i) Farms are square.
(ii) Farmhouses are on the edge of the farm.
(iii) Two main roads cross the area.
(iv) Roads pass along the edge of the farm.

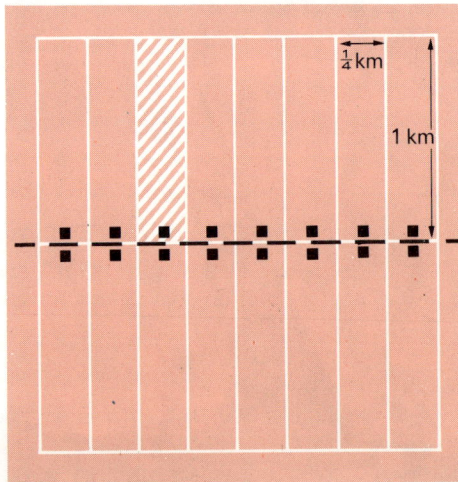

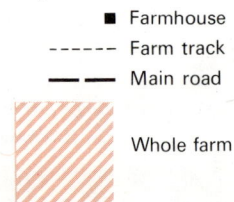

Key
■ Farmhouse
----- Farm track
– – – Main road

▨ Whole farm

Plan D
(i) Farms are square.
(ii) Farmhouses are in the corner of the farm and arranged in a group with neighbouring farmhouses to form a hamlet.
(iii) Roads are the same as in Plans B and C.

Plan E
(i) Farms are the same size as before, but oblong.
(ii) Farmhouses are at the end of the farm by the road.
(iii) Only one main road crosses the area.

Planning a polder

One of the main difficulties in establishing a polder is deciding on the most suitable plan for it. Fig. 2.4 shows five different ways in which a small part of a new polder called Scroogeland might be laid out. Each plan shows farms, farmhouses, and main roads which will lead to villages and the local town.

Some of the people who are going to live and work on the polder are:

(i) The farmers who need a farm which is easy to get round from the farmhouse in order to save time and effort, and which has good access to a road.

(ii) The farmers' wives who need to get easily from the farm to the local village or town for shopping or to take the children to school.

(iii) The postman who needs to get to all the farmhouses as quickly as possible in order to get through his deliveries in a reasonable time.

(iv) The local council which is responsible for building and maintaining all the main roads, and wants to keep its costs as low as possible.

2   Which of the five possible plans shown in Fig. 2.4 will each of these groups of people prefer?
(a) Read *all* the information given in Fig. 2.4 carefully.
(b) Read again the needs of each of the four groups of people who are going to settle on the polder. You may be able to think of other needs to add to those already given.
(c) On a copy of Fig. 2.5, fill in what you would expect to be the order of preference of each group of people.

	Plan A	Plan B	Plan C	Plan D	Plan E
Farmers' order of preference					
Wives' order of preference					
Postman's order of preference					
Council's order of preference					
Total					

Fig. 2.5 Table for Exercise 2

(d) Add up the numbers scored by each plan in your table. The plan with the lowest total, that is, the plan which comes closest to being everybody's choice, is the one that is most suitable.

Mr. Playfair, the planner must decide which plan should be used for the Scroogeland polder.

*3   Imagine you are Mr. Playfair. Design another plan which you think would be better than the one chosen in Exercise 2. Call it Plan F. Write a few sentences pointing out its advantages and disadvantages for each of the four groups of people.

*4   Use all the information given in the chapter so far to hold a public inquiry. Various members of the class should take the parts of the farmers, their wives, the postman, councillors, and planners. Each should put forward his point of view, and a vote should be taken to decide which plan should be adopted.
(b) Write up the proceedings of the public inquiry in the form of either a journalist's article for the local newspaper, *The Scroogeland Times* or a full front page for the newspaper.

Fig. 2.6 Plan of a small area in the North-East Polder

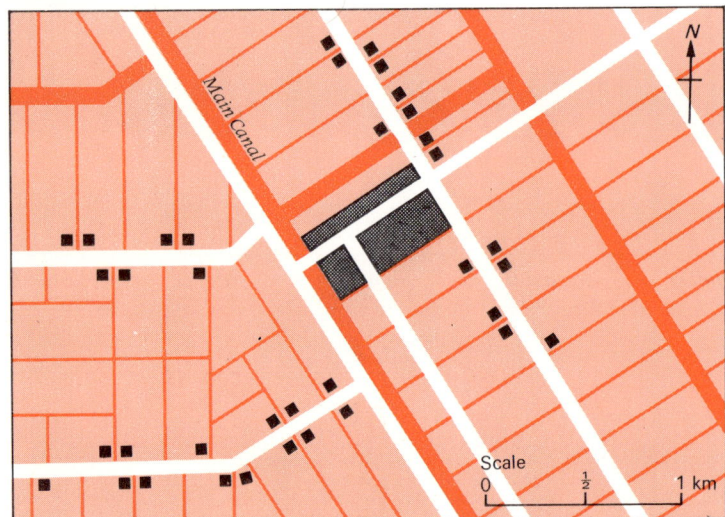

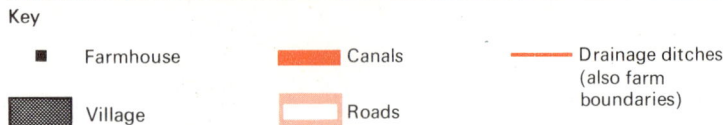

Key

■ Farmhouse   ▬ Canals   ▬ Drainage ditches (also farm boundaries)

▨ Village   ▭ Roads

Fig. 2.8 The North-East Polder

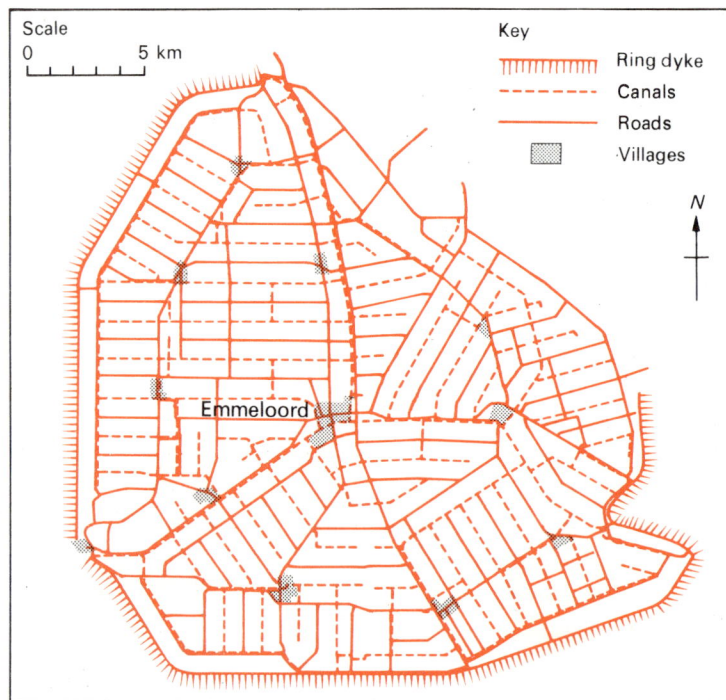

Key

▥ Ring dyke
╌╌ Canals
── Roads
▨ Villages

Fig. 2.7 The layout of the North-East Polder as seen from the air

Living on a polder

5   Describe the pattern of farms and fields in Figs. 2.6 and 2.7. Is it like any of the plans shown in Fig. 2.4?

The map in Fig. 2.8 shows the whole of the North-East Polder. The pattern of roads is centred on one town, Emmeloord, which is in the middle of the polder. The town is surrounded by a ring of smaller villages, so that no farm is more than 5 km away from a settlement.

For the first five years after a polder has been drained, the government organizes the farming. Then the land is divided up and rented to farmers. Sometimes as many as twenty-five farmers apply for each farm, and only the best farmers are chosen. As all the farmers are new to the area, they help each other out and share both the work and the farm machinery.

The farming landscape of the polders is planned for efficiency, not beauty. The land was built with the aid of machines, for machines to work efficiently on. Sometimes people who come to live on the polders, particularly young people, find it lonely and remote, and they try to move away.

Although the early polders are used mainly for farming, the situation is changing. The Netherlands is short of space for other things too, and today there is some argument as to how to make best use of the newer polders.

In Flevoland (Fig. 2.2) this is beginning to show. East Flevoland is still more or less similar to the North-East Polder. It is mainly agricultural, but it has larger areas in the towns for industry and services and larger recreational zones, which are also being used by people from outside the polder. South Flevoland, the most recently completed polder, is even more different. It has a much larger area of housing and industry in the western corner which is close to Amsterdam, a busy and expanding large city. There are also much larger areas set aside for recreation than in the early polders.

6 (a) Mr. Playfair has the job of planning the land use and layout of the projected Markerwaard Polder. Imagine you are Mr. Playfair. Draw a map of Markerwaard and show on it where you would locate: a town and villages, farmland, industry, housing, and areas for recreation.
(b) Write a short paragraph to explain the reasons behind your plan.

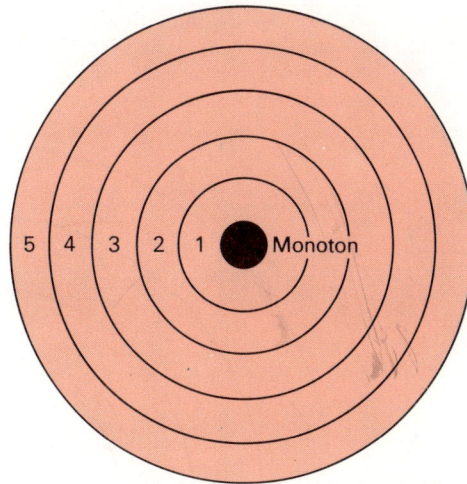

Fig. 2.9 The land around the town of Monoton

Fig. 2.10 Table for Exercise 7

Land use around a town

Fig. 2.9 shows the imaginary town of Monoton which, as its name suggests, is the only town in the middle of a monotonous flat plain. There are no differences in climate or soils anywhere on this plain.

All the farmers in the plain sell their produce in Monoton, which has the only market. Among the most important things that the population of Monoton needs are:
Fresh fruit and vegetables—*market garden* crops.
Fresh milk—a *dairy* product.
Wheat—an *arable* crop.
Beef—a *livestock* product.
Wood—a *forestry* product.

It is more difficult and therefore expensive to transport some of these goods to the market than others.

7 Copy Fig. 2.10 and fill in what you think is the order of difficulty of transport for the different products. For example, if you think that fruit and vegetables are the most difficult to transport because they are easily damaged and must reach the market while they are still fresh, put a '1' in the box by the side of fruit and vegetables. Then put a '2' against what you think is the next most difficult, and so on.

8 Make a copy of Fig. 2.9 and fill in the five zones with the land uses in the order you gave for Exercise 7. Use the symbols from Fig. 2.10.

*9 Apart from the cost of transport can you suggest why the outer, bigger rings are more suitable places for growing wheat, or rearing beef cattle than the small inner rings.

The example of Monoton is very simple, and has been used to show that some crops need to be grown closer to the market while others can quite sensibly be grown further away. The real world however is likely to be rather more complicated than this. In Fig. 2.11, three changes have been introduced to make the situation a little more realistic.

10 Look at the north-east zone of Fig. 2.11, and read the information carefully.
(a) What effect do you think a nearby main road providing faster travel to the town might have on a farmer's choice of crops?
(b) Re-draw the north-east zone of the diagram, showing the changes if any, which will take place in the neat pattern of rings due to the presence of a fast main road.

11 Look at the south-west zone of Fig. 2.11 and read the information carefully.
(a) What effect do you think the presence of a small town with its own market will have on the crop choice of the nearby farmers?
(b) Re-draw the south-west zone showing the resulting changes in the ring pattern.

*12 Look at the south-east zone of Fig. 2.11 and read the information carefully.
(a) What effect are the areas of poor soil and good soil likely to have on a farmer's crop choice?
(b) Are they likely to affect the choices of farmers in the areas outside them?
(c) Re-draw the south-east zone to show the changed land-use pattern.

Fig. 2.11 The land around a city

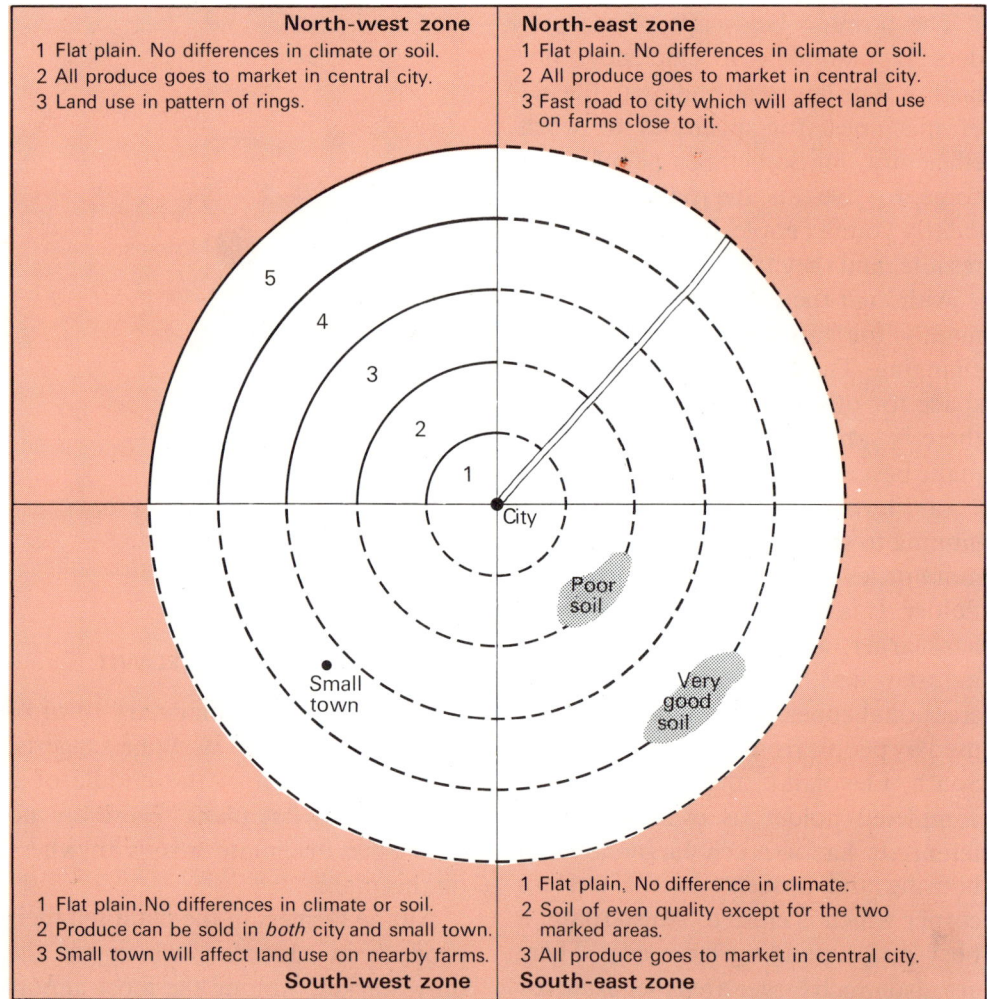

North-west zone
1 Flat plain. No differences in climate or soil.
2 All produce goes to market in central city.
3 Land use in pattern of rings.

North-east zone
1 Flat plain. No differences in climate or soil.
2 All produce goes to market in central city.
3 Fast road to city which will affect land use on farms close to it.

1 Flat plain. No differences in climate or soil.
2 Produce can be sold in both city and small town.
3 Small town will affect land use on nearby farms.
South-west zone

1 Flat plain. No difference in climate.
2 Soil of even quality except for the two marked areas.
3 All produce goes to market in central city.
South-east zone

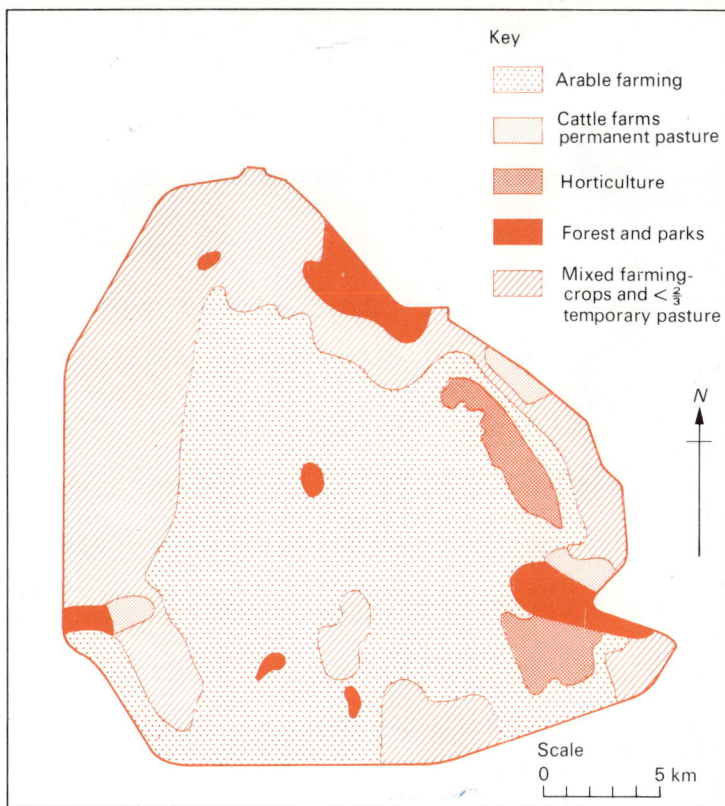

Fig. 2.12 The land use of the North-East Polder

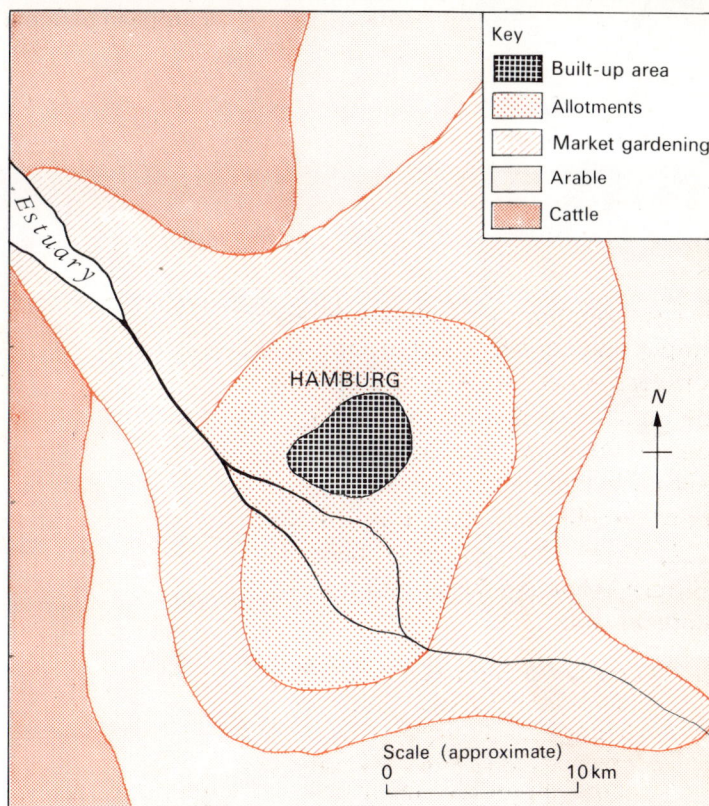

Fig. 2.13 Land use around the port of Hamburg

Local land-use patterns

Now let us look at some actual examples of land use, starting with a small area that we have studied before. Fig. 2.12 shows the land use of the North-East Polder.

13 (a) How far is the longest distance across the polder from north to south?
(b) How far is the longest distance from east to west?

As you can see from your answer to Exercise 13, the polder is small and so all parts of it have a similar climate. Because it is formed from the floor of a shallow lake it is also almost flat. It has one town, roughly in its centre. In all these ways it is very similar to Monoton.

However, the quality of the soil is not the same all over the polder. Some parts have sandy soils, while others have clay, depending on what the original lake floor was made of. Also, and perhaps even more important from a farming point of view, water has to be pumped out of the polder continually. Thus drainage is not equal all over the area, and some of the soils are wetter than others.

The pattern of farming is almost entirely due to these soil differences. Arable land is found where the soil is well drained, and pasture for cattle where it is wetter. Areas where the soil is particularly poor are forested, and the very best soils are used for market gardening.

An example of an area around a large city is shown in Fig. 2.13, a map of land use around Hamburg, a large port in northern Germany.

14 Market gardeners are usually full-time farmers. Allotment holders tend their crops in their spare time.
(a) What kinds of crops are produced on an allotment?
(b) What kinds of crops are produced by a market gardener?
(c) Describe and try to explain the pattern of allotments and market gardens around Hamburg.
*(d) The pattern of arable and live-stock farming is not in the form of rings. From what you learned from the polder example, can you suggest why the zone near the sea is used for cattle, while crops are grown inland?

35

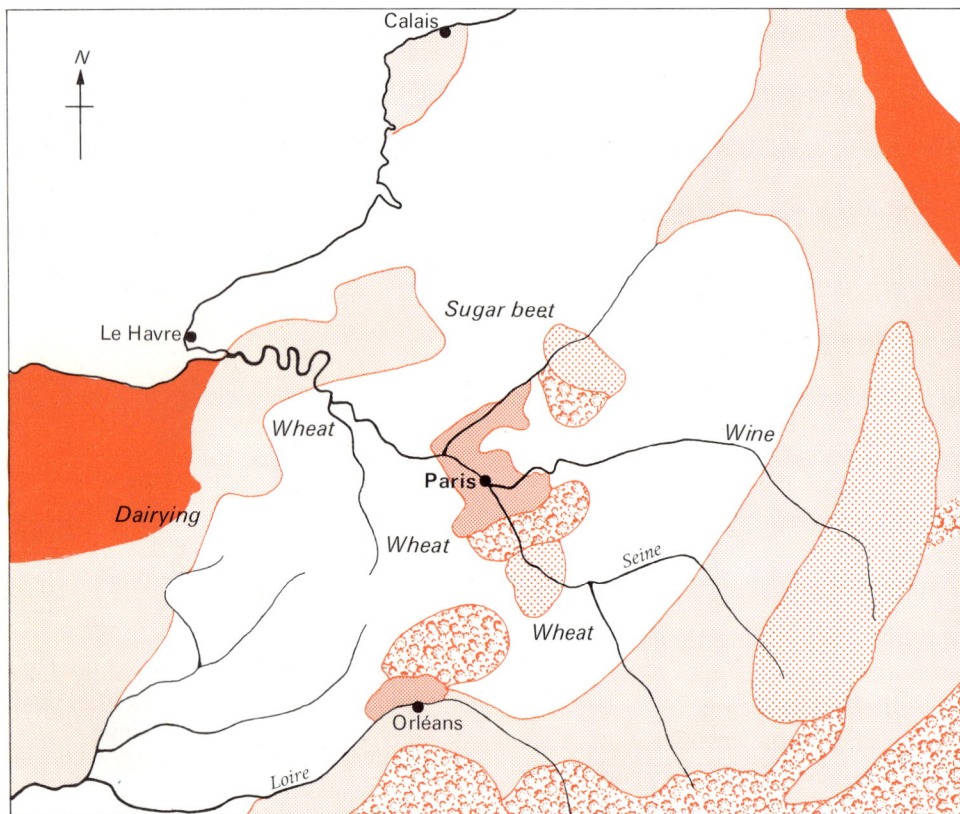

Fig. 2.14 The land use of the Paris Basin

Key

- Mainly permanent pasture
- Mixed farming
- Mainly arable
- Market gardening
- Land classified as poor agriculturally
- Forest

Areas which specialize in certain types of land use have been marked

Scale

0   50   100 km

Regional land-use patterns

The Paris Basin, shown in Fig. 2.14, is big enough to contain a number of large towns. Paris however, is much the biggest of these, and lies in the middle of the area.

15 How big is the area shown on Fig. 2.14?

Fig. 2.14 gives the impression of a land-use pattern of elongated rings centred on Paris. This is what you would expect from the work we have done so far. Let us look at the map in more detail.

16 (a) Where on the map is market gardening found? Is this where you would expect to find it? Why?

*(b) Why do you think there are some areas of forest very close to both Paris and Orleans?

*(c) Why do you think that dairy farming is not found in a ring around the market gardening zones?

The areas we have been looking at are of increasing size. It has been possible to find some part of the original ring pattern centred on the largest town in the area. Physical features like soil and drainage have caused disturbances in the pattern.

Intensity of land use

If we tried to look at the farming pattern for the whole of Europe, we should have a very complicated map. It would include areas of dairying, market gardening, arable farming, and stock rearing. If we then put on all the large cities as well, the map would become very confusing indeed.

To find a European pattern, we need to simplify our information in two ways.

(a) Instead of large towns we will use a map of density of population (see Fig. 1.15 on page 23), because

Fig. 2.15 Population density of Europe

most farm produce is needed where most people live. In other words, the area of highest population density will now be the main market, instead of a single city.

(b) You will have found that for activities like dairying and market gardening you can get a great deal of produce from a small area of land. In other words, this kind of farming is **intensive**. For arable farming, beef rearing, and forestry more space is needed to make a living. These kinds of farming are more **extensive**.

From what you have done so far, it is logical to expect that the higher the density of population, the more intensive will be the agriculture.

To see if this is true for Europe, look first at Fig. 2.15. The numbered dots on this map give the density of population per square kilometre in each European country. The lines on the map are **isolines**, lines joining points of equal density. Follow the 100-line round the map and you will see that it divides the countries with densities greater than 100 people per square km from those with less. Those points above 100 are inside the curve, and those below 100 lie outside it. Isolines for higher densities are also shown, and the areas between the lines have been shaded to make the pattern clear.

Fig. 2.16 is a map of Europe showing the intensity of agriculture for each country. The higher the figure, the greater the crop yield per hectare. The

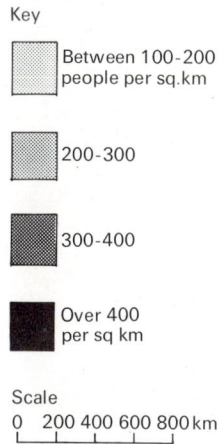

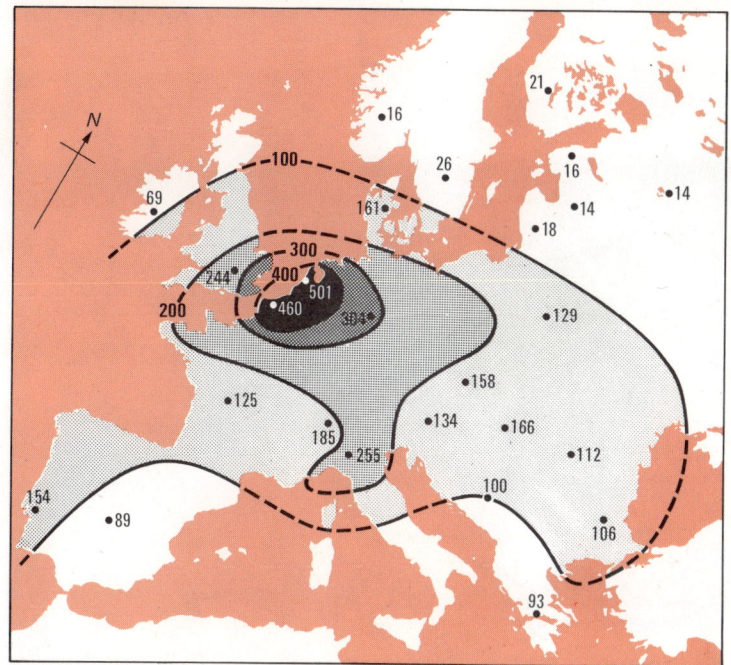

Key

Between 100-200 people per sq.km

200-300

300-400

Over 400 per sq km

Scale
0   200 400 600 800 km

Fig. 2.16 Index of intensity of agriculture

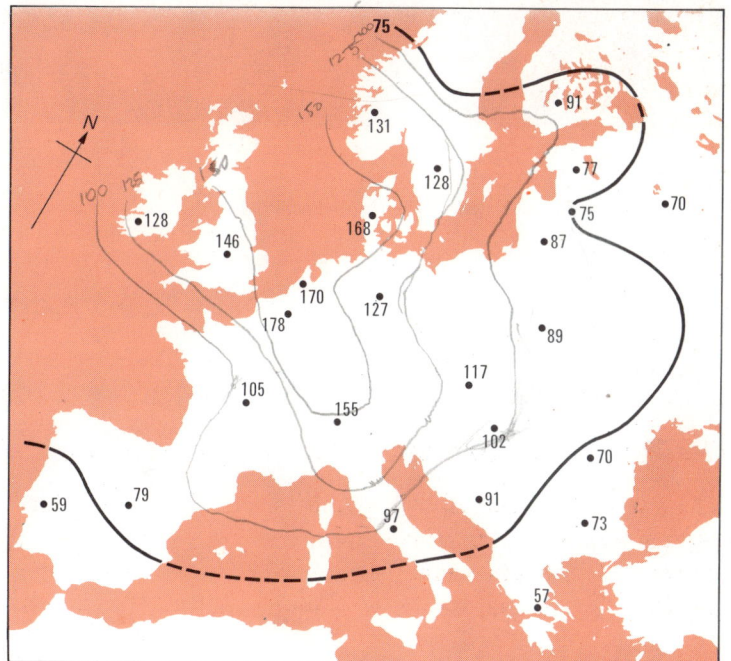

Key

Between 75-100

100-125

125-150

Over 150

Scale
0   200 400 600 800 km

isoline for the figure 75 has been drawn for you, but the map needs to be completed before a pattern can be seen.

17 (a) Trace Fig. 2.16.
(b) Draw on your tracing three more isolines, for the figures 100, 125 and 150.
(c) Shade the areas between the lines,

as has been done in Fig. 2.15, and give your map a key.
(d) Title your map 'Intensity of agriculture in Europe'.

18 Comparing your map with Fig. 2.15, is it true that in Europe the higher the density of population the greater the intensity of agriculture?

Fig. 2.17 The valley of the Geul in the south of the Netherlands

Workback

19 The photograph in Fig. 2.17 shows a very different farming area from the polders. It too is in the Netherlands, but in the south of the country, well away from the sea, and the big crowded cities.

(a) Write a paragraph describing the main differences you can see between the landscapes in Figs. 2.17 and 2.18.

(b) If you had to live on a farm in one or other of these areas, which would you prefer? Why?

20 Explain why land-use zones in the real world do not form exactly the same patterns as they do around an imaginary town like Monoton.

Fig. 2.18 The village of Nagele in the North-East Polder

Summary

This chapter has looked at the problems involved in planning the layout and land use of a completely new area of farming land in the polders of the Netherlands. You have also tried to predict the pattern of land use that would be found in a simple imaginary area of farming land. You then compared this simple pattern with actual land-use patterns around European cities to see how it could help you to explain and understand patterns in the real world.

3 Farming

In Chapter 2 we were looking at the way in which similar patterns of land use could be found in areas taken from various parts of Europe. This chapter will consider different ways of farming in Europe. Each of the areas chosen has had its own particular problems to face. Some farmers have been able to adapt quickly to changing conditions while others are still facing great difficulties.

Denmark

Denmark is made up of a long, low sand bar facing the North Sea, and a group of islands in the Baltic Sea. Its highest point is only 200 m above sea level, and nowhere is further than 50 km from the sea. The climate is similar to that of East Anglia, and it is good grain growing country. Until the late nineteenth century Danish farmers earned their living selling grain to nearby European countries.

1 In this exercise we look at the way Danish farmers have solved some of their problems in the past; you are to make their decisions for them:
(a) The date is 1870. You are Danish farmers growing wheat for export on farms about 20 hectares in size. But vast amounts of grain have begun to reach Europe from the United States, Canada, and Russia which are selling at a price which is less than it costs you to grow your wheat.
Hold a meeting, and decide on the advantages and disadvantages of:
(i) Asking the government to put a tax on all imported grain to bring the price up to yours.

(ii) Asking the government for money to help you to produce wheat at the same price as the imported grain.
(iii) Changing to pig farming and dairying to take advantage of the cheap imported grain as animal feed to produce and sell bacon, butter, and cheese.
At the end of your meeting, take a vote to decide which course to follow.
(b) It is now 1882. Your farms are so small that it is very difficult to produce dairy goods at a price people can afford. There are three options open to you:
(i) Max E. Miser, a millionaire who has made his money from pro-

cessed cheese, has offered to buy your farm at a very low price to save you from ruin.
(ii) Some of the neighbouring farmers have had the idea of setting up their own dairy to produce cheap butter and cheese in bulk. They have asked you to join them and form a **co-operative**.
(iii) Carry on as before and encourage your neighbours to sell their farms.
Decide which option to take and write a few sentences explaining your choice.

2 What evidence is there in Fig. 3.1 to show that grain production was once more important than dairying?

Fig. 3.1 Farm scene in Denmark

The first dairy co-operative was set up at Hjedding in 1882, and the first co-operative bacon factory at Horsens in 1887. Fig. 3.2 is a table showing the advantages of co-operatives.

3   Fit the words in the list below on to a copy of the right-hand column of Fig. 3.2.

efficiently	power
warehouses	large
low	shared
market	farming
lower	new

*4   Remembering that profit is equal to market price minus production and transport costs, use the information in Fig. 3.2 to write four paragraphs showing the effect of co-operatives on:
(a) Production costs.
(b) Transport costs.
(c) Market price.
(d) Profits.

5   Look at the information in Fig. 3.3. Which of the following statements is most likely to be correct:
(a) Co-operative dairies have proved such a failure that their numbers are falling?
(b) Co-operative dairies have become bigger and more efficient so fewer are needed?
(c) There are fewer farm workers in Denmark, so not so many dairies are needed?
Write a short paragraph to explain your choice.

Farm and food products such as bacon, butter, and cheese form nearly one-third of Danish exports. The Danish government did not help their farmers financially until the 1960s. At that time prices were so low that farmers were leaving the land, or changing from dairying to beef rearing or barley growing which did not need so much labour. In 1973 Denmark joined the European Economic Community (the Common Market), and its farm prices were raised to the levels of the Community.

By changing their products and modernizing their farming methods over the years, Danish farmers have been able to keep up with economic changes and remain successful.

Fig. 3.2 The advantages of co-operatives

Buying and selling	Small farmer	Co-operative
Buying cattle feed, seed, fertilizers:	Buys in small quantities at a higher price. Has little or no room for storage so he has to buy when he needs the goods rather than when the price is low.	Buys in ▓▓▓ amounts at a ▓▓▓ price. Can buy when the prices are ▓▓▓ and store goods in ▓▓▓ until they are needed.
Using tractors, milking machinery, and other equipment:	Must either use old, inefficient machinery, hire from commercial firms at high rates, or buy his own machinery	Members can share cost of ▓▓▓ machines and share their use so that they are used more ▓▓▓.
Raising money:	Must borrow from banks or finance companies at high interest rates.	Members can borrow from co-operative funds at low rates. Interest stays in ▓▓▓ rather than going to money lenders.
Selling produce:	Has little power to bargain for a good price. Must either provide own transport or hire it.	Has larger share of the ▓▓▓ so more ▓▓▓ to obtain good price. Transport costs are ▓▓▓ so cheaper.

Fig. 3.3 Table for Exercise 5

Year	Number of co-operative dairies in Denmark	Year	Number of farm workers in Denmark
1934	1400	1965	205698
1970	200	1973	140810

Fig. 3.4 Danish dairy farming
a Butter being taken from a large stainless steel churn
b A modern Danish milk tanker and dairy
c A milking parlour
d Trimming the carcass in a bacon factory

a
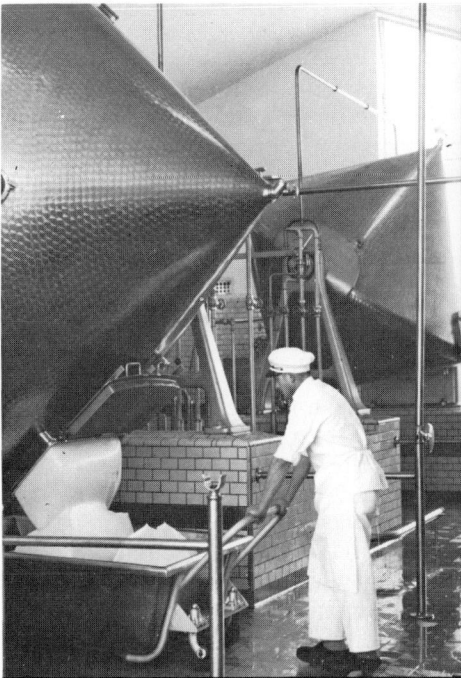

b

c

d
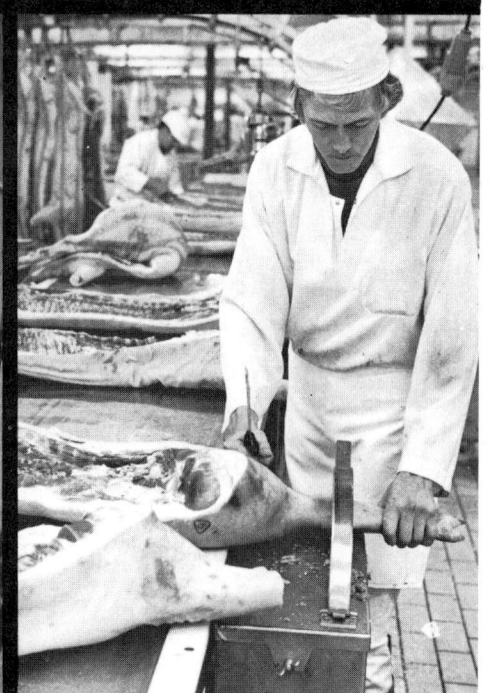

Poor farms in France

Many farms in southern France are only now changing from their old farming methods. They have a number of problems to solve, one of the most important of which is the practice of **monoculture**. This is when the farmer grows one crop year after year.

The grape vine is a crop well suited to the south of France; but the farmer is risking everything on the success of this crop alone, and there has been a specialization on it at the expense of many others.

By growing one crop only, in a good year the farmer can earn a high income but if the crops fail because of a late frost, strong winds, or developing a disease, then his income can fall disastrously. In the south of France the summer can be relied upon to bring sunshine, but the winter and spring can bring weather which causes havoc to the vines. When more than one crop is grown the risks are spread, and although in good years earnings might not be as high as with monoculture, it is unlikely that all the crops will be damaged by the weather.

6 Using the information for Marseille in the table of climatic data on page 124, say in which months of the year the French farmer is likely to be worried about:
(a) A risk of drought?
(b) A risk of frost (in growing vines)?

Fig. 3.5 Growing conditions table for the Monoculture game

Number on dice	Growing conditions	Return per hectare in francs		
		Vines	Olives	Winter wheat
2	Drought	500	450	450
3	Average growing conditions	1500	1400	1350
4	Above average growing conditions	2000	1700	1700
5	Good harvest	3400	3500	3500

Monoculture game

The following exercise demonstrates some of the dangers and benefits of monoculture.

7 Three farmers, M. Lenoir, M. Lebrun, M. Leblanc, each farm 12-hectare holdings in the south of France. M. Lenoir grows only the vine; M. Lebrun has 6 hectares of vines and 6 of winter wheat; M. Leblanc has 4 hectares each of vines, winter wheat, and olives.
(a) Make a copy of Fig. 3.7 extending for 10 years. (Omit the figures written

Fig. 3.6 The grape harvest

in white.) Copy the three parts of Fig. 3.8 onto separate sheets of card. Write CHANCE on the back of each, shuffle them, and lay them face downwards.
(b) Now throw a die once to decide the weather conditions for year 1. If you throw a 2, 3, 4, or 5, look at Fig. 3.5 to find the return per hectare for each crop in the different growing conditions. Let us assume you throw a 4. This means above average conditions. You would fill in year 1 as shown in white on Fig. 3.7. Vines show a return of F.2000 per hectare, so M. Lenoir does well with his 12 hectares of vines.
(c) If you throw a 1 or a 6, take a chance card. M. Lenoir may not be so lucky this time.
(d) Throw again for year 2 and fill in the table again. Continue to year 10. Add the 10 year totals for each farmer to see who has the highest income. How do your results compare with those of the rest of the class?

8 (a) Using the work you have done in this game, say in how many years did the monoculturalist earn (i) the highest income, (ii) the lowest income.
(b) How true is it to say the monoculturalist risks taking a low income in a few seasons in the hope of doing very well in most years?

Fig. 3.7 Earnings table

	M. Lenoir	Profit in Francs	M. Lebrun	Profit in Francs	M. Leblanc	Profit in Francs
Year 1 Weather Conditions Above average	12 Hectares of Vines	2000 X12 = 24000	6 Hectares of Vines	2000 X 6 = 12000	4 Hectares of Vines	2000 X4= 8000
					4 Hectares of Winter Wheat	1700 X4= 6800
			6 Hectares of Winter Wheat	1700 X6= 10200	4 Hectares of Olives	1700 X4= 6800
	Total	F24000	Total	F22200	Total	F21600
Year 2 Weather Conditions	12 Hectares of Vines		6 Hectares of Winter Wheat		4 Hectares of Vines	
			6 Hectares of Vines		4 Hectares of Winter Wheat	
					4 Hectares of Olives	
	Total		Total		Total	
Total for 10 years						

Fig. 3.8 Chance cards for the Monoculture game

1 *Vines* ruined by disease

   =NO RETURN per hectare

Olives survive

   =F 1100 per hectare

Wheat survives

   =F1000 per hectare

2 *Vines* and *olives* ruined by frost.

   = NO RETURN per hectare

Wheat survives

   = F1000 per hectare

3 Bumper harvest for *Vines*, but glut on world market reduces returns

   = F 2500 per hectare

Olives

   = F 3750 per hectare

Wheat

   = F 3500 per hectare

The transformation of Languedoc

One region in southern France which relied too heavily on growing grapes is Languedoc. Here the problem of monoculture was made worse because the wine made from the grapes was not of high quality but only *vin ordinaire*. This wine does not bring a high profit to the growers even in a good year. France began to import cheap wine from Algeria in North Africa in the 1960s. This caused a great fall in wine prices and the farmers faced ruin.

The task of solving the problem and bringing farming up to date has fallen on the French government. Over the past ten years a great deal has been done to encourage and to help farmers to turn from vines to a wide variety of fruits, salad vegetables, and dairy products. This **diversification** of farming takes a long time and is expensive because of two other problems.

The vine grows well in the Mediterranean climate. It thrives in the dryness of the summer. The new crops do not; they need water all year. **Irrigation** is needed over the whole area (Fig. 3.9). Water for this comes from rivers or reservoirs (Fig. 3.10) and it has to be taken by newly built canals to the dry fields to feed the crops (Fig. 3.11). Only the government can afford to do this over such a large area.

A modern farm needs to be at least 20 hectares in size if it is to give the farmer a fair income. Apart from providing for his family he has to earn enough from the farm to pay for fertilizer, seed, and equipment. The

Fig. 3.9 Irrigation in Languedoc

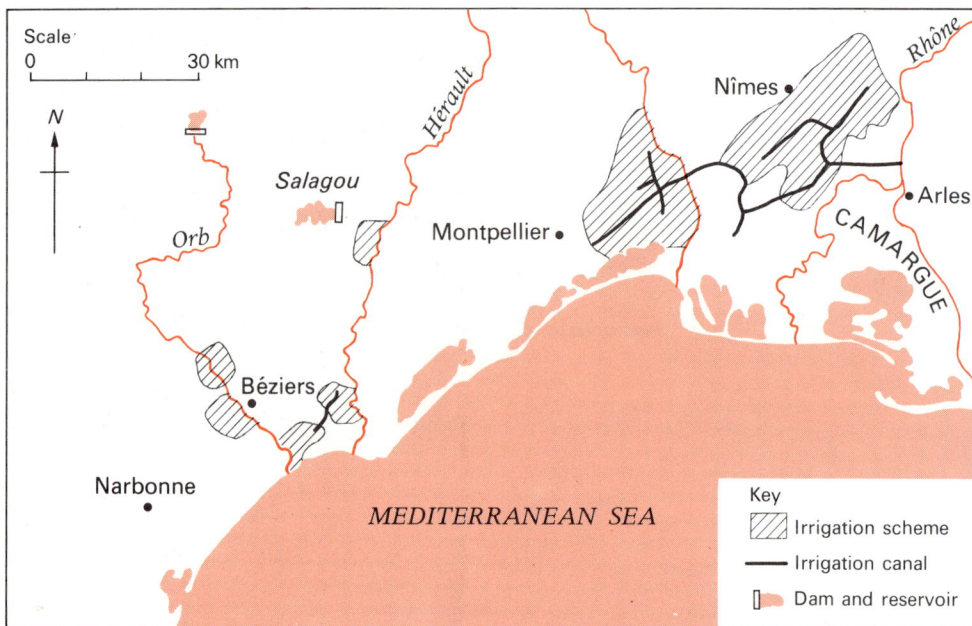

Fig. 3.10 Salagou reservoir

farms in southern France are too small. They are also split up into tiny fields which are separated from each other or **fragmented**.

9 Look at Fig. 3.12.
   (a) What disadvantages does this pattern of fields have for the farmer?
   (b) Redraw the diagram to show what you think would be a better way of laying out each farmer's land. (You may move the farmhouses if you wish.)
   (c) What would be the advantage to the others if one of the farmers gave up farming and got a job in a nearby coastal resort?

The government is encouraging the joining of scattered fields into more easily worked farms. This is known as **consolidation**. It takes many years, as farmers do not like giving up the land they know. In the last ten years over 500 000 hectares of farmland have been consolidated and crop production from areas like Languedoc is rising.

Irrigation, consolidation, and the joining of farms into even larger ones has made diversification possible. The Camargue area of the Rhône delta (Fig. 3.9) now produces all the rice needed in France, and the other irrigated areas on the map are growing more and more fresh food to supply the local seaside towns.

Fig. 3.11 Irrigating peach trees

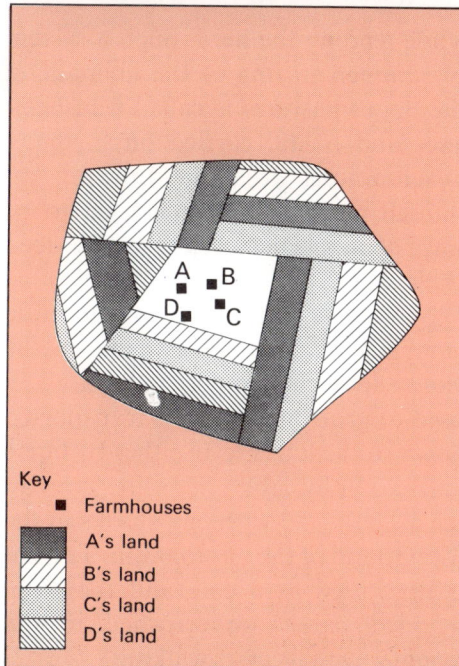

Key
■ Farmhouses
▨ A's land
▨ B's land
▨ C's land
▨ D's land

Fig. 3.12 Diagram of fragmented farms

Land use in the Austrian Tyrol

Fig. 3.13 shows the village of Mayr-hofen in the Ziller valley in the Austrian Tyrol, not far from the Italian border.

10 (a) Make a list of the types of land use you can see in the picture.
    (b) Put a piece of tracing paper over the photograph and draw in the outlines of the hills and the zones of land use which you can see. Label these on the tracing, using your list as a check.
11 Look at the map extract of Mayr-hofen at the end of the book. Do the villages tend to be found in the bottom of the valley, towards the edge of the valley, or on the slopes of the valley? Why do you think this is?

The photograph was taken in summer when only the tops of the highest mountains are covered in snow. In the winter snow covers the entire area shown in the picture and it stays for far longer on the high valley slopes, where it is too cold for trees to grow.

The wooded slopes shown in the picture are too steep and the soils are too thin for farming. As a result there is a shortage of good land for crops and pasture for the animals. The farmers in the area need to make as much use of the available land as they can. In the short summer, when the high pastures or 'alps' are not covered in snow, the farmers used to lead their herds of cattle and flocks of sheep up the steep paths of the mountainside to let them graze on the grass of the upper slopes. The little hut on the top of the slope is where they used to live in the summer

Fig. 3.13 The countryside around Mayrhofen in the Austrian Tyrol

while tending the herd. Such a system of summer grazing of the animals on the upper pastures is called **transhumance** and is still carried on in many mountainous areas in Europe, although much less than it used to be since some farmers prefer to stall-feed their cattle.

Nowadays on many farms the cattle generally remain in the fields on the valley floor. The upper slopes are still used to grow hay which is transported down to the lower level either by horse and cart or by cable goods lift. You can see a small field with hay-stooks in the foreground of the photograph. The hut is now used as a café and the steep wooded paths are crowded in the summer with tourists walking.

12 Look at the map extract. The alp or high upland pasture is labelled 'alpe'. Make a list of the names of the alpe and give an approximate grid reference for each.
13 What percentage of the map extract do you think is covered by forest? Does it occupy hill tops, valley sides, or the valley floor?

46

Fig. 3.14 Farm consolidation or remembrement in the regions of France

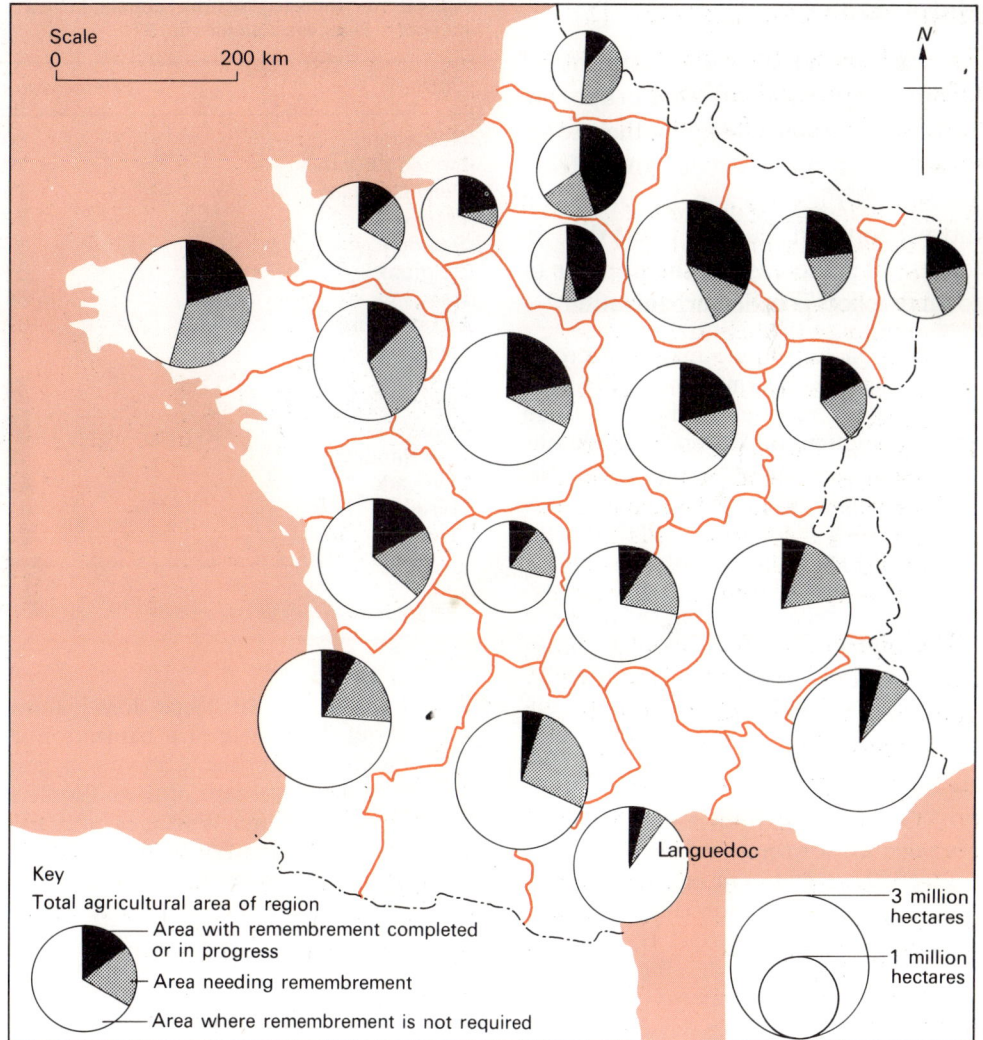

Workback

14   (a) Explain in your own words the difference between monoculture and diversified farming.

  *(b) If growing a variety of crops on a well laid out farm is such an improvement, why do you think it is difficult to get farmers whose families have grown vines for hundreds of years to make the change?

15   Look at Fig. 3.14. **Remembrement** is the French word for farm consolidation.

  (a) In which parts of France has the greatest amount of remembrement taken place? Use an atlas to help you.

  (b) Which parts of France have the greatest areas which still need farm consolidation?

  (c) How does the progress of remembrement in Languedoc compare with the rest of the country?

Summary

In this chapter we have looked at the ways in which farming methods have changed. In Denmark farmers have always been able to change their ways to keep up with the times. In southern France they have kept on with old-fashioned methods until very recently when the problem became so great that the government had to deal with it. In the Alpine areas the physical conditions in the high mountains strongly affect the farming life.

47

4 Land use in towns

Urbanization

Having looked at some patterns of farming and rural life in Europe, we need now to concentrate on the people who live in towns. As you can see from a glance at Figs. 4.1 and 4.2, more and more people in Europe today live in towns. This increase in the number of town dwellers is called **urbanization**.

1   (a) On an outline map of Europe, using the information in Fig. 4.2, draw a map entitled 'The urban population of Europe'. Shade the countries on the map using the following key:
less than 50 per cent in a light colour
50–69 per cent in a medium colour
70 per cent and over in a dark colour.
(b) Is it true to say that the further a country is away from the United Kingdom, the less it is 'urbanized'?
(c) How does the pattern of urbanization compare with the pattern of population density in Fig. 1.15 on page 23?

2   On your map draw a line round the countries with an urban population of 70 per cent or more. Look back at Fig. 2.16 which shows the intensity of agriculture in Europe. Is there any similarity between the patterns shown on the two maps?

Fig. 4.2 The percentage of urban population in a number of European countries in 1971

Country	Percentage
Netherlands	80
United Kingdom	77
West Germany	70
France	70
Sweden	67
Belgium	67
Italy	64
Luxembourg	62
Switzerland	59
Austria	51
Finland	51
Spain	51
Irish Republic	49
Denmark	45
Norway	43
Portugal	24

*3   Look at Fig. 4.1. What does it show about the growth of urbanization in the three countries? Can you suggest why the percentage of town dwellers in the U.K. and West Germany has gone down between 1950 and 1971?

4   Would you prefer to live in the town or in the country? Make a list of the advantages and disadvantages of town life. Do most of your class agree or disagree with you?

Reasons for urban growth

The growth of towns and cities can be shown in a simple diagram as in Fig. 4.3.

Stage 1

During stage 1 most people lived in small villages and worked on the land. Transport was slow and limited. The villages were largely self-supporting, growing their own food and with local craftsmen carrying out such industries as weaving. These were on a small scale in their own homes and became known as cottage industries. Small towns provided local centres for trade and entertainment on weekly market days, or for defence in times of danger.

Stage 2

The mid-eighteenth century in Britain saw the beginning of the Industrial Revolution, which later spread to the rest of Europe. By the second half of the nineteenth century, Belgium, Germany, and France were all major industrial countries. The new industrial towns grew up on the coalfields in these countries.

The development of machinery, for example power looms for weaving, made large-scale production possible. At the same time, the growth of the railways enabled manufacturers to sell their goods further away. Large-scale production became highly profitable, and factories were built.

Meanwhile, new methods of farming

Fig. 4.1 The percentage of the population living in towns since 1800

Country	1800	1850	1900	1950	1971
France	23	30	41	51	70
West Germany	21	30	56	71	70
United Kingdom	33	50	70	80	77

Fig. 4.3 Diagram of urban growth

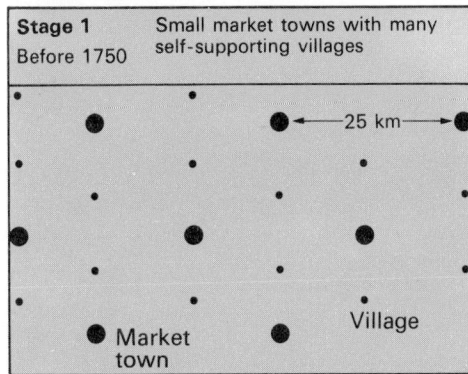

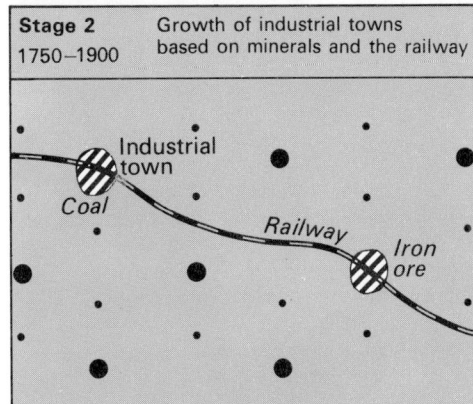

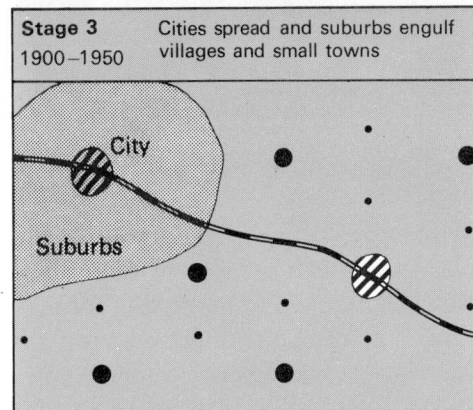

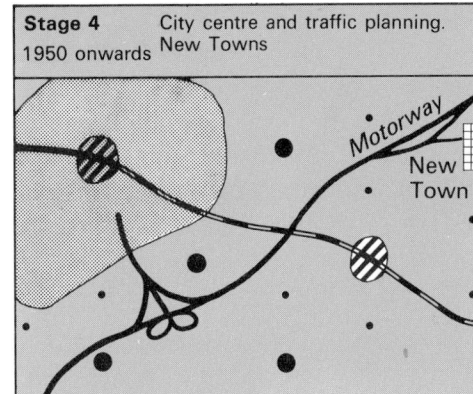

Stage 1
Before 1750

Small market towns with many self-supporting villages

←— 25 km —→

Market town

Village

Stage 2
1750–1900

Growth of industrial towns based on minerals and the railway

Industrial town

Coal

Railway

Iron ore

Stage 3
1900–1950

Cities spread and suburbs engulf villages and small towns

City

Suburbs

Stage 4
1950 onwards

City centre and traffic planning. New Towns

Motorway

New Town

a

b

c

d

49

and the use of machinery on the land made agriculture more efficient. Fewer farm workers were needed, so people had to look for work in the factories. Towns grew up around the factories and mines. But the towns could not grow fast enough to cope with the inrush of people. As a result of this:

(a) Existing houses became over-crowded and unhealthy slums.

(b) Rows of densely packed, cheap houses were put up, which also became overcrowded.

Conditions in the overcrowded towns were made still more unhealthy because there was no pure water supply, no mains drainage, and no organized collection of rubbish. The factories were powered by coal, and houses were heated by coal. This produced smoke which polluted the air and laid thick layers of dirt on the buildings.

Stage 3

This was an extension of stage 2. All through the nineteenth century the drift of people to the towns had continued and the towns grew larger and larger.

Then in the twentieth century the development of train services enabled richer people to move to new houses further away. They commuted to the town centre to work each day. This growth of suburbs around large towns swallowed up previously separate villages and smaller towns to form vast built-up areas.

Some efforts were made during this time to clear the worst slums, and conditions slowly improved.

*5   Draw a three-stage diagram to summarize the changes in people's lives in stages 1, 2, and 3, beginning:

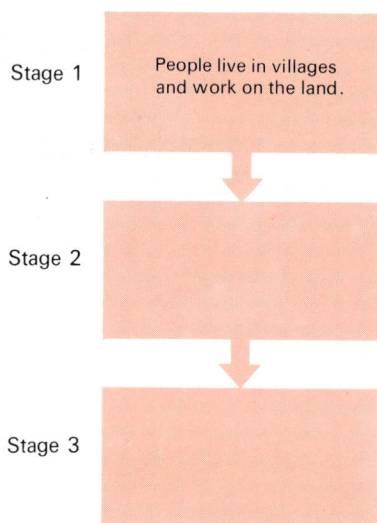

Stage 1 — People live in villages and work on the land.

Stage 2

Stage 3

Stage 4

The flow of commuters which began during stage 3 has resulted today in congestion in old city centres in the daytime. At night these same city centres are empty and deserted. In some parts of Europe a fourth stage has begun, a stage of re-planning and designing city centres, building new towns, and dealing with traffic problems.

The patterns of land use in European towns today are the combined result of

Fig. 4.4 The medieval walled town of Rothenburg-auf-der-Tauber

these stages of growth. Sometimes the older parts of towns have been completely destroyed to make way for new development. Sometimes new growth has just been added on. Some smaller market towns did not grow at all, and have remained almost untouched by stages 2, 3, and 4 (Fig. 4.4). Perhaps they were not in the right place to be on a rail route, or they did not have nearby deposits of important minerals like coal or iron ore to help the growth of industry.

6   Complete your diagram from Exercise 5 by adding a fourth stage.

Fig. 4.5 The site on which Evry New Town has developed: the main road to the left is the A6, marked in Fig. 4.8

The pattern of land values in Evry New Town

On the land shown in the photograph in Fig. 4.5, the French Government is building a new town at Evry, outside Paris. It is one of several new towns shown on the map in Fig. 4.6.

The area for development is shown in Fig. 4.7. Imagine that the French Government has offered this land for sale by auction to development companies who can choose to build either factories or houses in each square kilometre of land they buy. We will see what pattern of land use emerges for the new town.

7 The class should divide into development companies, each with four members. Each company has 1 000 000 francs to spend on buying land in the auction. The land will be sold in lots of 1 square kilometre. These squares are numbered on Fig. 4.7. The minimum increase at a time for each bid is 10 000 francs.

Each of the numbered squares

Fig. 4.6 New towns around Paris

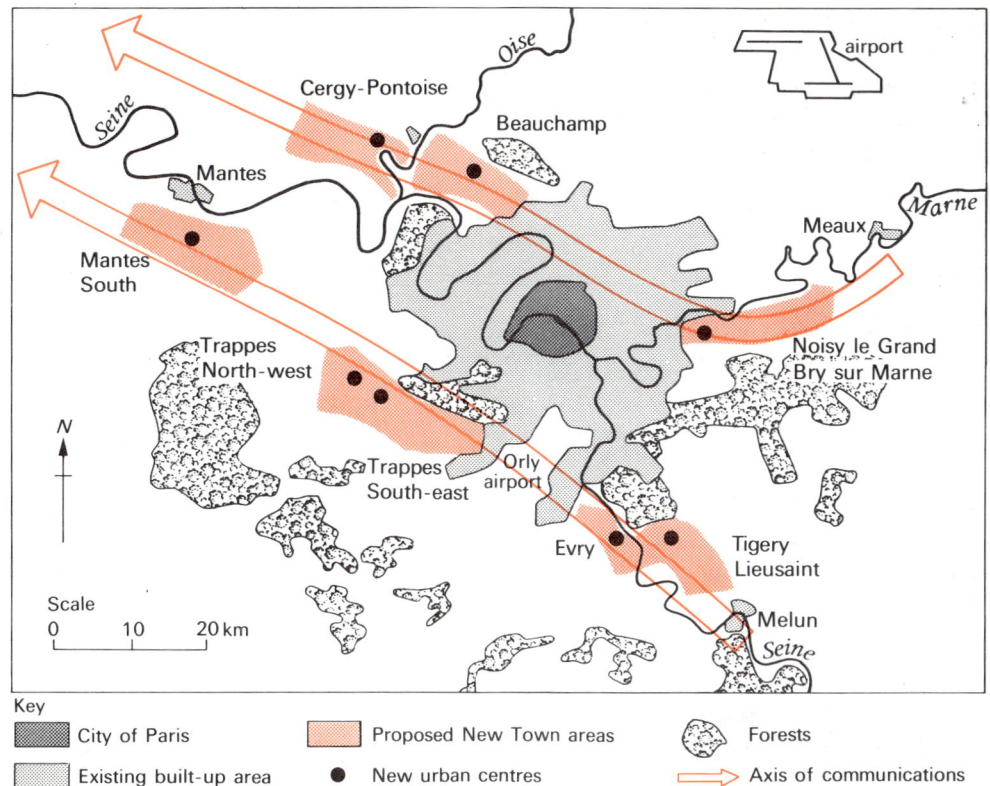

Key

■ City of Paris

▨ Existing built-up area

▦ Proposed New Town areas

● New urban centres

🗿 Forests

⇨ Axis of communications

51

counts as a whole square, regardless of whether it is already partly built up or contains some countryside. Some squares will turn out to be of a higher value and more profitable for development than others.

Each development company should have:

(i) A bidder.

(ii) A company cartographer who will record on a copy of Fig. 4.7 the price each square reaches.

(iii) A company accountant who will work out how much money the company has left after each purchase.

(iv) A financial adviser who will work out how much money each of the other companies has left after each purchase.

As in all auction rooms there must be silence while bidding is in progress, but between each sale of a square of land, the auctioneer will allow a brief period for members of the company to consult.

8 When the auction is over, look very carefully at the map your company cartographer has drawn.

(a) On a copy of Fig. 4.7 shade in each square sold according to the following key:

over 300 000 francs: black or a dark colour

100 000–300 000 francs: red or a medium colour

less than 100 000 francs: yellow or a light colour

(b) Can you see any pattern in these prices? For example, do prices tend to rise near the centre, and do squares with road junctions tend to fetch a higher price?

(c) Write a brief note describing the pattern in the company minutes, and attempt to explain why there should be this pattern in the price of land.

Fig. 4.7 The Evry New Town auction

Fig. 4.8 The centre of Evry New Town

Land use in Evry

9 The development companies must now choose between housing and industry for each of their squares. Housing should not be placed in the same square as industry, because although nearness to work is important, being too close can lower the quality of housing because of noise and traffic.

The company's profits will depend on the income they can make from their chosen land use. This is worked out as follows:

(a) *Factory squares*: a T-junction in the square counts as 3. A cross-roads counts as 4. Multiply the total for each square by 1 000 000 francs to find the profit. Why do you think cross-roads and T-junctions increase the value of factory squares?

(b) *Housing squares*: What is the distance in whole kilometres from each of your housing squares to the nearest factory square (each square represents 1 km²)? Divide 5 000 000 francs by the number of kilometres distance.

10 (a) When the land use has been chosen for each square, the companies should fill in their choices on a large display copy of Fig. 4.7.

(b) Each company should add the profit from its squares to the money it has left over from the auction. The company with the largest total will be the winner.

Fig. 4.8 shows a larger-scale plan of the centre of Evry as it has been developed. The black area in the centre of this plan is the area marked with a large red dot on Fig. 4.7. Notice that the shopping centre is surrounded by housing and office areas which radiate from it.

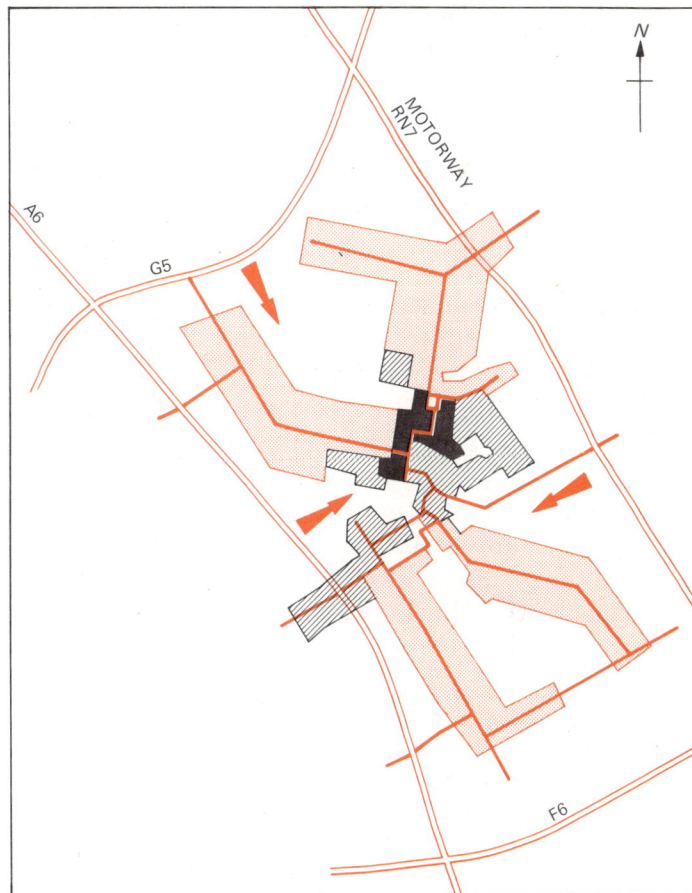

Fig. 4.9 Part of Evry showing housing and newly landscaped open space

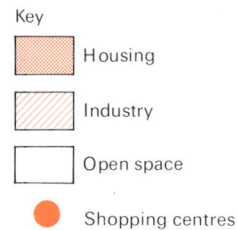

The auction has shown how:

(i) land values are forced up when competition is fierce.

(ii) the need to be profitable can affect the use to which land is put.

These two factors are important in the production of land-use patterns in towns but they are not the only ones. In the case of Evry, the land-use pattern of the actual town (shown in Fig. 4.10) was planned beforehand so that it included areas of open space to make the town more attractive as a place to live.

Open space in towns is unprofitable and unless it is planned from the start in new towns, or protected where it survives in old towns, it would disappear due to business pressure.

11 Compare your land-use map with the one shown for the real Evry in Fig. 4.10. Bearing in mind that your choices were made with the one intention of making the biggest profit for the company, why should the real land-use map not be exactly the same as yours?

12 In what ways is Evry similar to the English New Town of Hemel Hempstead studied in Book 1 with respect to:
(a) The position of shops and offices?
(b) The location of industry?
(c) The position of housing?
(d) The provision of parks and open spaces?

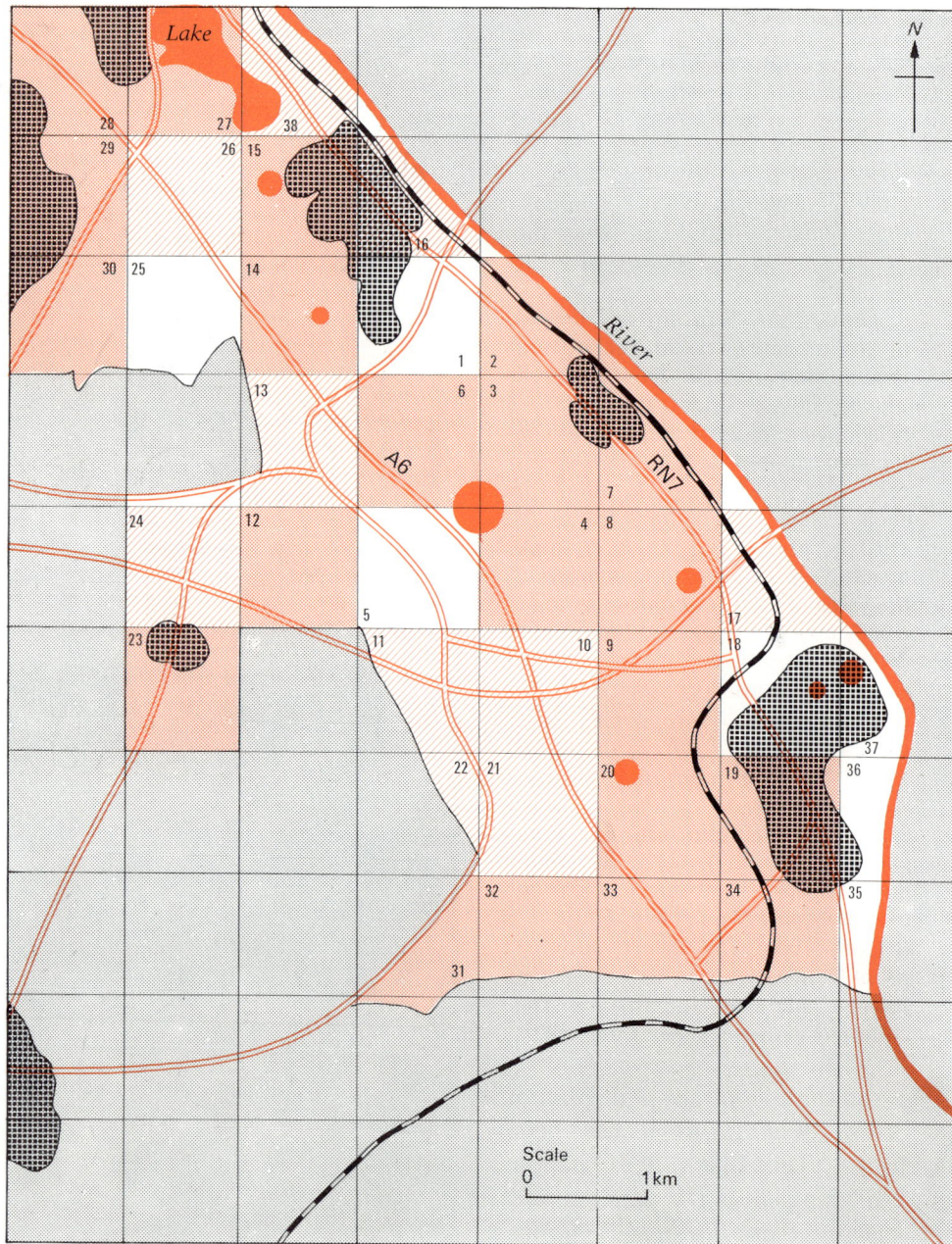

Fig. 4.10 Evry—the actual pattern of land use

Patterns of urban land use

Some people say that competition for land in towns is a matter of businesses trying to get a site at the centre. The centre is seen as the most important part of the town. It is the place most people can get to, and where the most important routes meet.

There is not room for everyone in the middle, so the price of central land is forced up. Only those types of business which can make a lot of money in a small space, that is by having multi-storey buildings like shops and offices, can afford the prices. The rest must find sites further away. This will result in a land-use pattern of rings around the town centre or **central business district** (C.B.D.). See Fig. 4.12a.

On the other hand, it is said that businesses will compete for sites along main routes as well as in the centre, because their positions are also accessible. If this is the case then the land-use pattern would be more like a star with its rays stretching out along the main routes (see Fig. 4.12b) from the centre which still has the main area of shops and offices.

Fig. 4.11 The central business district of Rotterdam

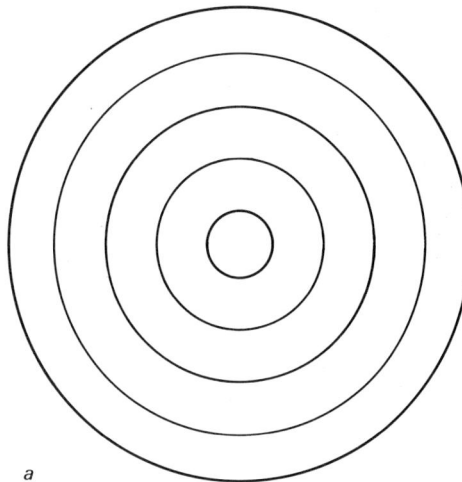

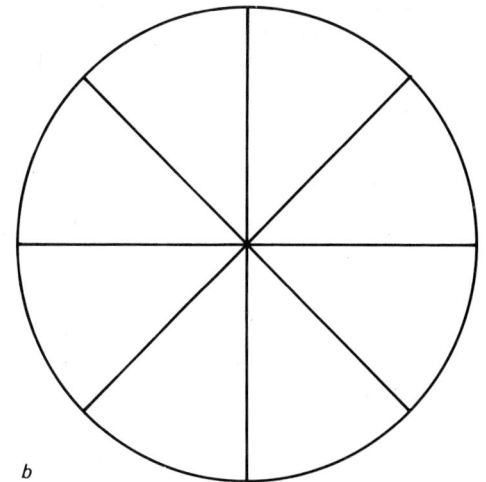

a   b

Fig. 4.12 Patterns of land use in the city

Fig. 4.13 Land-use pattern of Paris

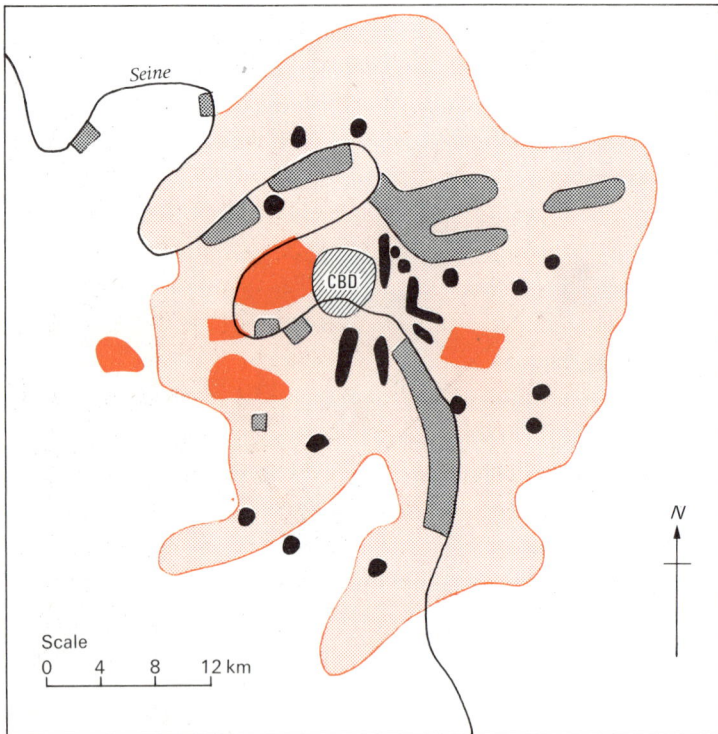

Fig. 4.14 Land-use pattern of Hamburg

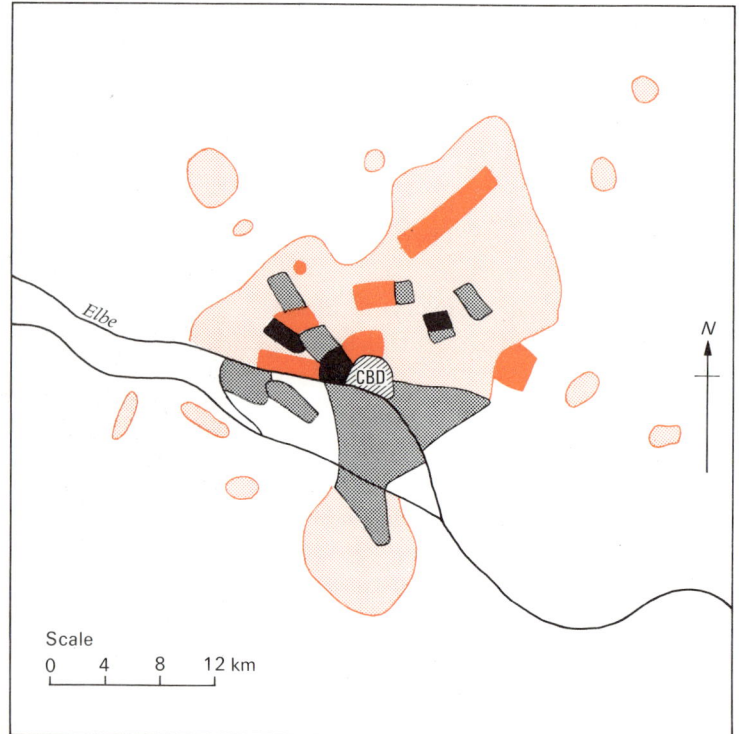

13 Look at the land-use maps in Figs. 4.13 and 4.14 and the key below.

(a) Describe the location of industry on each map; does it appear to be influenced at all by the presence of the rivers?

(b) How close to the centre of Paris are the parklands? What area do they cover? Where are the parks of Hamburg?

*14 (a) Trace the two shapes shown in Fig. 4.12 and lay them over the map in Fig. 4.14 in order to help you decide whether Hamburg has a sector or ring-like pattern. This has already been done for Paris in Fig. 4.15 to give you the idea.

(b) For Hamburg, draw a circle and try to divide it up into sectors and rings to show its simplified land-use pattern.

Key

Industry

Shops

Parks

Houses

Scale
0   4   8 km

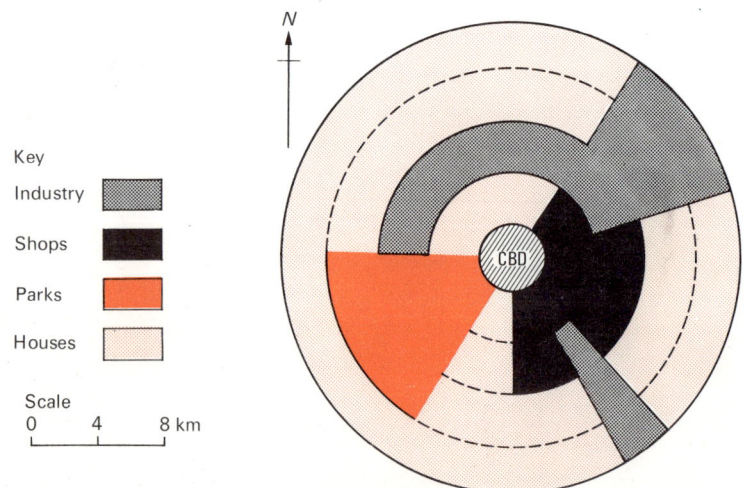

Fig. 4.15 Simplified land-use zones of Paris and key for Figs. 4.13 and 4.14

Fig. 4.16a Sussex Square, Broad Marsh, Nottingham—now demolished

Workback

15 Figs. 4.16a and b show the harsh living conditions in towns in the nineteenth century.
(a) How many homes have been built in the area shown.
(b) How is the courtyard entered?
(c) How many houses share each lavatory?
(d) Are there any gardens?
(e) What do you notice about the position of the houses?
(f) Describe what problems living in the courtyard might present for a family of five. Use Fig. 4.16a to guide your imagination.
(g) Which stage of the diagram of urban growth do you think this exercise is about?

16 (a) Why are tall office blocks found in the centre of most large cities?
(b) Where in towns are you likely to find long-established industries?
(c) Why is new industry often on estates near main roads to the city?
(d) Why are large housing estates not usually near the C.B.D.?

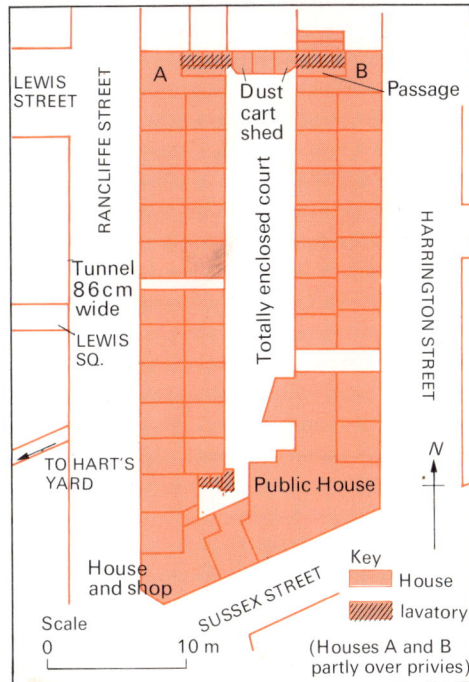

Fig. 4.16b Plan of Sussex Square built in the middle years of the nineteenth century

Summary

In the middle ages small towns grew up as centres of trade and for defence. With the rapid growth of industry in the nineteenth and early twentieth century came the massive increase in the numbers of city dwellers which is still going on in Europe today.

As towns have grown, competition for land within them has forced land prices to rise in the centre and to a lesser extent in the suburbs where major route junctions occur.

In studying the land-use patterns that have arisen you have seen that similar patterns are to be found in different cities throughout Europe.

5 Inside three conurbations

As the towns of Europe have grown, some have become so big that they have swallowed up surrounding smaller towns. Other towns which were quite close to each other have joined together to make huge urban areas. Very large cities like these are called **conurbations**. This chapter looks at three European conurbations which are very different in some ways but which also have similarities.

The growth of Paris

Paris, the capital city and centre of government is by far the most important city in France. No other city can approach it. With a population of over 8 million, the conurbation is eight times larger than its nearest rivals, Lyon and Marseille. It employs nearly a quarter of all French industrial workers, and a third of those working in services and administration. It is the country's major entertainment centre and the biggest universities are also there. If you add to all this the city's rich culture and its international tourist appeal, it is hardly surprising to find that Paris is a severely congested city with a very high population density.

The way Paris has grown since the twelfth century has been a major reason for the very high density of its population. From the twelfth to the nineteenth century, a series of defensive walls was built round the city at different stages of its growth. The first walls (A on Fig. 5.1) enclosed a small area around the islands in the River Seine. The islands were the religious

Fig. 5.1 The growth of the City of Paris

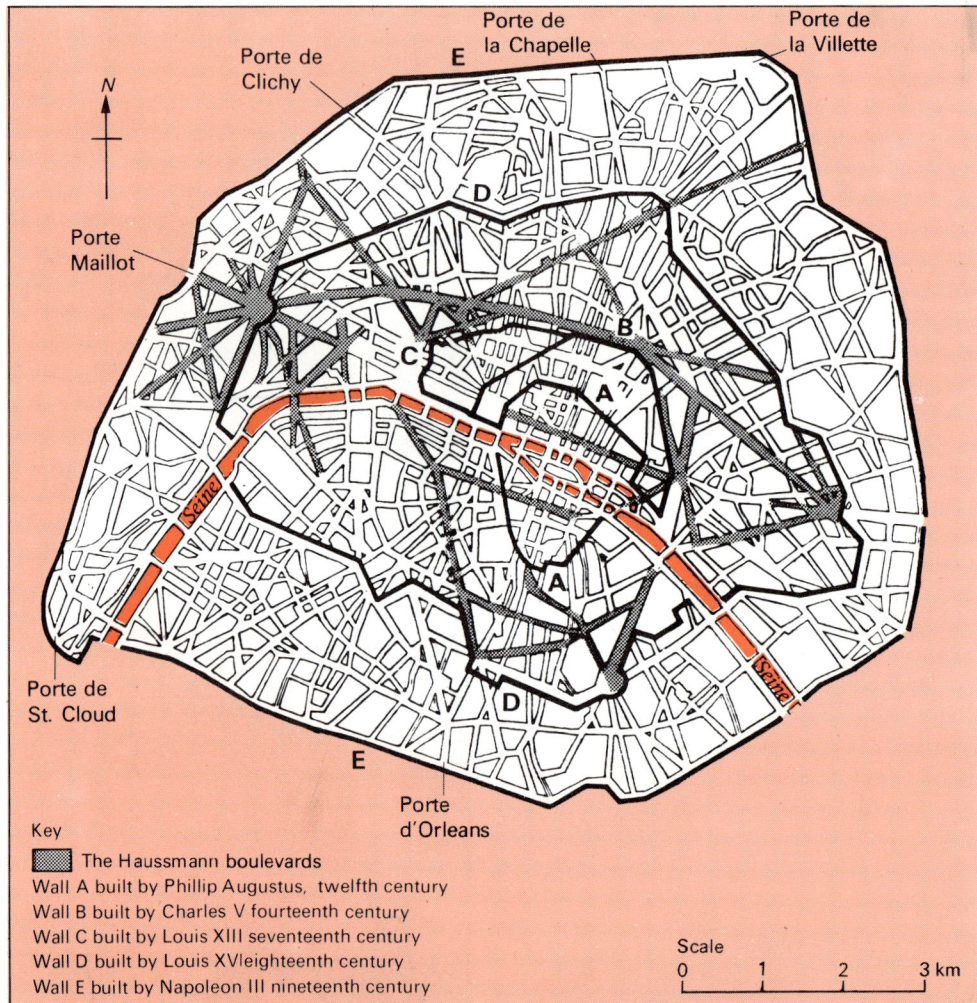

Key
▨ The Haussmann boulevards
Wall A built by Phillip Augustus, twelfth century
Wall B built by Charles V fourteenth century
Wall C built by Louis XIII seventeenth century
Wall D built by Louis XVI eighteenth century
Wall E built by Napoleon III nineteenth century

and administrative heart of the settlement. The south bank had a university and the north bank was the business area. By 1370 the city had spread outside these early walls especially to the north. New walls were built using an old meander of the Seine as a moat (B on Fig. 5.1). Again in 1631 new walls were needed to the west to guard a new royal palace (C on Fig. 5.1).

Louis XIV had the walls pulled down, and replaced by wide avenues which he called *grands boulevards*. He forbade anyone to build beyond the area marked by these boulevards. But his order was not effective; people continued to build outside the limits, in order to be close to the capital. By the eighteenth century Louis XVI had to construct new walls (D on Fig. 5.1).

Fig. 5.2 Paris at the beginning of the seventeenth century

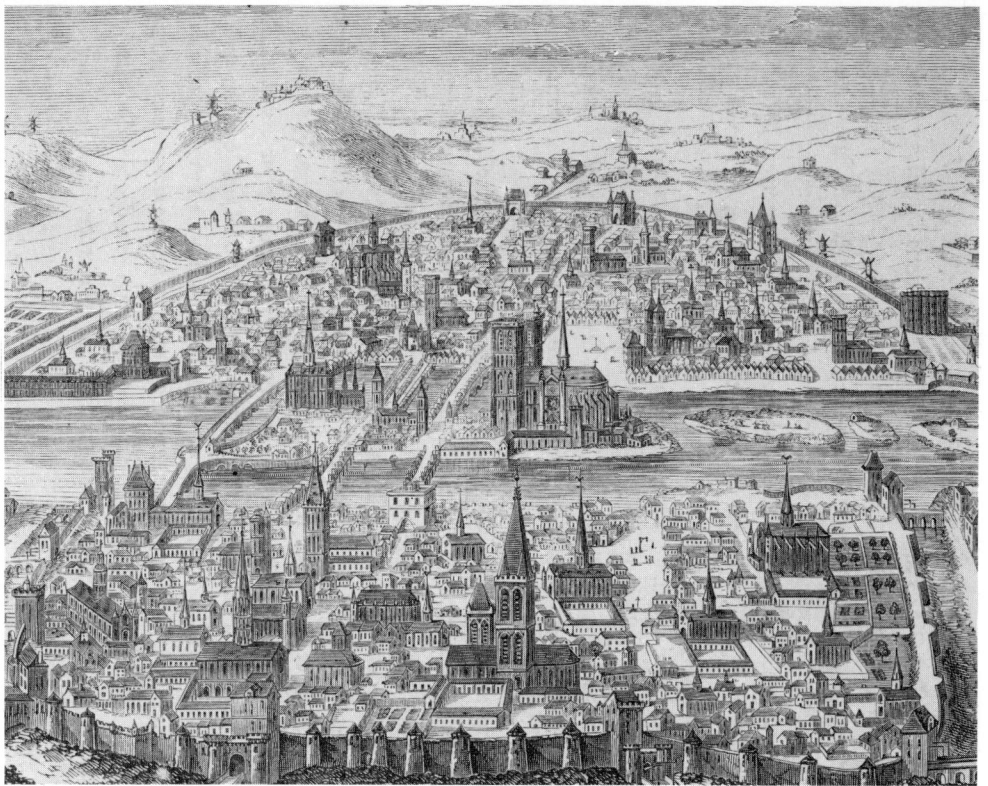

This repeated enclosing of the city squeezed most people inside the walls and created a high density of population. Each time the city became overcrowded, people moved outside the limits to live. After a while these people and their homes became so much part of the city that it became necessary to rebuild the walls further out. These in their turn encouraged overcrowding of people over a bigger area.

The last time this happened was in the middle of the nineteenth century under Napoleon III. His clerk of works, Baron Haussmann, was made responsible for improving and modernizing the city. Old city walls and large areas of housing were pulled down and a system of wide boulevards was built to open up the city (Fig. 5.3). The last walls to be built around Paris were put up in 1841–5, and lasted until the 1920s. Once again overcrowding took place inside them, and people spread outside into suburbs, over an ever increasing area.

The position of these walls (E on Fig. 5.1) still marks the boundary of the present City of Paris, the focus of the conurbation. When the Metro, the Paris underground railway system, was first built at the end of the nineteenth century the lines stopped at the city boundary, and the original terminal stations such as Porte de Clichy and Porte de la Villette still carry the names of the gates of Paris.

Fig. 5.3 Boulevard Haussmann looking west

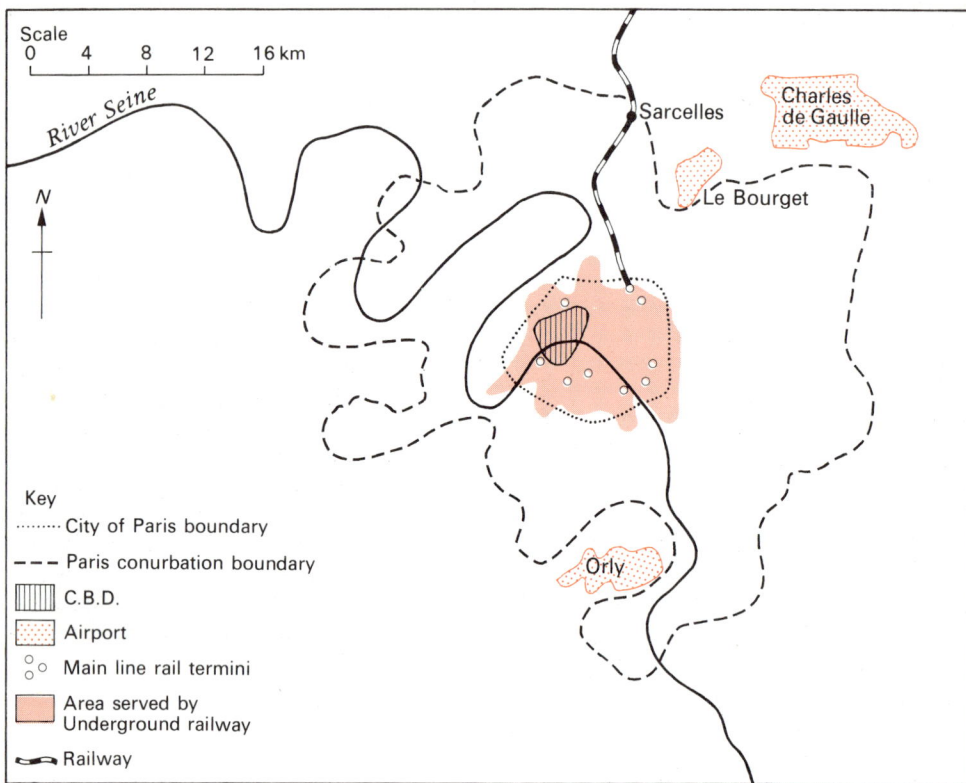

Fig. 5.4 The Paris conurbation

Fig. 5.5 The Greater London conurbation

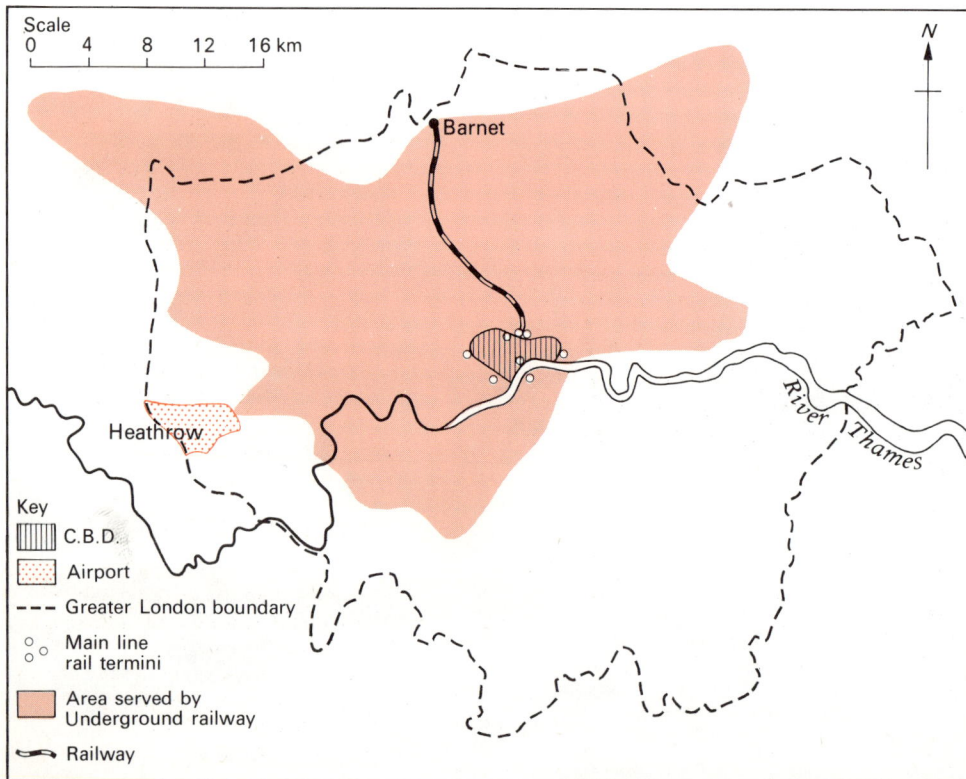

Transport in Paris

The City of Paris has remained congested. It is one of the most densely populated areas in Europe, and is also the place where over one-third of the inhabitants of the conurbation work, even if they live in the suburbs. All these people must somehow get to work.

The public transport routes which have grown up make it much more attractive to live in or near the City rather than to try to commute from the suburbs.

1   Look at the maps in Figs. 5.4 and 5.5.
    (a) What is the most obvious difference between the underground railways of Paris and London as shown on the maps?
    (b) If you lived in Sarcelles in Fig. 5.4 and worked in the C.B.D. of Paris, how would you get to work—by road, by rail, or by Metro?
    (c) If you lived in Barnet in Fig. 5.5 and worked in the C.B.D. of London, how would you get to work—by road, rail, or Underground.

The huge uncontrolled growth of the suburbs has not been followed by a similar growth in the public transport system. More and more people have taken to commuting to the City by car (Fig. 5.8), and this in its turn has shown up the shortcomings of the great boulevards built by Haussmann.

2   Look at Fig. 5.6.
    (a) What advantages did the Haussmann boulevards have when they were first built?
    (b) What is the main disadvantage of a road network like this for the smooth flow of traffic today?

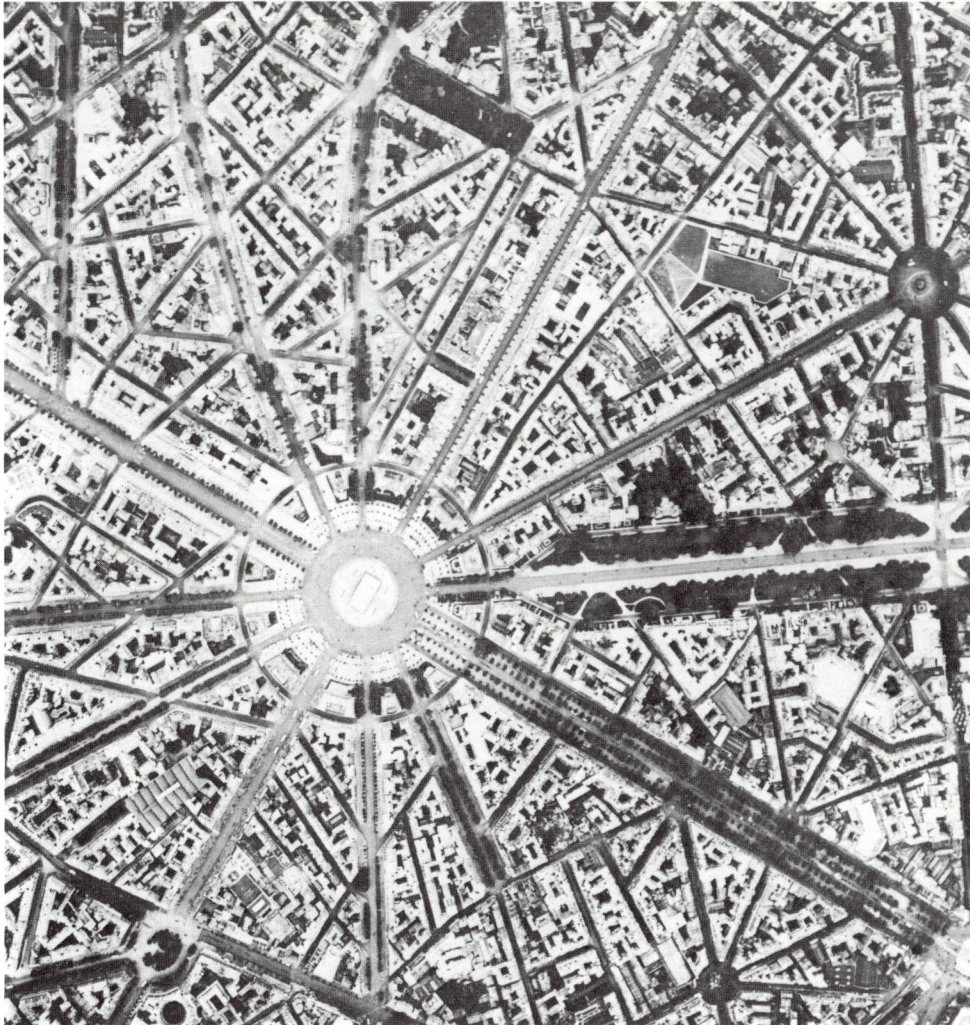

Fig. 5.6 Boulevards radiating from the Place de l'Etoile

3 Study Fig. 5.7.

(a) What do you think would be the benefits of each of the possible solutions to Paris's traffic problems?

(b) Do these solutions have any weaknesses?

(c) Which, if any, would you use in trying to overcome traffic problems in Paris? Your answer should be in the form of a sketch map of Paris.

*(d) Have you any other ideas apart from improvements in transport which might be useful?

Fig. 5.7 Transport in Paris

Problems

1 Metro only covers the City of Paris.
2 Rail routes end at the edge of the City.
3 Road pattern of boulevards focuses on nodes.
4 As suburbs grow, more people must commute.
5 People who both live and work in the suburbs also find getting to work difficult by public transport as routes all go towards the centre.

Far too many cars both in the City of Paris and using cross routes in the suburbs.

Possible solutions

1 Extend some Metro lines into the suburbs
2 Introduce railway express routes across the whole conurbation through the centre.
3 Build a fast ring road around the City of Paris with roads out to the suburbs.
4 Introduce double-decker buses.

Completed in 1973, a new ring motorway, the Boulevard Périphérique, now encircles the City of Paris (Fig. 5.9). This has made it easier to bypass the city but it has not helped those who wish to travel into the centre.

The Metro is being extended beyond the City into the suburbs. Some of these routes are shown on Fig. 5.10 to show how far they extend. A new railway line, the Regional Expressway, which is partly above and partly below ground has been built right across the City from one edge of the conurbation to the other (Fig. 5.10). This takes commuters quickly right to the C.B.D. without any need to change types of transport.

Traffic congestion is one of the most obvious signs of too much pressure on a city centre, and improving transport is very important. But other things can and are being done in Paris.

Fig. 5.8 Traffic in Place St. Michel seen from Notre Dame cathedral

Fig. 5.9 The Boulevard Périphérique near Porte de St. Cloud

Fig. 5.10 Planning in Paris

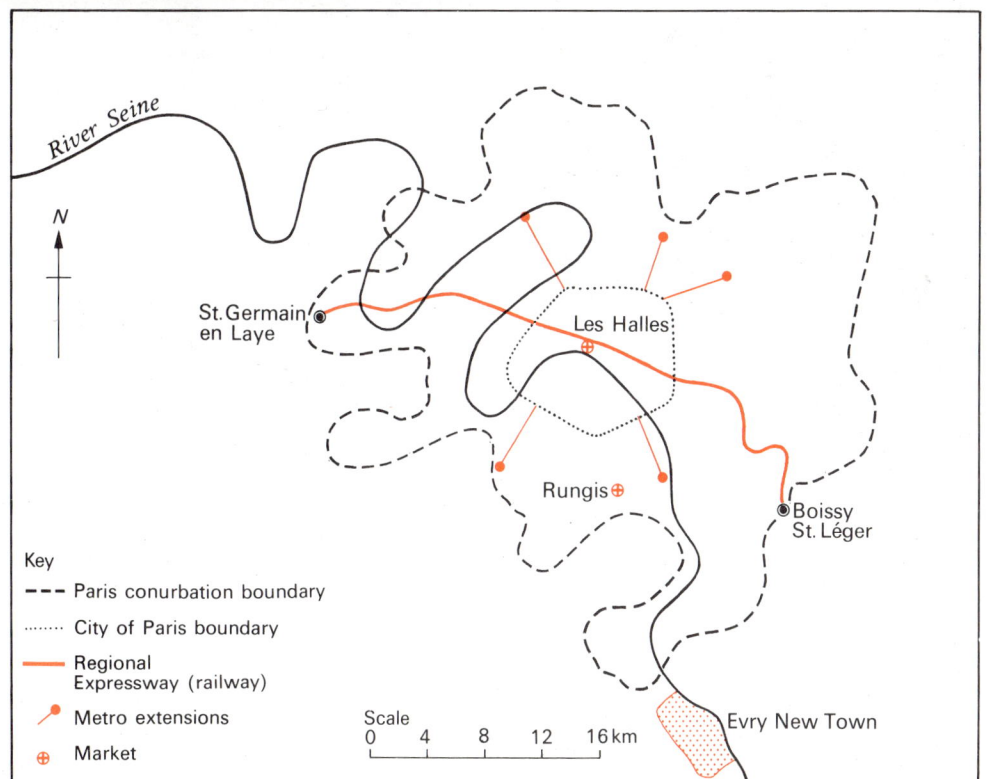

Key

- – – Paris conurbation boundary
- ········· City of Paris boundary
- ——— Regional Expressway (railway)
- Metro extensions
- ⊕ Market

Fig. 5.11 Construction work on the site of Les Halles

The planning of Paris

If you answered Exercise 3d you may have suggested ideas similar to these in this section. Planners are trying to make sure that new building in the suburbs and beyond takes place in certain areas which are provided with space for industry, good housing, schools and shops, and which have good routes into the City. New Towns like Evry, which we have already looked at in Chapter 4, are part of this kind of planning. Others can be seen in Fig. 4.6.

Also businesses and jobs are being moved out of the centre to new sites so that fewer people need to come into the centre to work. For instance, Les Halles, the fruit and vegetable market has been moved to Rungis (Fig. 5.10). The old site of Les Halles (Fig. 5.11) and the nearby Plateau Beaubourg site are being redeveloped for:

(i) A station and part of the new Regional Expressway line.

(ii) Road underpasses and junctions.

(iii) Landscaped open space.

(iv) The Pompidou arts centre (Fig. 5.12).

4   Describe the scene shown in Fig. 5.12. How many styles of building can you see? What are the main differences between them?

Fig. 5.12 The Pompidou Centre

Finally, some of the old areas of overcrowded houses in the City, like those of Le Marais (Fig. 5.13) are being restored, partly to preserve historic areas, and partly to provide modern homes in less crowded conditions (Fig. 5.14).

5 Describe the scene in Fig. 5.13 as vividly as you can. In what ways do you think Fig. 5.14 is an improvement?

Fig. 5.13 (left) Houses before restoration
Fig. 5.14 (below) After restoration

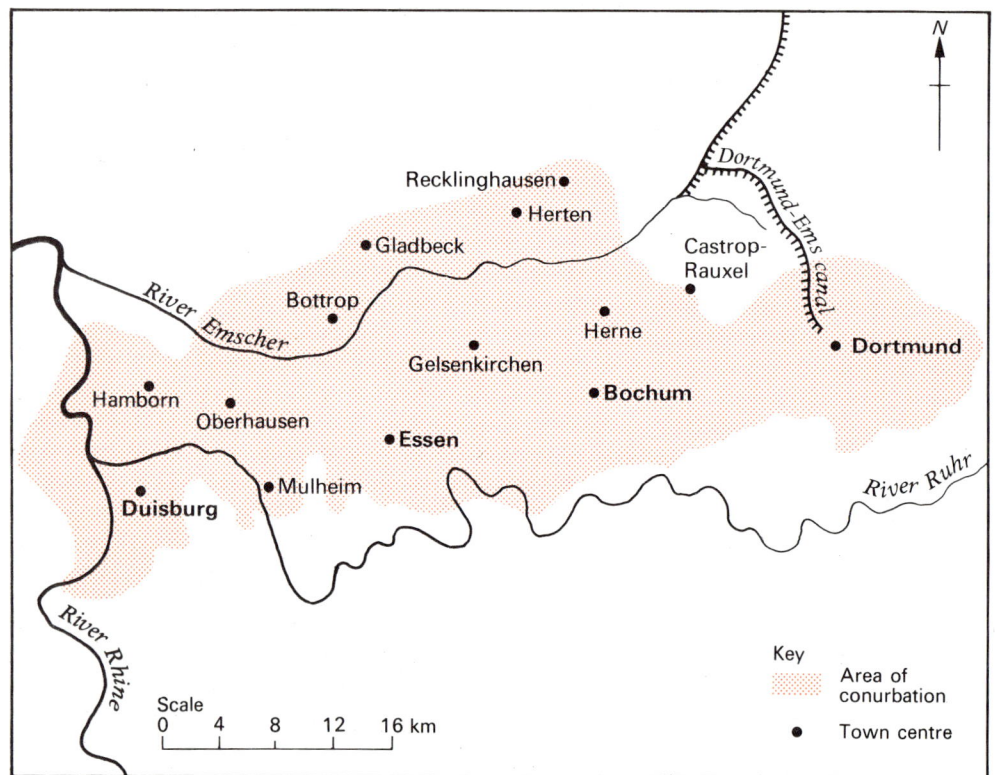

Fig. 5.15 The Ruhr conurbation

Fig. 5.16 Barges on the Dortmund–Ems canal

The Ruhr

Fig. 5.15 shows quite a different conurbation. People have been settling here for over a hundred years to find work in the coal mines and the iron and steel industry, which grew up on the large Ruhr coalfield.

As more and more people poured in to find work, a lot of cheap, badly built housing was put up for them. Canals were dug to link the factories to the navigable rivers. One of these is shown on the map in Fig. 5.15. They were the first means of transporting bulky heavy goods. After the canals came the railways and soon no place on the coalfield was further than 1 km from a line. The industrial towns grew until 'each town merged with the next, and there was no way of telling where the boundaries between Herne, Gelsenkirchen and Castrop-Rauxel actually ran. Along this broad strip known as the Ruhr, 70 km long and 40 km wide, lay eighteen large cities, so tightly wedged together that they appeared to be one great Ruhr metropolis.'

6   (a) Find Herne, Gelsenkirchen, and Castrop-Rauxel on Fig. 5.15.
(b) On an outline map of West Germany, mark the River Rhine, Duisburg, and Dortmund. Shade in the area of the Ruhr conurbation using Fig. 5.15 to help you.
(c) How is this type of conurbation different from Paris?

In the first half of the twentieth century the cities consisted largely of run-down industrial housing, like many British cities, but bombing during the Second World War left few buildings in the Ruhr standing. At this time the needs of industry changed. Improvements in technology meant that the amount of coal needed to make steel was reduced by two-thirds. The remaining coal seams were so thin and broken that they were very expensive to mine. Although coal is still mined, some industries have begun to use imported oil for power. The three hundred mines of a century ago have been reduced to about forty. The giant steel firms such as Krupp and Thyssen have lost money. The textile and metallurgical industries are also out-of-date. The prospects for the traditional industries of the Ruhr are not good. However, attempts are being made to improve the situation by introducing new industries making products such as plastics, chemicals, cars, and television sets. To improve living standards, much new housing is being built. There are strict laws to control air and water pollution, and the dumping of industrial waste. An ambitious plan to 'turn the Ruhr green' has been put into action by the Ruhr Planning Authority.

About 10 million people live in the Ruhr conurbation. In common with most Europeans few own their own houses, and most of them live in flats, so open spaces are very important. For years the big cities have laid out parks and gardens for older people who like peace and quiet. But young people need active pastimes like football, swimming, and dancing. For them the Ruhr Planning Authority is making a number of area parks in the most densely built-up areas along the River Emscher where coal is still mined.

7   Study the map in Fig. 5.17 carefully.
    (a) How many area parks are there to be?
    (b) How far apart are they?
    (c) What other kinds of open space are being planned?

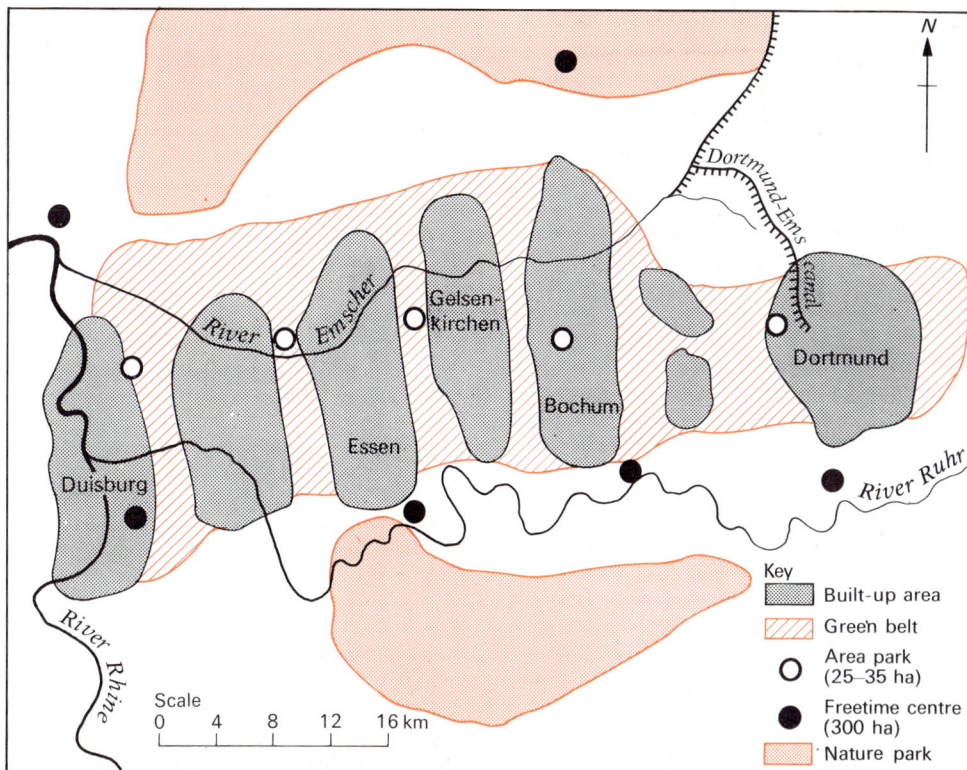

Fig. 5.17 Plans for recreation in the Ruhr

Fig. 5.18 Activities in an area park

| Activities | Top ten choices for | | | | Total |
	Families with children under 10 years of age	Teenagers	People 20 – 40 yrs	People over 40 yrs	
Outdoor swimming pool	9	2	6	6	23
Indoor swimming pool	10	3	7	9	29
Adventure playground	8	7			8
Indoor and outdoor ice rinks		7	10	10	27
Football pitches	7	7	1	1	16
Water playground	6				6
Zoo	0				0
Go-cart track		10	5	7	22
Cinema	2	6	4	2	14
Discotheque		9			9
Commercial area (fairground mini-golf etc.)	5	5	3	4	16
Multi-purpose building (gymnasium, sauna etc.)	4	4	9	5	22
Table tennis			3	3	7
Pony riding	3				3
Restaurant	1		8	8	16
Roller-skating rink		8			8

These area parks cost millions of deutschmarks each to create. A competition for the detailed planning and building of each park is held to find a design. Then the local people who will use it are consulted before the final building is done. The parks are intended to provide many different facilities, especially for those who want to stay all day.

Fig. 5.19 People enjoying the sun in Vonderort area park, Oberhausen

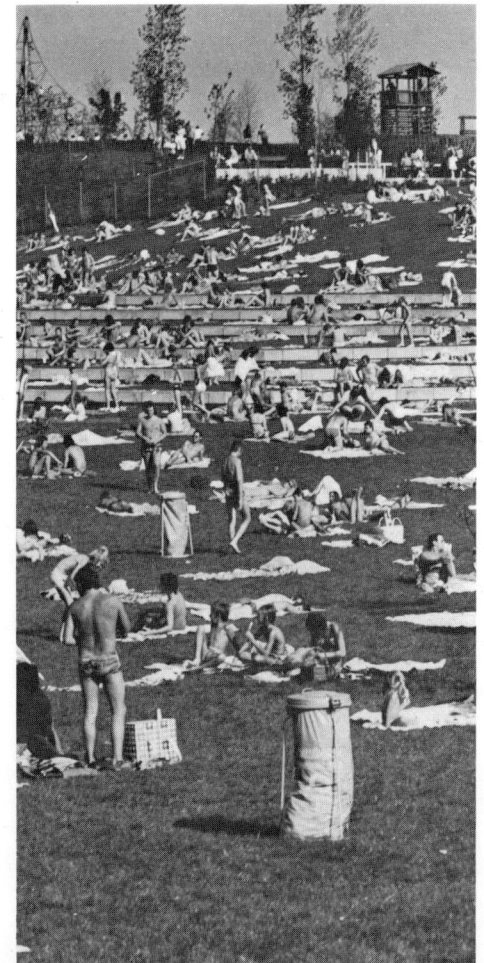

Fig. 5.20 Outline of Mattlerbusch area park

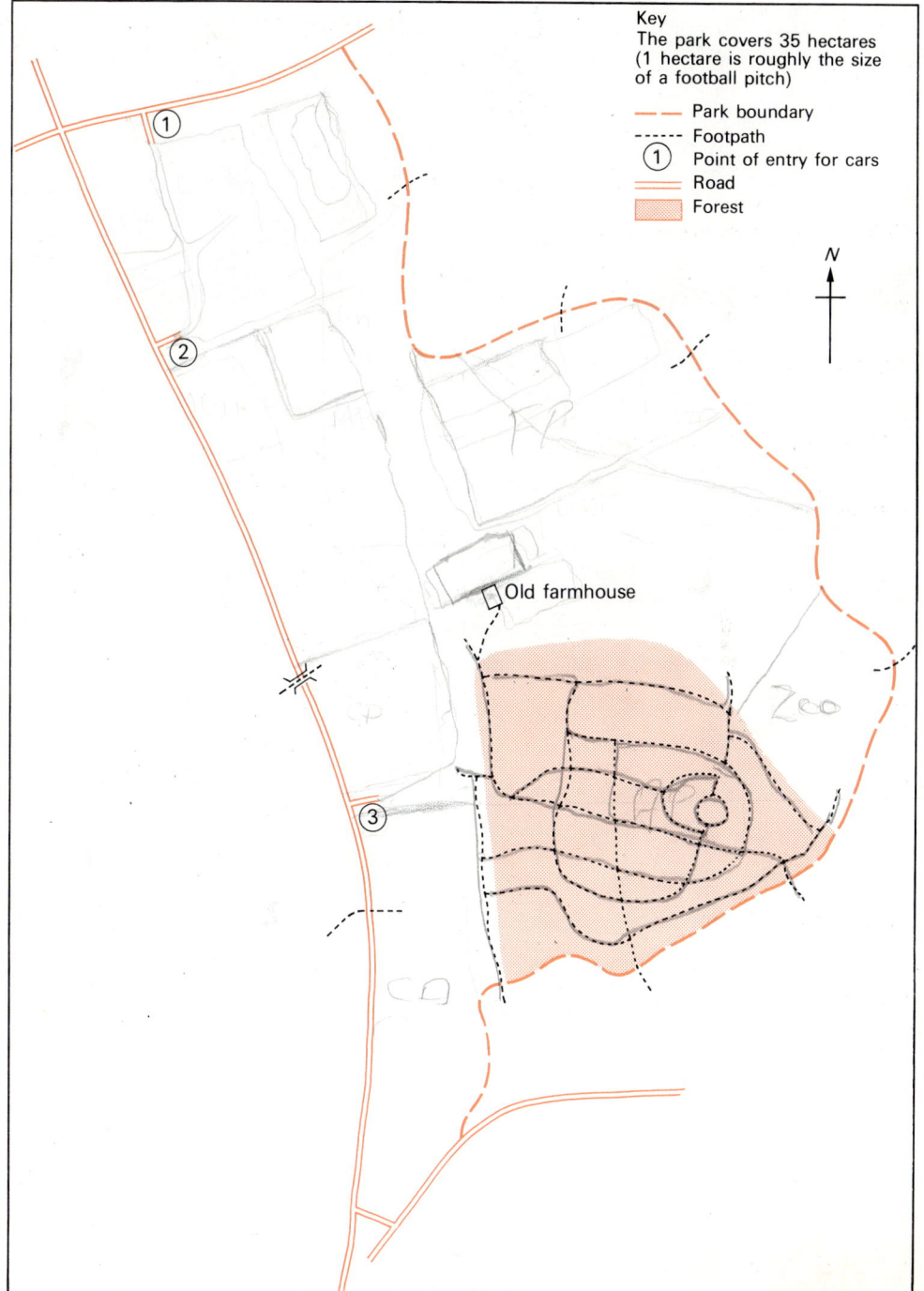

Key
The park covers 35 hectares
(1 hectare is roughly the size
of a football pitch)

– – – Park boundary
· · · · · Footpath
① Point of entry for cars
══ Road
▨ Forest

N

Old farmhouse

8 The table in Fig. 5.18 shows a list of some of the activities the people living around Duisburg want to see in their park at Mattlerbusch.

(a) Imagine you are part of a family with children under the age of ten. Pick out the ten most important activities from their point of view. On a copy of Fig. 5.18 fill in the column for the young family, giving 10 points to the most important activity, 9 for the next, and so on.

(b) Do the same thing for each of the other columns, trying to work out what each age group might be looking for.

(c) Add up the marks for each activity. Put this in the total column. How does your order of preference compare with other members of the class?

(d) Is your final order at all like that of the original list of activities, which has in fact been written in the order of preference of the people who actually live around the park?

As you can see from the outline of the park in Fig. 5.20, part of it is already covered by woodland crisscrossed with paths that will provide for those who wish simply to walk. It also shows points at which cars can enter, and a much larger number of entrances by footpath for pedestrians.

9 On a copy of Fig. 5.20 draw a design for the Mattlerbusch area park to include:

(i) Paths, roads, and car parks.

(ii) Those activities you consider to be most important from your answers to Exercise 8.

Fig. 5.21 Gysenberg area park at Herne

The area parks provide very important, although still quite small open areas in the heart of the conurbation. As can be seen from the photographs in Figs. 5.19 and 5.21, they are very heavily used.

Randstad Holland

In Paris all the usual capital city functions such as the home of government, the law courts, the main theatres and entertainment centres, and chief company headquarters are found within a few square kilometres. In Randstad Holland this is not the case. It is a conurbation made up of cities that are growing towards each other. Each has its own identity and character, and the capital city functions are spread among them. Amsterdam is the financial, commercial, and main entertainment centre. Rotterdam is the country's leading port and industrial centre. The government is in the Hague (Fig. 5.22).

Fig. 5.22 Government buildings in The Hague

Fig. 5.23 Population of six cities in Randstad Holland 1850–1963

10 (a) Fig. 5.23 is a graph showing the population of the Randstad cities from 1850 to 1963. If the cities continue to grow at the rate shown on the graph, what will be:

(i) The population for each city in the year 2000?

*(ii) The population of the six cities together in both 1980 and the year 2000?

(b) Estimate the number of grid squares covered by built-up area in Fig. 5.24. Then copy and complete the following statement:

In 1963 ...... million people lived in the cities of Randstad Holland, and the built-up area covered ...... square kilometres. If the growth of population continues as shown in the graph we would expect a population of ...... by the year 2000. If the amount of space taken per person was the same, the built-up area would then cover ...... square kilometres.

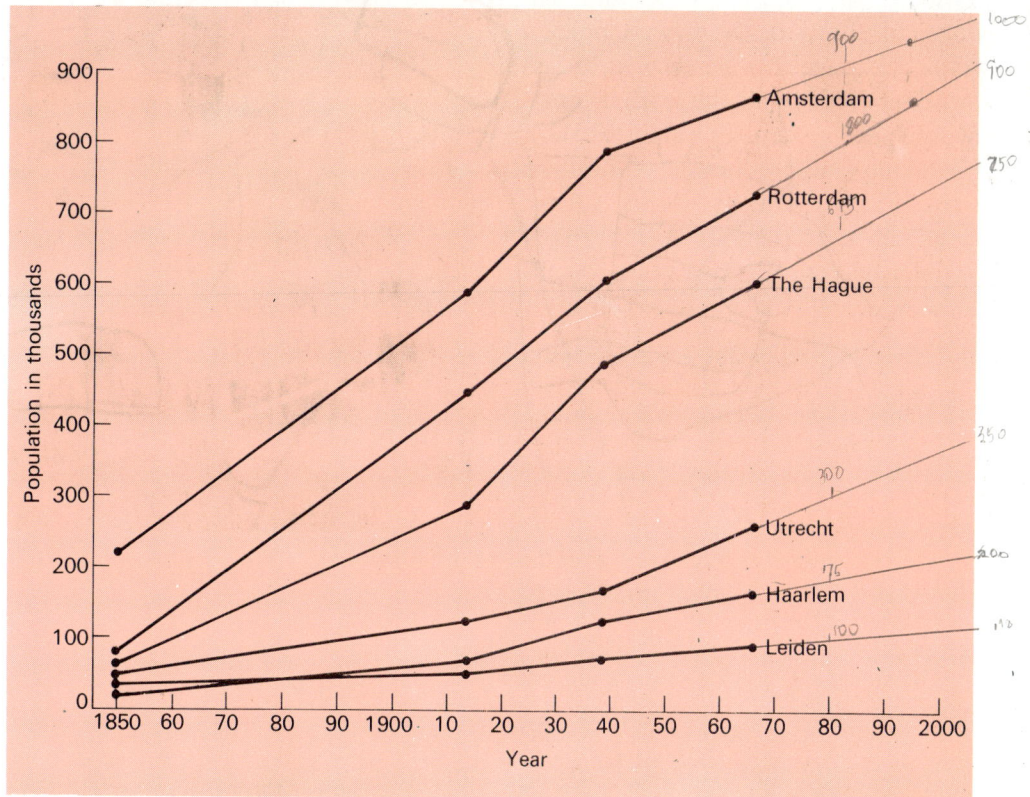

11 Suggest what disadvantages might result if the cities of Randstad were allowed to merge without control.

The large estimates of population increase foreseen in the 1960s created a problem for the planners. In the centre of Randstad is an area of very valuable agricultural land (Fig. 5.24 and 5.25) which was threatened by development.

To preserve this it was planned to expand other towns well away from the existing built-up area of Randstad. These were to act as independent centres with enough industry to keep journeys into the conurbation as few as possible. Such towns were Groningen, Arnhem, Nijmegen, Breda, and Tilburg. In addition, the newest polders (Fig. 2.2, page 27) were to have less farming land than the earlier ones. More space around Lelystad (Eastern Flevoland) and Almere (Southern Flevoland), the new polder towns, would be used to house the overspill population from the cities of northern Randstad.

12 Even if such plans were successful there would have to be some extension of the existing built-up areas. Imagine that you have the power to decide where this should take place.
(a) Trace the coastline and built-up area from Fig. 5.24.
(b) Keeping your tracing laid over the map shade each square according to which of the following groups it falls into:

Light green—land which should *not* be built on.

Darker green—land which is too far away from Randstad to be under threat of development.

Fig. 5.24 The area called Randstad Holland

Fig. 5.25 Intensive agriculture in the heart of Randstad Holland

Fig. 5.26 Growth of six of the Randstad cities (population in thousands)

	1971	1977
Amsterdam	820	738
Rotterdam	679	601
The Hague	538	471
Leiden	100	102
Utrecht	278	245
Haarlem	173	163

Light red—land which is suitable for the expansion of already existing towns.

Darker red—land which is suitable for building new towns or industrial areas.

(c) Write a few sentences to explain where the red squares are, and why you would allow building to go on in them rather than elsewhere.

13 (a) On a copy of Fig. 5.23 add the actual population figures for the years 1971 and 1977 from Fig. 5.26.

(b) How do these real figures compare with the ones you predicted in Exercise 10?

The fact that the population has not risen as expected has caused the Dutch planners to think again about their policy for Randstad. There have been worries that if development is discouraged and people move away, the cities would suffer socially and would lose their cultural life and their industrial strength. Also it was feared that too few good-sized areas of open land would remain in the rest of the country. The inner cities are already suffering from traffic congestion as people commute from suburbs in to the centres for work. Old houses in the inner cities are decaying, or becoming used for other purposes.

14 In the light of the actual changes in population would you wish to revise the position of the red squares on your map? Explain any changes you would like to make.

Fig. 5.27 The narrow old streets in the centre of The Hague are closed to traffic and have been turned into a series of shopping precincts

Workback

15 In designing your area park in Exercise 9, you were interested in providing a lot of activities in a small space. The freetime centres marked on the edge of the conurbation (Fig. 5.17) are much bigger, and based on large lakes. What facilities do you think they will provide for people coming:
    (i) for the day?
    (ii) for the weekend?
16 What are the difficulties of using past figures of population growth when you are trying to plan for the future?

Summary

The conurbations studied in this chapter are of three different kinds. In Paris all the growth is focused on one city centre, a capital city. The conurbation of the Ruhr showed the problems of many smaller cities which have grown into each other since the nineteenth century to create a vast, industrial sprawl. In the Netherlands the cities of the Randstad have not yet merged completely, and perhaps it will be possible to prevent the extreme problems of Paris and the Ruhr from occurring again there.

The policy now is to concentrate future development within Randstad rather than to disperse it about the country. New housing within the cities is being actively encouraged, along with the renovation of older houses and the creation of traffic-free zones (Fig. 5.27). New development in suburban areas is now to take place on the inner side of the horseshoe at Gouda, Alphen aan de Rijn, Woerden, and Gorinchem (Fig. 5.24). Buffer zones between the cities are to be left without further development to prevent them joining together.

6 Industrial location

This chapter will look at how industry is distributed in Europe, and try to find reasons for its location. There are so many different industries that it is useful to group them together in some way in order to study them.

(a) **Primary industries**. These provide the raw materials which are used by other industries. They include mining, farming, fishing, and forestry.

(b) **Secondary industries**. These use the products of primary industry and change or process them into other things. Iron ore is made into steel which can be shaped into massive girders, or tiny screws. Oil is refined into a great range of things from petrol to paint. Timber from the forests can be cut, shaped and then assembled into furniture, or it may be pulped to make paper. So secondary industries either make things by processing raw materials or assembling component parts produced by other secondary industries.

(c) **Tertiary industries**. People who work in this group do not produce anything. They provide a great variety of services for the other industries and the rest of the community. Doctors, teachers, businessmen, shopkeepers, lorry drivers, are examples of these people.

1   (a) In which group of industries do the following people work: a soldier, a deep-sea fisherman, a footballer, a factory worker, a baker, a lawyer, a carpenter.
(b) Can any of these people be put into more than one group?

Iron-ore mining in Sweden

Northern Sweden is a remote, cold, empty part of Europe, but it has the continent's largest deposits of iron ore. The mining area is inside the Arctic Circle. Summers are cool and short, and in the winter it is dark all day as well as all night, with snow and continuous frost. The Baltic Sea and all the rivers are frozen from November until May. Across the mountains to the west in Arctic Norway, however, the climate is not so severe. The North Atlantic Drift, an ocean current which has crossed the Atlantic from the warm Caribbean Sea, reaches the Norwegian coast and prevents the sea water from freezing. Winds from the Atlantic bring warm air to Norway and keep the winters milder than on the Baltic coast. The high mountains between Norway and Sweden prevent this warm air reaching the Swedish side.

2   (a) Find the Norwegian towns of Bodo and Bergen, and the Swedish towns of Haparanda and Uppsala in your atlas. Mark them on an outline map of Norway and Sweden. Add the Arctic Circle to your map.
(b) Copy the graph in Fig. 6.1 which shows the temperature throughout the year in Bodo, extending the temperature axis down to $-12°C$.
(c) Draw on your graph another line to show the temperature in Haparanda using the table on page 124.
(d) What is the main difference between Bodo and Haparanda in the winter months?
(e) What do you notice about the temperatures in the two places during the summer?
*(f) Draw another graph to show the changes in temperature for Bergen and Uppsala using the figures on page 124. What are the main differences and similarities between their temperatures? How do they differ from the temperatures shown on your first graph?

Fig. 6.1 The temperature at Bodo

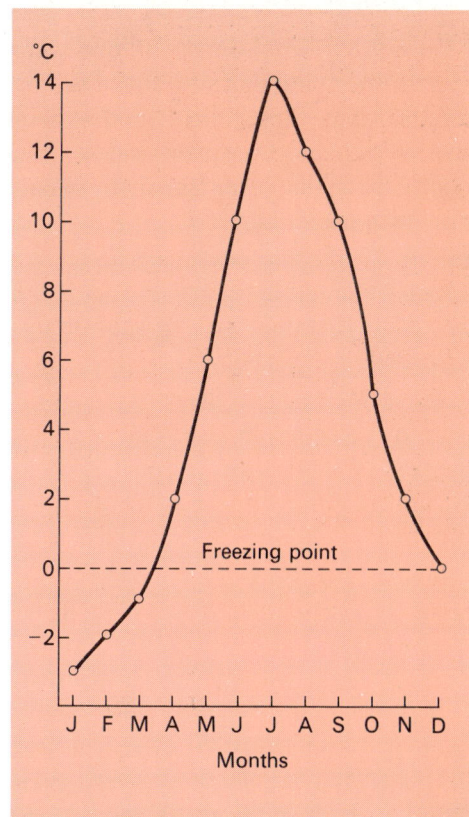

Fig. 6.2 Iron-ore mines in northern Sweden

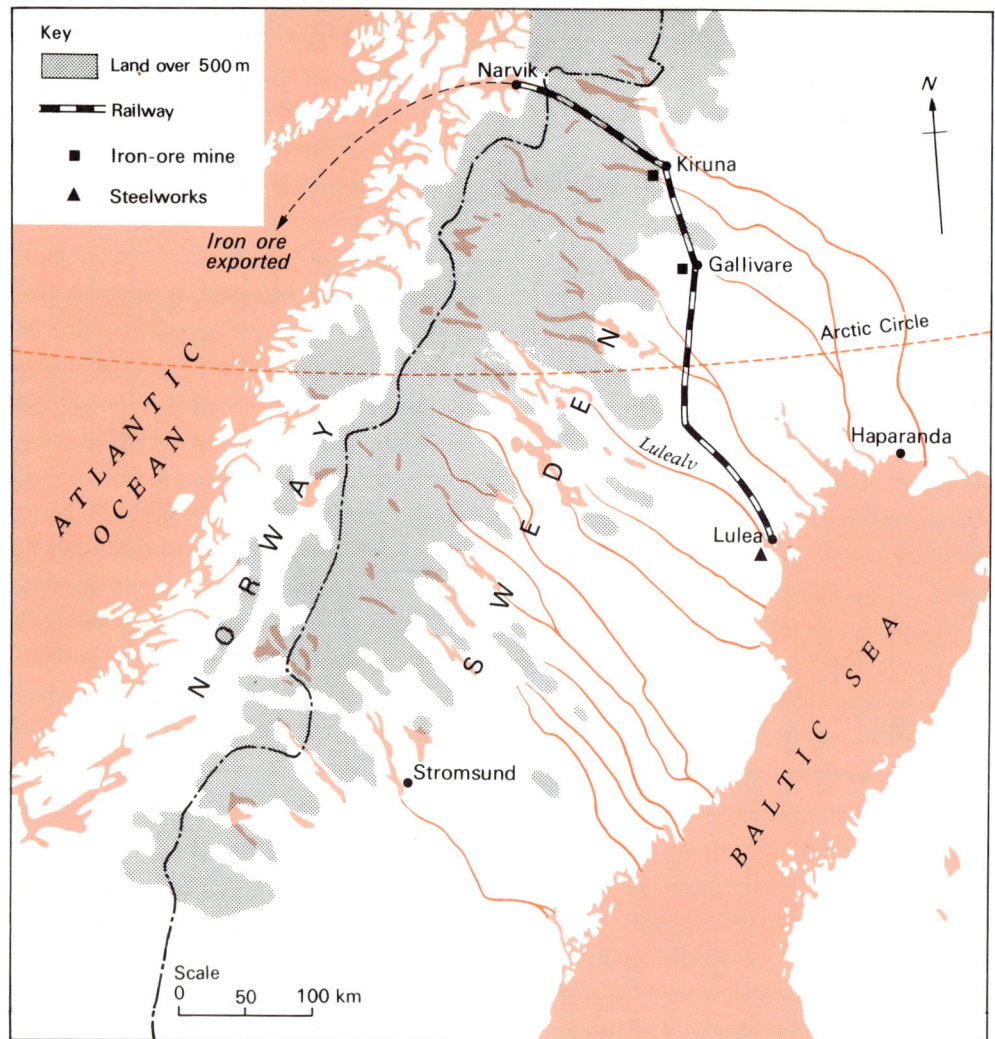

Key

Land over 500 m

Railway

■ Iron-ore mine

▲ Steelworks

Iron ore exported

Narvik
Kiruna
Gallivare
Arctic Circle
Haparanda
Lulealv
Lulea
Stromsund

ATLANTIC OCEAN

NORWAY

SWEDEN

BALTIC SEA

Scale
0   50   100 km

In 1704 a vast iron-ore mountain was discovered at Gallivare (Fig. 6.2). The nearest ironworks was at Stromsund and the only means of transport was by reindeer.

3   Find Gallivare in your atlas. Mark it on your map of Norway and Sweden. How far north of the Arctic Circle is it:
(a) In kilometres?
(b) In degrees latitude?

4   (a) Using Fig. 6.2 decide how many river valleys would have to be crossed on the shortest route from Gallivare to Stromsund.
(b) What is the chief hazard of a route that avoids all the larger river valleys?

In 1818, 1250 tonnes of ore were mined. Carrying this amount of ore by reindeer was very difficult and expensive. A scheme was proposed to join Gallivare to the River Luealv by canal, but this was not adopted.

5   Bearing in mind the relief and climate of the area, what are the main drawbacks to canal transport in this part of Sweden.

In 1860, because the cost of transport by reindeer was so high, only 50 tonnes of iron ore were mined. It became obvious that some other form of transport had to be found if mining was to continue. Until 1878 the Gallivare ores were not much in demand. They had a high iron content but they also contained phosphorus. When iron ore containing phosphorus is made into steel in an old-fashioned blast furnace the result is a very brittle metal. The invention of the 'basic' process in 1878 solved this problem, and there was fresh incentive to provide better transport.

The North European Railway Co. Ltd. was given the right to build a railway from Gallivare to Lulea; this was completed in 1887. The Swedish government extended the railway to the new iron-ore mines at Kiruna, and later to Narvik on the Norwegian coast in 1902. This line has now been electrified (Figs. 6.3 and 6.5).

The railway line therefore runs to two ports, Narvik in Norway and Lulea in Sweden. The Kiruna mines are the largest (Fig. 6.4) and produce over 16 million tonnes a year. Most of the iron ore mined there is exported through Narvik. The mines around Gallivare produce about 9 million tonnes a year which is mainly exported through Lulea. About 1 million tonnes of this remains in Lulea to be used in the steelworks which were founded there in 1906. From this it can be seen that Narvik is by far the most important port for iron ore export.

6   Can you suggest why less iron ore is shipped through Lulea than Narvik?

The importance of the iron ore at Gallivare and Kiruna was realized in the 1960s. At this time demand for iron ore all over the world was increasing

Fig. 6.3 The building of the railway line from Kiruna to Narvik at the turn of the century. Notice the absence of machinery

Fig. 6.5 The electrified Gallivare to Lulea line today

Fig. 6.4 The mining town of Kiruna in northern Sweden

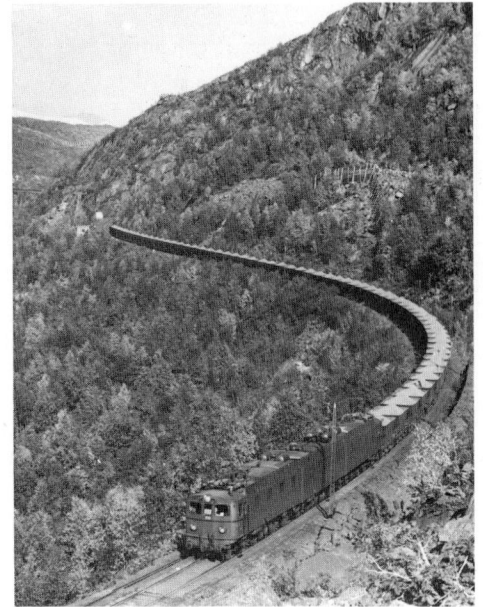

rapidly. The Swedish ore was available in large quantities and it was also high quality ore with more than 60 per cent iron content. The area in which the iron ore is found, however, is an area of difficulty for mining, transport, and living.

Sweden has few unemployed people, so workers cannot easily be persuaded to move into the Arctic areas to mine or use the ore. Also Sweden has little coal. Even so it has been found worthwhile to smelt some of the ore to make Sweden's own steel in Lulea. It is doubtful if smelting would be at all economic if it were not for the hydro-electric power (H.E.P.), that is electricity produced by the force of moving water.

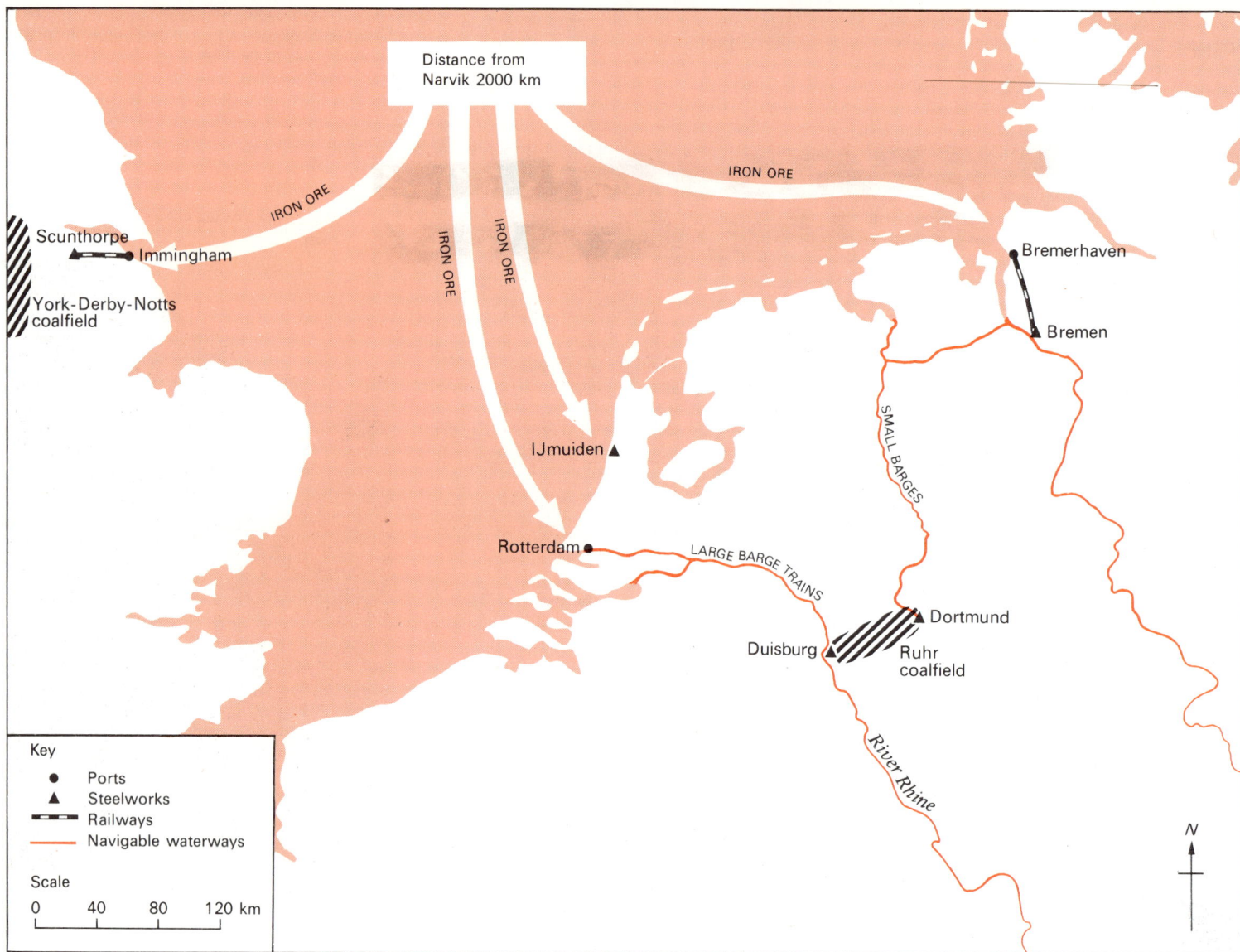

Key

- ● Ports
- ▲ Steelworks
- ▪▫▪ Railways
- — Navigable waterways

Scale

0   40   80   120 km

7 (a) Suggest reasons why you would not immediately choose to work for a mining company at Gallivare.

(b) What would persuade you to go to work in such an area?

8 Once the necessary machinery has been installed H.E.P. is very cheap to produce, but there is a difficulty in producing electricity by this method in northern Scandinavia. What do you suppose it is?

Ore is mined in northern Sweden because it is valuable high-grade ore that is worth the extra cost of transport to markets in the south. It seems unlikely that this region will develop into a major steel-making area because of its climate and remote position. For the future, workers will be paid high wages, **wages of attraction**, to come from the southern towns such as Stockholm and Malmo to work for four- or five-month periods; after which they are likely to return to spend their earnings in the south. Primary industry will continue to be all important in the north.

Iron and steel location in Europe

The Swedish iron ore which is exported from the ice-free port of Narvik (Fig. 6.2) has a long way to travel to the European steelworks which need it. Only the high quality of the ore makes this expensive journey worthwhile.

A long journey from the mines to the steelworks can be covered most cheaply if:

(a) The loads carried are as large as possible.

(b) There are few changes of types of transport because unloading and loading is an additional expense and wastes time.

Fig. 6.6 shows some of the steel works in Europe that use imported Swedish iron ore. Duisburg and Dortmund have had steelworks for a long time. They use coking coal from the Ruhr coalfield in their blast furnaces, but have to bring in iron ore.

9 (a) How far does iron ore have to travel from Kiruna to:
   (i) Duisburg through Rotterdam?
   (ii) Dortmund through Bremer-haven?
   (b) How many times does the ore have to change types of transport on these two routes?
   *(c) Look carefully again at both routes on Fig. 6.6 and at the photographs in Figs. 5.16 and 6.7. Which of these two steelworks should get its iron ore most cheaply? Why?

Newer steelworks are being located closer and closer to the coasts to try to reduce the cost of transport of the iron ore.

10 Look at Fig. 6.6.
   (a) How far does ore travel from
   (i) Kiruna to Scunthorpe?
   (ii) Kiruna to Bremen?
   (b) How many times does the ore change types of transport on these two routes?
   (c) How much shorter are these journeys than those to Duisburg and Dortmund?
   (d) Where do you think the steelworks at Scunthorpe and Bremen get their coal from? Which is closer to a coalfield?

11 (a) Which two steelworks on Fig. 6.6 have the most economical sites for bringing in Swedish iron ore?
   (b) Where do you think they are likely to get their coal from?

Coastal sites for steelworks are becoming important as more high-grade iron ore is imported not only from Sweden but also from as far away as West Africa and South America. Apart from the Swedish ore, most other European deposits like those in Lorraine in France and the East Midlands of England have a very low iron content. They are not rich enough in iron to be worth transporting across Europe to supply the many steelworks and are only used locally.

As trade between countries creates new markets in which to sell goods and provides new sources of raw materials, road, rail and port facilities change. This affects the costs of an industry. The factors that led to the original siting of a factory may change. For instance, an iron and steel firm sited in the Ruhr on local coal and iron ore might become unprofitable once new

Fig. 6.7 Barge train on the Rhine

iron-ore deposits are used and coal is required less. A new site would be more profitable and may be developed.

But once a firm has built its factory at great cost, it will remain in an area long after the initial attractions of the area have gone, because it is so expensive to move. This is called **industrial inertia**.

The car industry

The making of steel from iron ore is only the first stage in a chain of industrial processes. Very often, component parts made from steel together with others made from wood, rubber, glass, and other man-made materials need to be put together or assembled, to make complicated machines like cars.

Since the Second World War, more and more people have become car owners. The car industry and the industries associated with it form the largest manufacturing industry in Europe.

12 Fig. 6.8 shows the location of some of the main car assembly plants in Europe. On a copy of this map and using an atlas to help you, add the following car-making centres:
Great Britain: Merseyside, Coventry, Oxford, London.
France: Paris, La Rochelle, Lyon.
The Netherlands: Eindhoven.
West Germany: Dusseldorf, Mannheim, Bochum, Munich.
Italy: Turin, Milan.

Factors of location

(a) The average car is made up of 20 000 different components, made by 2000 firms. Only a few days' supply of parts can be held in stock at the assembly plant at any one time. It is therefore useful for the assembly plant to be located near to the *major raw material* and *component suppliers*.

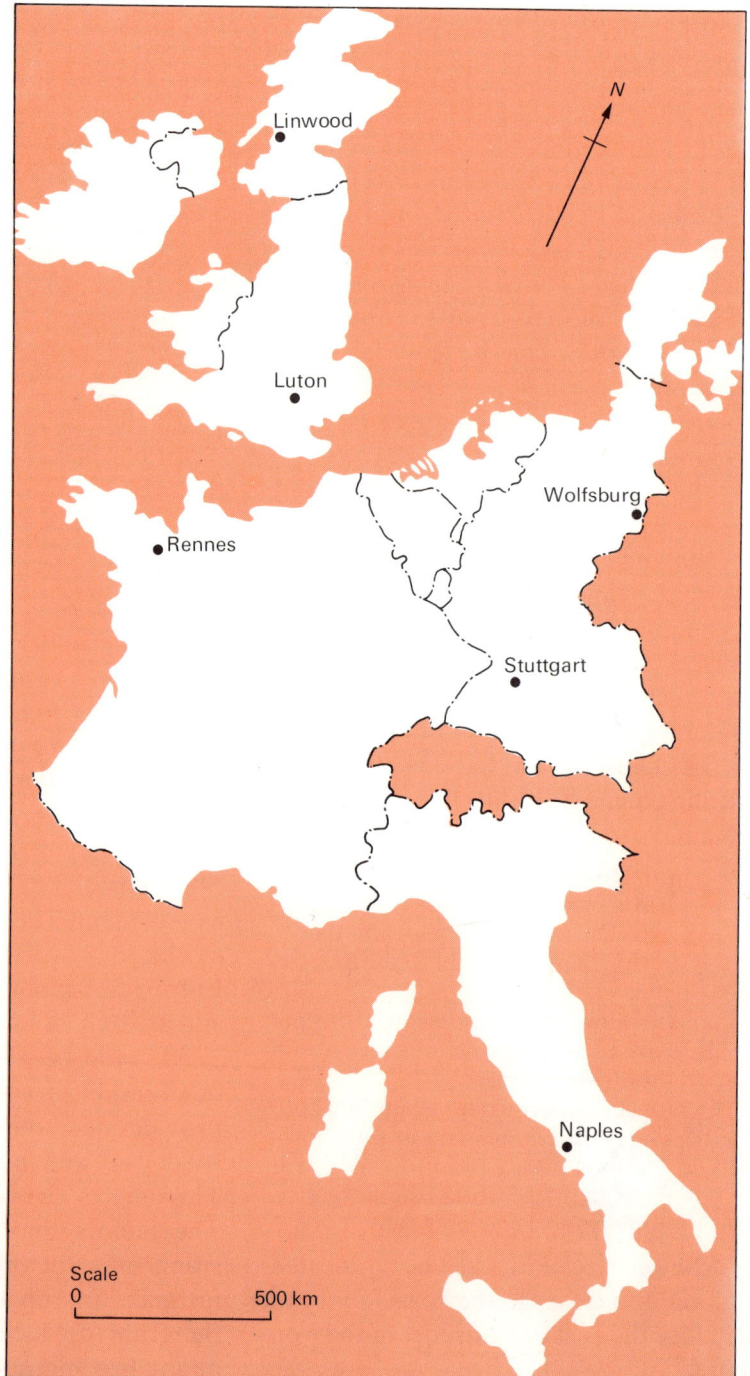

Fig. 6.8 Some European car assembly towns

Fig. 6.9 Renault cars being taken down the River Seine from Billancourt

Fig. 6.10 A Renault assembly line at Le Havre-Sandouville

(b) *Nearness to markets* is also important and these markets are the main conurbations of Europe.

(c) The industry employs very large numbers of people, so a reliable *supply of labour* is needed. Cars are assembled on a production line and output can only continue as long as every link in the chain is working properly. A strike in one component factory, making perhaps headlights, can result in the whole car production line being halted. New ways of production are being tried in order to make jobs more satisfying, interesting, and varied.

(d) If the industry and its various suppliers *concentrate* in the same locations, the *mass production* of cars should be cheaper. The car assembly factories, if they become large enough, can attract the makers of component parts to locations nearby who can then reduce the cost of transporting the parts.

13 (a) Describe what you understand by the term 'a car assembly plant'?
(b) What is a component supplier to the car industry? Give an example.

*14 Describe in your own words why it is important for a car manufacturer to have good labour relations.

The location of the car industry in France

The French car industry has expanded steadily. In 1976 about 3 500 000 vehicles were made. There are three main companies: Renault, Citroen/Peugeot, and Simca. Renault produces about 42·5 per cent of French cars, Citroen/Peugeot 41 per cent, and Simca 16·5 per cent.

The first cars were made by coach builders and craftsmen skilled in the handling of wood, metals, and fabric. They were to be found chiefly close to Paris. The Jura mountains area also had local skilled craftsmen and the

town of Montbeliard is now the home of Peugeot. So the present distribution of the car industry owes a lot to history.

Most of the French car plants are located in the south-western and western suburbs of Paris. Here the land is flat and the industry is well served by river, rail, or road transport. A large labour force is available and there is a major market in Paris itself.

The French government has been very much aware of the influence a successful car industry can have on other firms. It has been estimated that if an assembly plant is located in a town, then for every job which exists in the plant, a further ten will be created in related industries in the town. The government has been trying to persuade car manufacturers to build new assembly plants away from Paris, to try to spread the wealth more evenly throughout France. As the government now owns the Renault Company it can influence its location directly.

Fig. 6.11 Renault factories in France

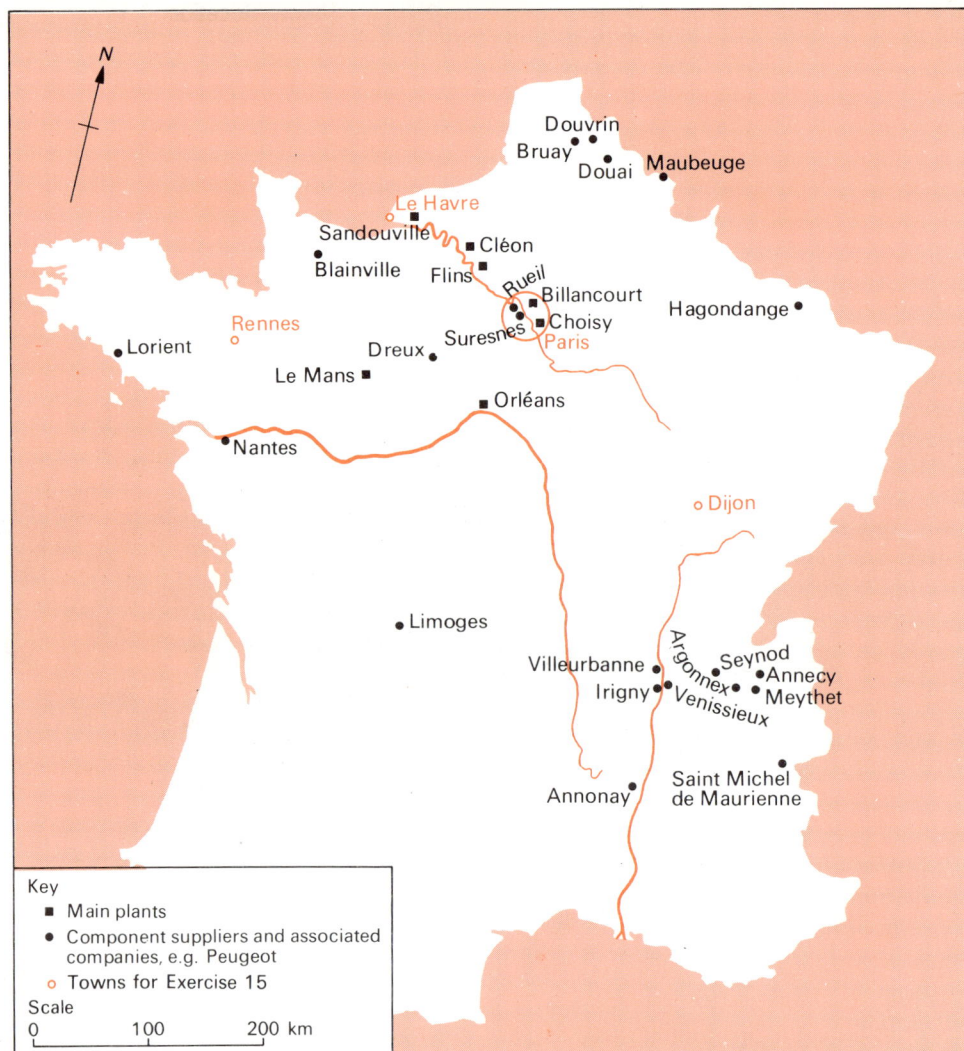

15 Imagine that you are a car manufacturer with an assembly works in Paris. You wish to expand, but the government says you cannot do it in Paris but must move to Rennes, Le Havre or Dijon. These places are shown on Fig. 6.11. Look carefully at Fig. 6.12. It gives information about the costs of car production in each of the three places.

(a) If you have to sell your cars at 21 000 francs each, which of the three towns would be the most profitable site for your new factory?

(b) Which of the three towns would the government like you to choose?

*(c) What other information would you like to have about the towns before finally going ahead?

(d) Describe in a few sentences the advantages and disadvantages of your choice compared with the other two towns.

Renault has four sites along the River Seine between Paris and Le Havre. It also has factories on the banks of the River Loire and at Le Mans. They produce 7000 motor vehicles every day. As the firm has expanded the newer sites have been located closer to Le Havre and further away from Paris. The siting of the Renault factory at Le Havre is a good example of the government exerting its influence to **decentralize** the industry away from Paris. The new site still has the advantages of the old one in being on the banks of the Seine which allows easy export of the finished cars to markets abroad (Fig. 6.9). Renault altogether employs 150 000 workers and is the largest industrial company in France.

Fig. 6.12 Car production costs in francs per car

	A Rennes	B Le Havre	C Dijon
Cost of component parts	15 000	15 000	15 000
Cost of transporting parts to assembly plant	1500	2100	2100
Cost of transporting cars to market	900	1200	1500
Fixed costs of production—e.g. electricity, cost of site	1500	1500	1500
Cost of labour	1800	1500	1200
Additional costs caused by strikes and lost production	600	300	600
Grants given by Government to encourage producers to locate outside Paris	600	1200	1800
Profit needed on each car to stay in business which must be added to production costs	1500	1500	1500

Tourism

The workers in this industry very often owe their jobs to the success of primary and secondary industries in creating wealth. Shorter working hours and longer paid holidays mean that families in Europe are spending more and more money on recreation and entertainment and so it is not surprising that tourism is one of the fastest growing industries in Europe.

Three types of holiday location have been chosen to show how they provide both a service for the holiday-maker and income and employment for local people.

A Mediterranean coastal resort

Fig. 6.13 shows an area in the south of France before it was developed for tourism. It is in Languedoc on the Mediterranean coast. The shallow lagoons were infested with mosquitoes, and there were few roads.

16 Look carefully at the photograph in Fig. 6.13 and the map in Fig. 6.14.
(a) What do you think makes this area attractive to the land developer who wants to build a tourist centre?
(b) What advantages would a tourist centre like this have for:
  (i) the holiday-maker?
  (ii) the local inhabitants?
  (iii) France?

In 1961 the French Government bought 4000 hectares of land along this stretch of coast, and was able to control the use of another 30000 hectares inland. A major programme of land reform followed to turn the coastal

Fig. 6.13 The site of La Grande Motte before tourist development

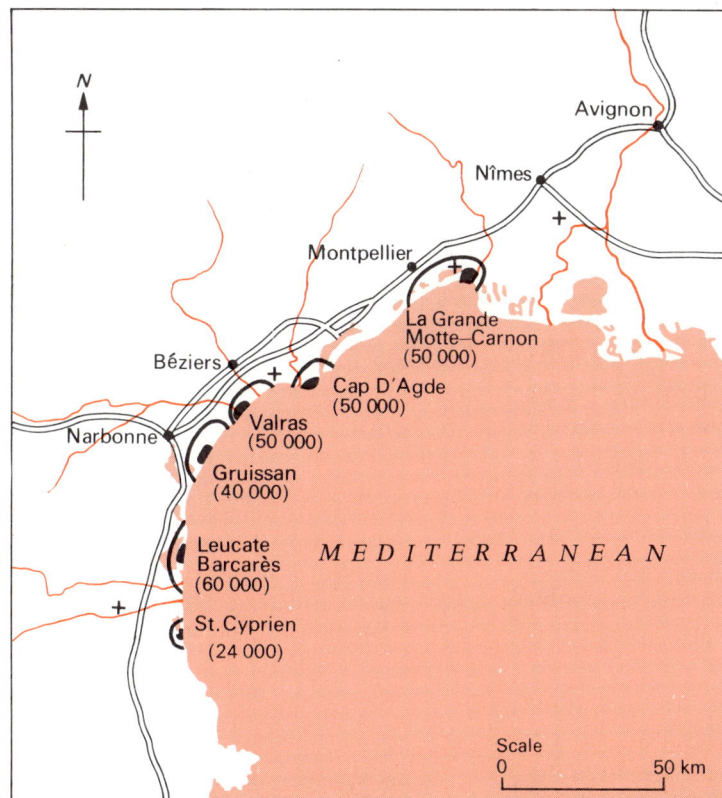

Fig. 6.14 Tourist development in the Languedoc area of southern France

Key

⬭ Tourist areas

🔴 New resorts

(50 000) Proposed capacity for new resorts (numbers of beds)

═══ Main roads

+ Airport

Fig. 6.15 La Grande Motte today

wasteland into a fine tourist area, with agricultural land behind it to grow a wide range of crops under the Mediterranean sun to supply the needs of the tourists. We have already looked at farming in this area in Chapter 3. Marshes were drained and new roads were built; the resorts which were established are shown on Fig. 6.14.

These developments have provided a great deal of employment. There is work on the farms to produce food, jobs in the hotels and restaurants serving the holiday-makers, and jobs building the roads, homes, and hotels. The road building has made it possible for people living in large cities such as Lyon, to reach this part of the Mediterranean quickly. Because of the long hot summers, what was once a poor, under-used and remote area has become prosperous (Fig. 6.15).

There is however an employment problem during the cool winter months. At this time only the builders and farmers have work. The hotel owners have to lay off staff, and there are not many jobs available in local industry. This is one of the dangers not just for Languedoc but also for any holiday location in Europe which depends on the sun for attracting holiday-makers.

17 (a) If an average temperature of 15°C is needed to attract holiday-makers in search of the Mediterranean sun, how many months will the tourist season in Languedoc last? (It has temperatures similar to Marseille. See the climatic tables, page 124.)
    (b) Which food items would you expect local farmers to try to grow to meet the needs of the holiday-makers? Look back to Chapter 3 which may help you.

A Tyrolean resort

Mayrhofen is the largest settlement in the valley of the River Ziller in the heart of the Austrian Tyrol. You have already seen a photograph of it in Fig. 3.13. The mountainous area around the village is attractive to tourists in summer for walking and climbing. Chair-lifts have been constructed to help people up to the old transhumance pastures, which, besides having many beautiful Alpine flowers, also offer breath-taking scenery. In the winter months a great deal of money is still taken in fares on the chair-lifts, for the gentle upper slopes are covered in snow. This attracts the tourists who now visit the area in increasing numbers for winter sports.

If you answer the following questions on the map extract, you will learn more about the area.

18 What is the highest point on the map extract at the end of the book and what is the lowest?
19 Why does the road from Zell am Ziller to Hainzenberg have so many hairpin bends? What other examples can you find of roads taking similar courses?
20 The 'Penkenseilbahn' is a cable-car enabling tourists to reach quickly the upper slopes of the Penkenberg, a mountain to the west of Mayrhofen. What other methods of quickly climbing steep slopes can you identify from the map and what places do they connect?
21 Draw a cross-section along the route of the Penkenseilbahn. To do this:
    (a) Measure the length of the cable-car route from Mayrhofen to Lapch-

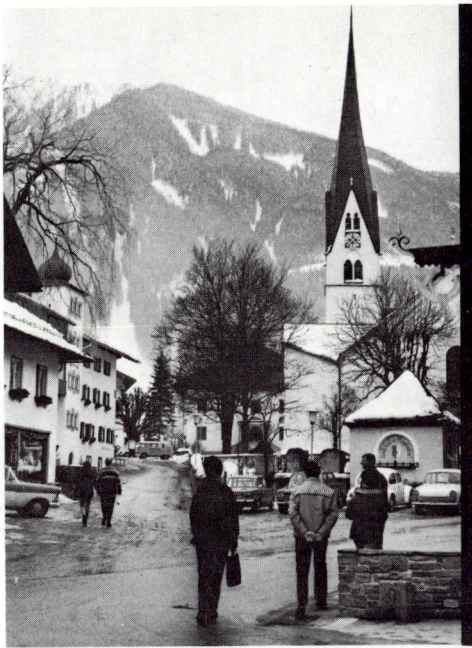
Fig. 6.16 Mayrhofen in winter

Fig. 6.17 Skiing in the Tyrol

berg and draw a horizontal line of the same length on a piece of graph paper.

(b) Lay the edge of another piece of paper along the line of the cable-car route and mark each point where it crosses a contour line, labelling each contour line with its height.

(c) Lay the edge of the same piece of paper along the line you have drawn on your graph paper and transfer each contour point to the graph paper.

(d) Draw four lines parallel to the original horizontal line 10 mm apart; these lines stand respectively for 500 m, 1000 m, 1500 m, and 2000 m above sea level.

(e) Draw little crosses at the right height above each of your contour points and join these up; the line you have now drawn represents the surface of the land below the cable-car route.

22 Draw another cross-section from the k of 'Penkenseilbahn' on the map to the top of the Hollenzberg mountain north-east of Mayrhofen. Mark on your section the position of the roads, the railway, and the river and show by shading or by little tree symbols the wooded section. Show settlement by little houses.

23 The little 'H' symbols on the map stand for bus stops; why are these found more often on the minor roads parallel to the main road between Hippach and Mayrhofen?

*24 The goods lift running from the west to Schwendau carries large buckets full of magnesium ore from mines about 8 km to the west. At Schwendau the ores are washed and concentrated ready for transport; what two reasons can you suggest for this being done at Schwendau?

You have read the map extract in some detail. Now use this information to make the decisions required in the next exercises.

25 If you were going for a holiday to the area shown on the map extract which town would you choose to stay in: Zell am Ziller, Mayrhofen, or Finkenberg
(a) In summer?
(b) In winter?
Write two paragraphs to explain your choice.

26 Decide on a site, somewhere on the map extract, for a new hotel. The following list will give you an idea of what the site will need to have:
(i) Access to a settlement for labour and entertainment.
(ii) Access to a road or railway for bringing in supplies and people.
(iii) Access to ski-lifts for winter sports.
(iv) Access to cable-cars and chair-lifts for summer visitors.
Explain your choice.

27 Land suitable for skiing must be high up, yet gently sloping and above the treeline. Such areas are called 'alpe'. There are many of these on the map extract. Suggest a route for a new ski-lift in the area shown on the map.

85

Fig. 6.18 Sightseeing boat, Amsterdam. Each year over a million tourists see the beauties of the city this way

An historic town

Amsterdam's main role is still that of the commercial and administrative centre for the Netherlands (see Chapter 5), but during the spring and summer months it attracts an increasing number of visitors. The tourists come not because of the climate or the scenery, but because of the reputation of Amsterdam as an entertainment and cultural centre, a city with beautiful historic buildings, old canals, and good hotel accommodation. We have looked earlier in the book at the problems of cities, but Amsterdam in spite of its difficulties has kept its charming character (Figs. 6.18 and 6.19). Many other famous cities offer varied interests to visitors—Venice, Rome, Copenhagen, Brussels, Munich, Vienna, Barcelona, as well as London and Paris.

28   The growth of tourism has led to an increase in many kinds of jobs in tertiary industry. Make a list of some of the industries you would expect to benefit from the increased numbers of tourists in a city like Amsterdam. Explain why you think they would benefit.

Fig. 6.19 Dam Square, Amsterdam—a favourite place for young foreign tourists to congregate

Government influence on location

Industries and therefore industrial wealth are not evenly spread over a country. Some areas have never been attractive to industry. They may be too far away from centres of population or good roads and railways like southern Italy. Other areas perhaps once had successful industries which became out of date and lost money, creating unemployment. The Lancashire coalfield or the Ruhr coalfield in Germany are examples of this.

To even out regional differences in wealth and to allow poorer areas to have a fairer share in prosperity, the governments of most countries in Europe have tried to attract new industry to areas which need it. We have already seen how the French government has tried to move industries out of Paris in the early part of this chapter. Governments have offered tax refunds to firms prepared to move to poor areas. They have sometimes built factories ready for industry to move into and have improved roads and other means of transport into the areas.

In the areas which are already doing well and have more than their share of industry, governments have tried to discourage new industry by taxing them heavily and by refusing to give building permission for new factories.

There are good reasons for trying to relocate industry, but it is not a simple task. As we have seen earlier in the chapter, most firms cannot just locate

Fig. 6.20 Carrot and stick measures for industry

themselves anywhere, and still be profitable. This is the case for most of the car industry in Italy, France, and the United Kingdom. In Italy an Alfa Romeo plant has been sited near Naples in southern Italy. Component parts have to be brought all the way there from the north of the country, and the finished cars have a long way to go to the main markets which are also in the north. The result has been that the company has found it very difficult to make a profit at this new factory. In cases like this, other firms see the difficulties faced by Alfa Romeo and are unwilling to make such a move themselves, even though it would help the unemployed people in that part of Italy.

It is easier to move government departments and offices than secondary industries to poorer areas. No single location is vital to their success. They do not depend on being close to raw materials or a market to operate profitably.

29 Fig. 6.20 is a cartoon showing how a government might try to encourage industry to move by holding out a carrot, and discourage it from staying where it is by beating it with a stick. Copy the drawing and fill in the numbered gaps, using information from the above paragraphs.

30 Which two of the following industries do you think have the greatest freedom of choice of location?
   (i) Car industry.
   (ii) Mail order industry.
   (iii) Football Pools companies.
   (iv) Steel industry.
Write a paragraph explaining your answer.

Workback

*31 Using Fig. 6.11 and remembering what you have learned about the problems of commuting in Paris in Chapter 5, what advantages will the new sites towards Le Havre have for:
(a) the workers at Renault?
(b) the Renault company itself?

32 If you were the manager of two hotels, one in Languedoc, France, and the other in Mayrhofen, Austria, describe some of the differences you would expect with respect to:
(a) Seasonal income and employment.
(b) Services required of the hotel.

33 Using the list of missing words below, complete the following.
(a) Northern Sweden though rich in .... lacks .... industry. This can be explained by adverse .... conditions, remoteness, and .... difficulties. Gradually demand for Swedish ores has increased and the building of a railway from the main orefields of .... and .... to .... on the Norwegian coast and .... on the Baltic coast has led to a large export trade in iron ore. Lack of .... and scanty population leading to shortage of .... makes it difficult for Sweden to .... these ores in the north. Although .... provides much power in the area, northern Scandinavia is still economically an .... area in Europe.

Missing words:

Narvik	smelt
Lulea	Gallivare
Kiruna	labour

underdeveloped	transport
secondary	hydroelectricity
physical	iron ore
coal	

(b) Car .... lines provide not only many jobs but high wages. .... have adopted .... and .... measures to influence manufacturers to locate away from the .... areas. Some locations have marked advantages. .... the largest French car maker has centred much of its production along the .... where .... suppliers are nearby.

Missing words:

Governments	component
assembly	Seine
stick	Renault
prosperous	carrot

Fig. 6.21 A car factory in Turin, northern Italy

Summary

This chapter has looked at a variety of primary, secondary and tertiary industries, and their location in Europe. It has shown that some industries like iron and steel have more definite locational needs than others like offices, and that governments are beginning to take an interest in directing the future location of industry.

7 Ports

A port is a place through which there is an exchange of traffic between land and sea. This traffic may consist of freight (such as iron ore or manufactured goods) being **imported** into the country from overseas, or being **exported** to other countries. The traffic may also consist of people travelling on business or on holiday.

A large port which handles a great deal of traffic will become a very complicated built-up area. It will have all the land uses we have seen already which are common to any large town, plus others that are connected with its job as a port (Fig. 7.1). In cities such as Rotterdam and London the presence of the docks has encouraged the growth of industry.

1 Make a list of six important features you would expect to find in a port. Can you see any of these in the photograph in Fig. 7.1?

Fig. 7.1 Part of the docks at Rotterdam

The growth of a model port

Stage 1

Fig. 7.2 shows a river estuary on which a port has grown. In its first stage of development in the seventeenth century the port consists of warehouses, merchants' houses, banks, and the customs house. Ships anchor at quays built along the river bank close to the centre of the town, and may well be grounded on the mudflats at low tide.

2 Make as large a copy of Fig. 7.2 as you can in your exercise book.

3 Using the information on the map to help you, write a few sentences to say why you think the first port was sited in the position shown.

4 Why do you think that warehouses and other storage sheds are amongst the first port buildings?

Stage 2: the extension of the quays

5 What features shown on the map might limit the expansion of the port both upstream and downstream of the first site?

6 As ships arriving at the port become larger and more numerous, more quays are needed. On your copy of Fig. 7.2 shade in colour the banks where they are likely to be built.

Fig. 7.2 Estuary for the development of a model port

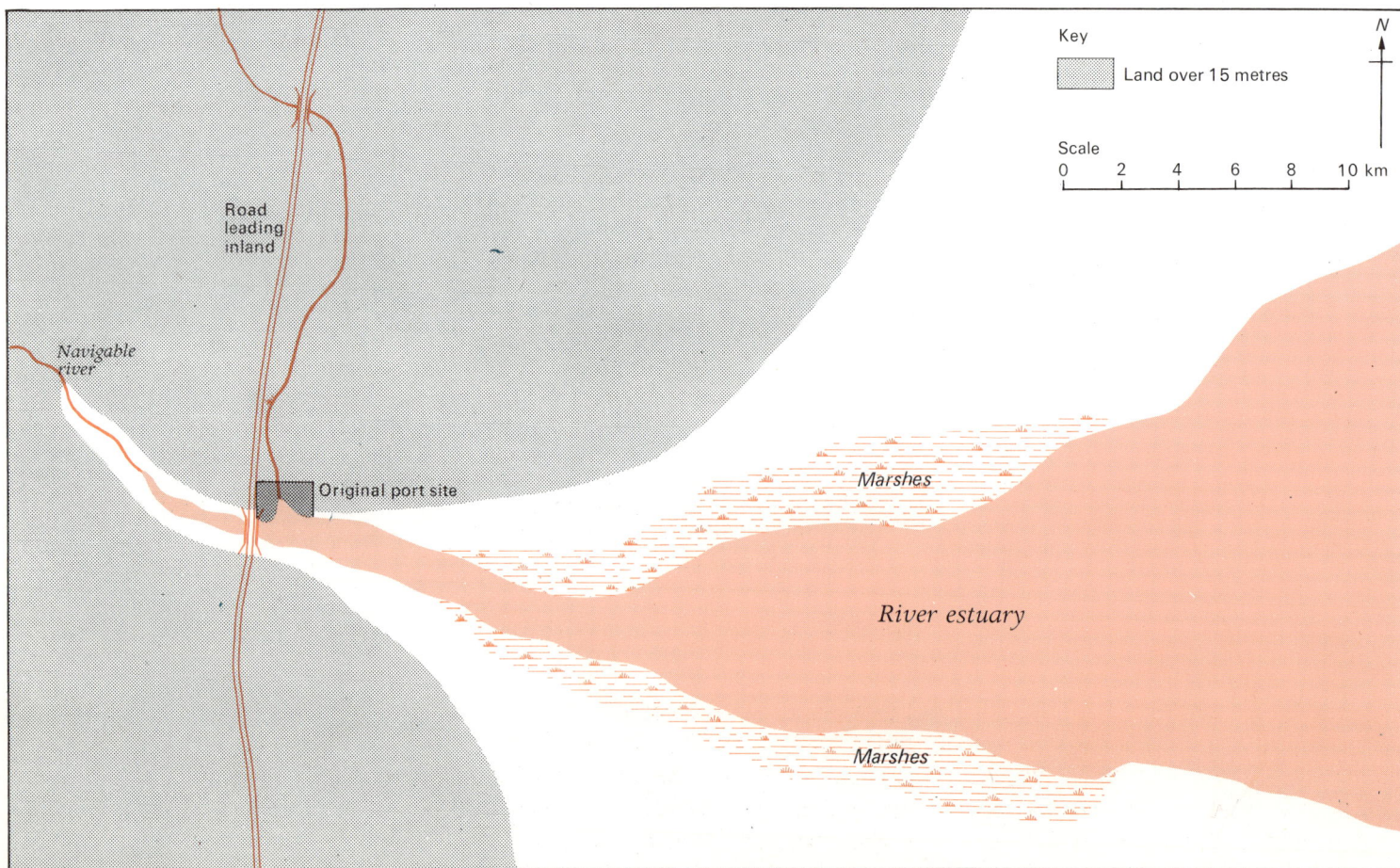

Fig. 7.3 Diagrams of docks *a* For stage 3 *b* For stage 4

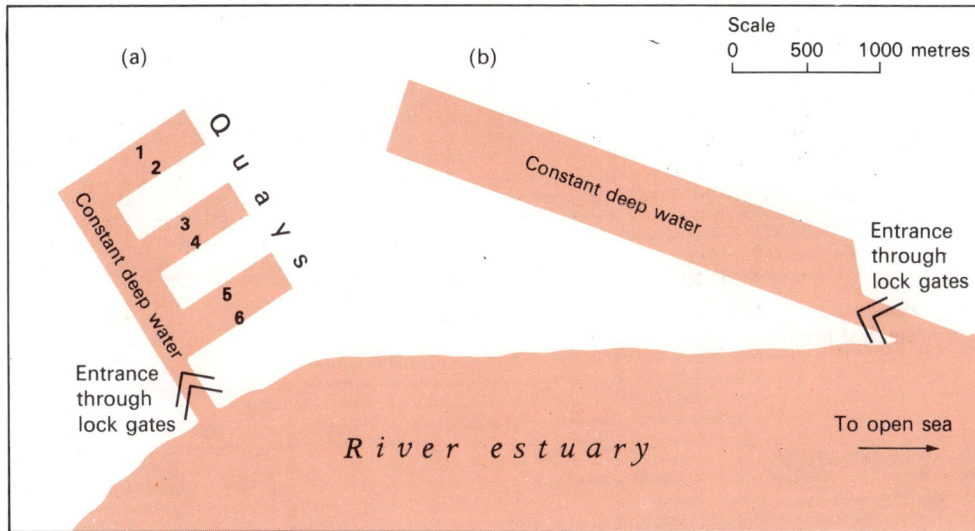

Scale
0   500   1000 metres

(a)

Q u a y s

1
2

3
4

5
6

Constant deep water

Entrance
through
lock gates

(b)

Constant deep water

Entrance
through
lock gates

R i v e r   e s t u a r y

To open sea

giving room for either one or two really large ships or several smaller ones. Even if they are still behind lock gates, they have to be easier to enter so that the ships do not have to swing round before they can berth (Fig. 7.3b). With the size of ships and cargoes still increasing, the storage space on the dockside, and its transport links have to be enlarged again too.

8   Add these larger modern docks to your map in suitable positions. They should be almost twice as big as the earlier docks. Use Fig. 7.3b to help you.

Stage 3: enclosed docks

As time goes on there are more ships, and they are bigger still so they take longer to load and unload. Congestion occurs as ships wait for the high tide to get to the quays. The port needs to expand again.

This time it is not done by just extending the quays which are open to the tides. Enclosed docks or dock basins are built. These are basins excavated in the river banks. When the tide comes in they are filled with deep water. Then the lock gates are closed (Fig. 7.3a). The deep water remains inside the dock as the tide goes out in the estuary. This means that ships in the dock can remain to be loaded and unloaded during low water. When the tide comes in again the gates can be opened and the ships can return to the river.

7   (a) Where would you build enclosed docks on your model port map? In a different colour draw diagrams of dock systems in suitable positions using Fig. 7.3a to help you. (This does not mean that the older quays will become disused. They are still satisfactory for smaller ships.)
(b) By this time the town around the port will have grown too, and some new transport links like railways will be needed to join the new docks with the town and areas inland. Draw in new town limits and roads and railways on your map.

Stage 4: new enlarged docks

By the mid-twentieth century even these dock systems are too small as the size of ships increases still further. Any new docks to take the largest vessels need still more space and deeper water.

The enclosed docks now need to provide long straight lengths of quay

Fig. 7.4 An oil tanker coming in alongside the deep-water terminal at Fos near Marseille

Stage 5: deep-water terminals

The port has now almost completed its growth in the second half of the twentieth century. However, one very important modern development remains to be added to your map. This is facilities for handling of goods such as wheat, oil, and iron ore in very large quantities. Special ships are designed to carry these goods cheaply and efficiently. They are some of the largest ships afloat and need very deep water. The goods they carry need very large, specialized storage areas and buildings at the dockside, like tall elevators for storing grain. The largest oil tankers may in fact never come to the shore, but remain in deep water at the end of a long jetty along which pipes carry the oil to storage tanks on land (Fig. 7.4).

Bulky general cargoes are being packed into metal containers (all of standard sizes) which can be unloaded easily and quickly with special cranes (Fig. 7.5). Container ports need large dockside space for the storage of containers, and to allow lorries or trains to fetch and carry them. Although the introduction of containers has meant many improvements in efficiency, it has caused a great deal of unemployment among dock workers. Younger dock workers can often be re-trained for a new job, but this is not always possible for older men. Progress such as this is often at the expense of those who have worked all their lives on the quayside.

Fig. 7.5 Container handling facilities at Bremerhaven in north Germany

9   As the final stage of growth on your map, mark on:
(a) A container port.
(b) An oil terminal.
(c) Grain elevators.
10 Draw lines across your finished map to divide it into the five stages of its growth. Number each stage clearly.

Although new docks have been built in each of these stages this does not necessarily mean that the old ones are abandoned immediately. Docks are expensive to build, and the older, less efficient ones will continue to be used for smaller ships for as long as possible.

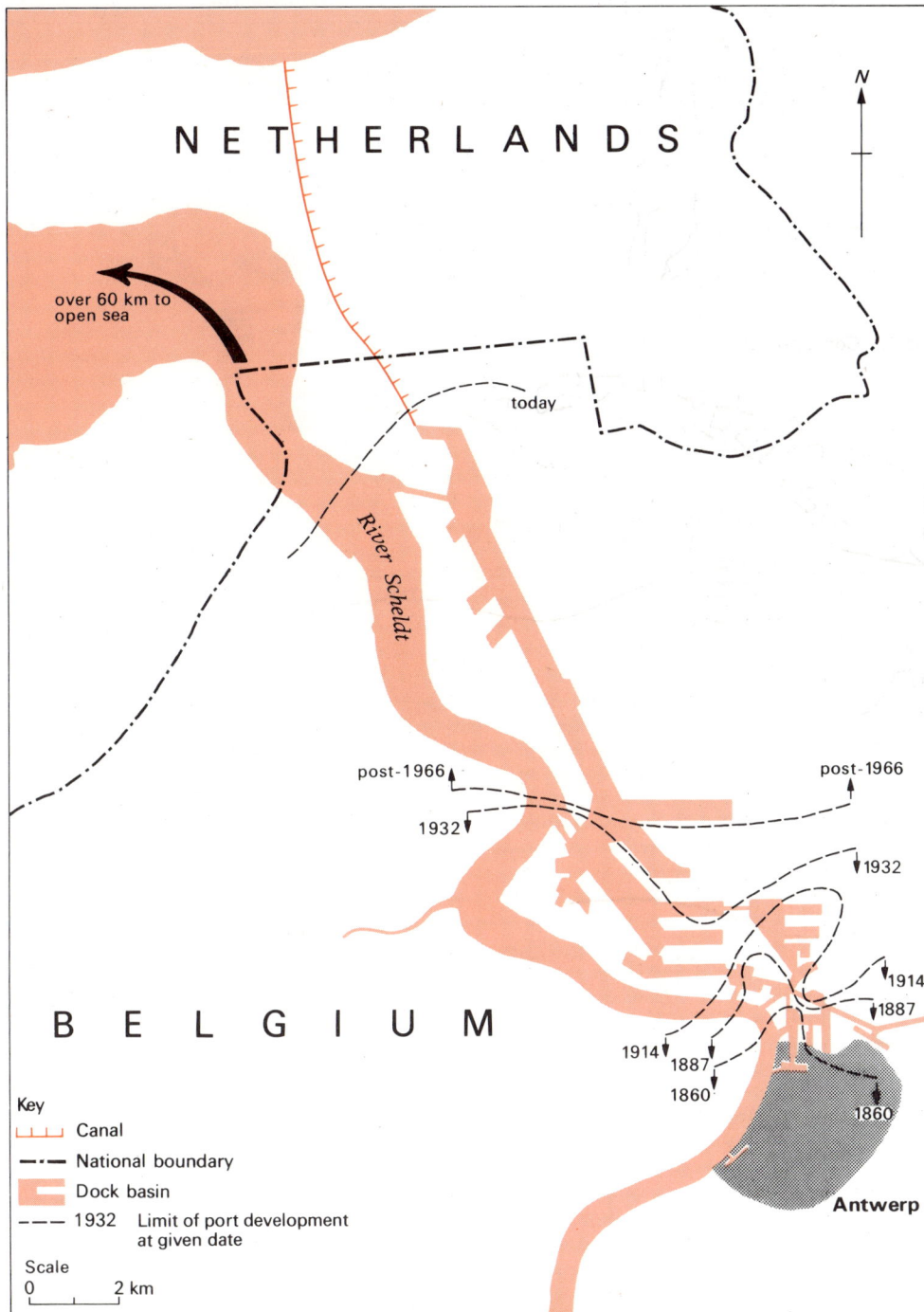

Fig. 7.6 The growth of the port of Antwerp

Antwerp's stages of growth

Having seen how a model port has developed it is now time to look at two European ports to see how they compare with the model.

The map in Fig. 7.6 shows the Belgian port of Antwerp, and the dates by which certain parts of it were built.

11 (a) Find Antwerp in your atlas. According to Fig. 7.6 when was the time of largest port growth in Antwerp?
(b) Which of the five stages of growth that you used in your model do you think are shown in Fig. 7.6?
(c) Which feature (which did not apply in your model) is likely to prevent further growth of the port of Antwerp towards the sea?

Fig. 7.7 The port of Rotterdam

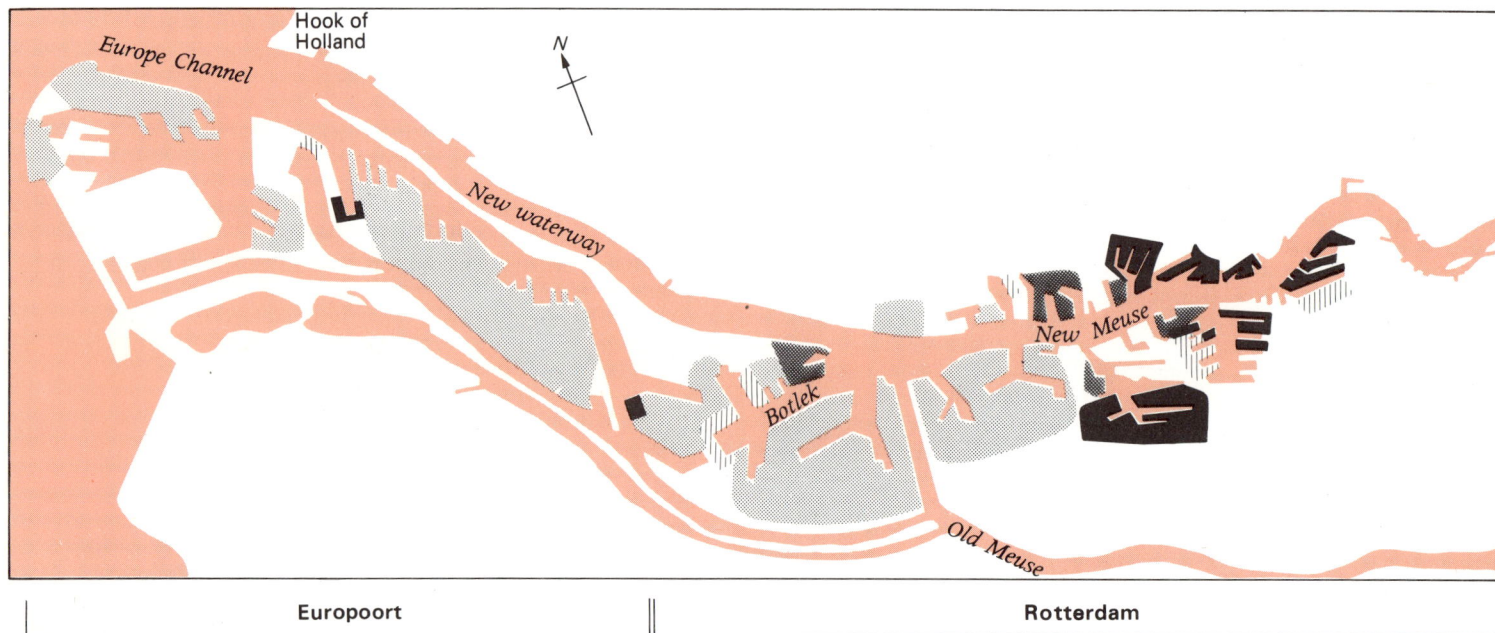

Europe Channel

Hook of
Holland

N

New waterway

New Meuse

Botlek

Old Meuse

Europoort | Rotterdam

Key to major port activities

General cargoes or containers

Bulk-handling facilities for ores, coal, grain, fertilizers

Petroleum handling facilities with refineries and chemical works

Shipbuilding and repairs

Scale

0 1 2 3 km

Rotterdam

Fig. 7.7 is a map of the port of Rotterdam. It shows not only the layout of the docks but the positions of some of the port's land uses. You can see how the docks are very much smaller and more complicated the further you get from the open sea. They get much larger and simpler towards the west. Notice how very much bigger the modern Europoort is than anything that has gone before.

Rotterdam has taken full advantage of its position at the mouth of the Rhine. The building of Europoort has been accompanied by a deepening and widening of the New Waterway so that the big ocean-going ships of today can reach more of the docks. Rotterdam

was in fact the first European port to be capable of handling the 250 000 tonne tankers which are now common.

12 (a) What are the main land uses and industries in the old complicated docks?
(b) Which of the areas shown black on the map are likely to be container ports? Why?

13 The shipbuilding and repair yards are a long way from the sea. How do you think this could be a disadvantage to a modern shipbuilding industry?

14 How do you think the port of Rotterdam is similar to, or different from, your model in each of the five stages?

The growth of ports

The graph in Fig. 7.8 shows the amount of cargo handled by ten European ports since the Second World War. From it you can see how they have grown. Some have expanded dramatically, like Rotterdam, while others like Rouen have increased their cargo only a little.

15   (a) Which countries have the three largest ports in Fig. 7.8?
(b) How much more cargo does Rotterdam handle than its neighbour Antwerp?
*(c) Which port has had the fastest percentage rate of growth over the last ten years as shown on the graph? Which three ports have the lowest rate of growth?

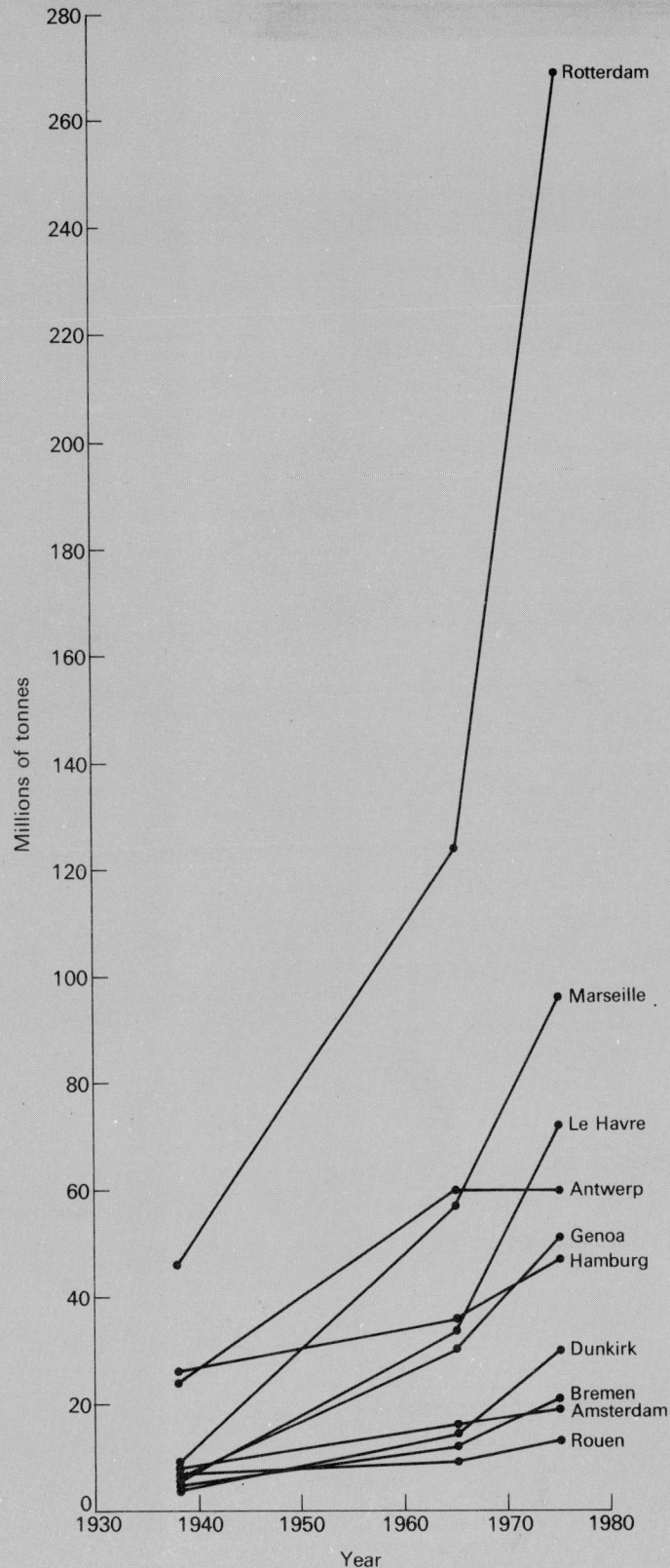

Fig. 7.8 Graph to show the cargo handled by ten European ports

Port hinterlands

Earlier in this chapter we defined a port as a place through which there is an exchange of traffic between land and sea. The port itself does not usually produce all the materials and goods that it exports. It imports goods which will then need to be distributed to other places inland. For instance, one of the things that Rotterdam handles in bulk is iron ore from northern Sweden. A great deal of this will be sent on up the River Rhine to the industrial region of the Ruhr in Germany. In the same way, although Rotterdam has oil refineries, some of the crude oil it imports is piped inland to be refined in other countries.

In order to grow, a port needs to be able to serve as large an area as possible. Such an area is known as its **hinterland**. The size of the hinterland mainly depends on how good the transport communications are from the port to the land around it. It follows that the port which handles the greatest amount of traffic is likely to have the largest hinterland.

16   (a) On an outline map of the part of Europe shown in Fig. 7.9 mark the following ports: Hamburg, Rotterdam, Antwerp, Le Havre, and Marseille.

(b) Draw on your map a circle to represent an ideal hinterland for Antwerp. The radius of the circle will represent the tonnage handled by the port.

The scale for the radius of the circle will be 1 cm for every 20 000 000 tonnes of cargo. The circle for Antwerp will have a radius of 3 cm

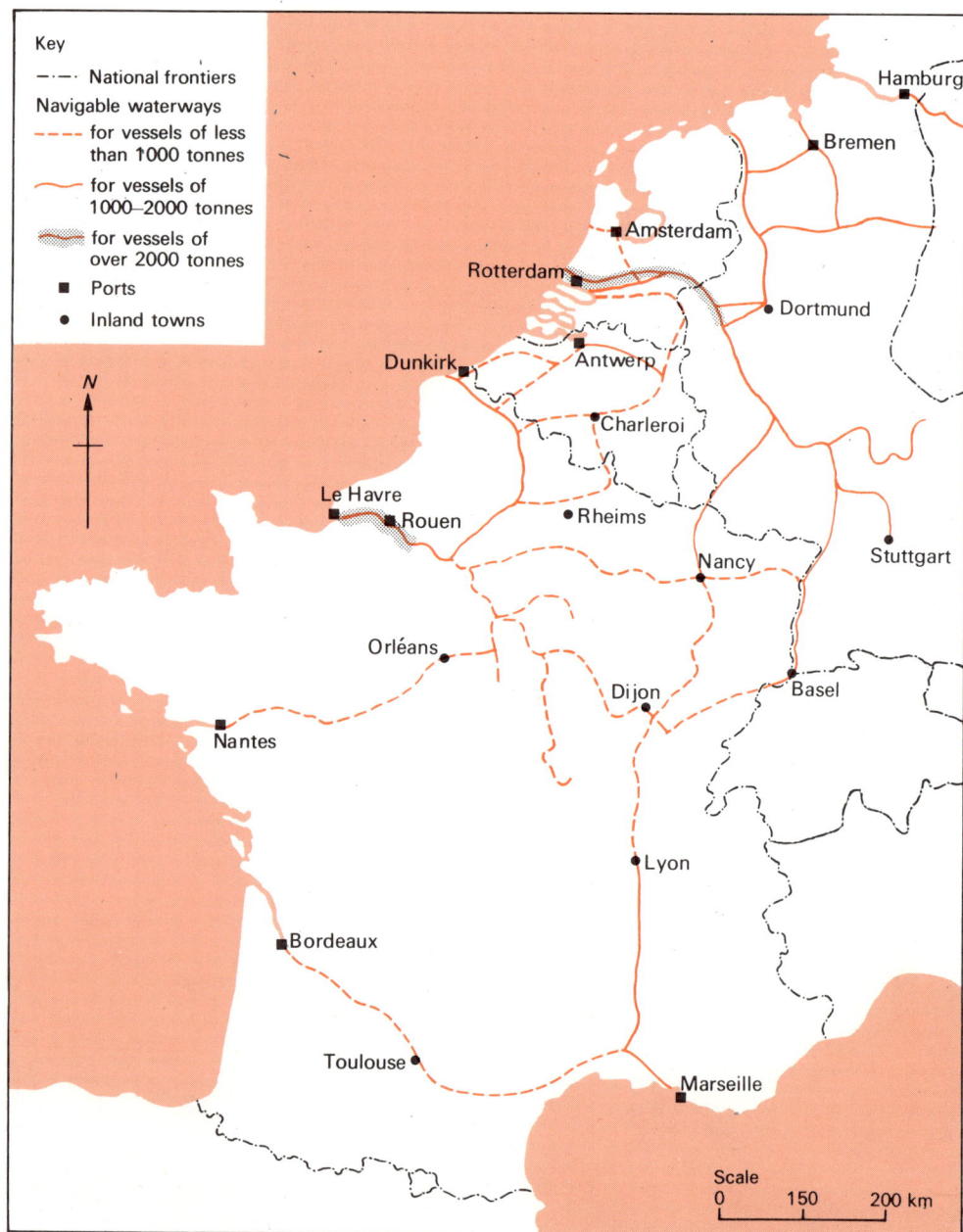

Fig. 7.9 Ports and main inland waterways of part of Western Europe

because it handled 60 000 000 tonnes in 1975. With the point of your compasses on Antwerp, draw a circle round it with a radius of 3 cm, omitting the parts of the circle which would run into the sea. This circle represents the area of the hinterland of Antwerp.

(c) Look up on Fig. 7.8 the tonnages handled by Rotterdam, Le Havre, Hamburg, and Marseille in 1975. Using the same scale as you did for Antwerp, draw in circles to show the hinterlands of these ports.

It can be seen from the map you have drawn that the hinterland of Rotterdam covers a far greater area than any of the others. In fact, the hinterland of Antwerp is completely inside it.

But you would only expect to have circular hinterlands if transport links were equally efficient all over the area. In fact, this is most unlikely to be the case. Fig. 7.9 shows the ports, together with the most important inland waterways that lead to them. It is important to remember that other European countries use their canals and rivers a great deal more for cargo than we do in the United Kingdom. You can see from the map that these waterways are by no means evenly distributed, and that transport links are better in some directions than in others.

17 Look at the ten inland towns marked on Fig. 7.9, noting particularly their positions in relation to water transport to the ports. Supposing you had a factory in each of these towns, and you wanted to export your products,

moving them to the coast by waterway. List the port or ports which you would use in each case.

*18 (a) Using this information draw on a second map rather more realistic hinterlands for the five ports you used in answer to Exercise 16. It does not matter if your hinterlands overlap, as some of the towns may find it equally easy to get to more than one port.
(b) Is the hinterland of Rotterdam still much larger than the others?
(c) How many countries have you included in the hinterland of Rotterdam?

Rotterdam has a double advantage. Besides having a large hinterland, the hinterland also contains most of the major industrial areas of West Germany. These are to be found all along the River Rhine and its tributaries. Its trade contacts across the sea are worldwide.

Look back at Fig. 7.8 again. The growth of the French port of Marseille has been faster than all the other ports except Rotterdam. It now handles more tonnage than Antwerp, yet in the maps you drew in answer to Exercise 18 you probably found that its hinterland was far smaller.

We need to look at the position of Marseille. Much of the port's recent growth can be accounted for by its position in relation to the oil-producing countries of the Middle East and North Africa. Marseille receives most of France's oil imports from North Africa to which it is very close. Of the total tonnage of cargo handled by Marseille, the vast majority are imports, and consist mainly of crude oil (Fig. 7.10).

Fig. 7.10 The growing importance of Marseille due to its position

Fig. 7.11 Rotterdam Europoort looking east, showing the New Waterway on the left

Workback

19 The map in Fig. 1.12 shows some European ports which are not marked on Fig. 7.9. What are the main differences in the traffic handled by the ports shown on the two maps?

20 (a) At which stage of the model port would you expect to find:
   (i) Container docks?
   (ii) Oil refineries?
   (iii) Enclosed docks?
   (iv) A customs house?
   (b) The photographs in Figs. 7.1 and 7.11 show two views of the port of Rotterdam. Look carefully at both of them and decide which stages of the model port they show. Write a short paragraph explaining your choice.

21 Bearing in mind the position of Antwerp, how would you explain its relative lack of growth since 1965?

22 Look back at Figs. 7.8 and 7.9 and the work you have done on hinterlands. Can you suggest any reasons why Rouen and Amsterdam should have grown so little compared to the other ports.

*23 Why do you think that it is so difficult to draw an accurate map showing the hinterland of a port?

Summary

Certain patterns can be detected in the way that ports grow. The volume of traffic—whether of people or goods, imports or exports—passing through European ports in recent years has been growing very fast. As a result docklands have also been expanding quickly. The size and nature of a port's hinterland determine its growth, these in turn depending on efficiency of transport, and the types of industry in the area.

8 Communications

Some roads lead to Rome

Many British roads run along the courses of Roman roads laid out 2000 years ago. Fig. 8.1 shows that English motorways have much the same pattern as the major Roman roads.

Roman roads were built mainly for military reasons so that the Roman legions could move rapidly through Europe in the event of trouble. Roads are only used if they lead somewhere useful, if there is a surplus of goods at one end and a need for those goods at the other end. The towns on which Roman roads focused are often not modern transport centres. In Spain the main focus was at Zaragoza which is not very important today. In France, Paris was where a single Roman road crossed the Seine, the main route centres being Rheims and Arles.

1 Identify the following Roman roads on Fig. 8.1: Watling Street, Ermine Street, Fosse Way, Stane Street.
2 On Fig. 8.1, with the help of an atlas, identify the positions of: Zaragoza, Madrid, Paris, Rheims, Arles.

Compare the pattern of roads in France on Figs. 8.1 and 8.2. In the nineteenth century the Emperor Napoleon planned roads that focused on Paris as the capital city. These roads still reflect the pattern of economic life.

Fig. 8.2 shows that Spain, Ireland, and Britain shared this pattern of routes meeting at the capital in 1850. Further east the network was complicated. Germany was not one nation, but was made up of many small states.

Fig. 8.1 The main Roman roads in Europe

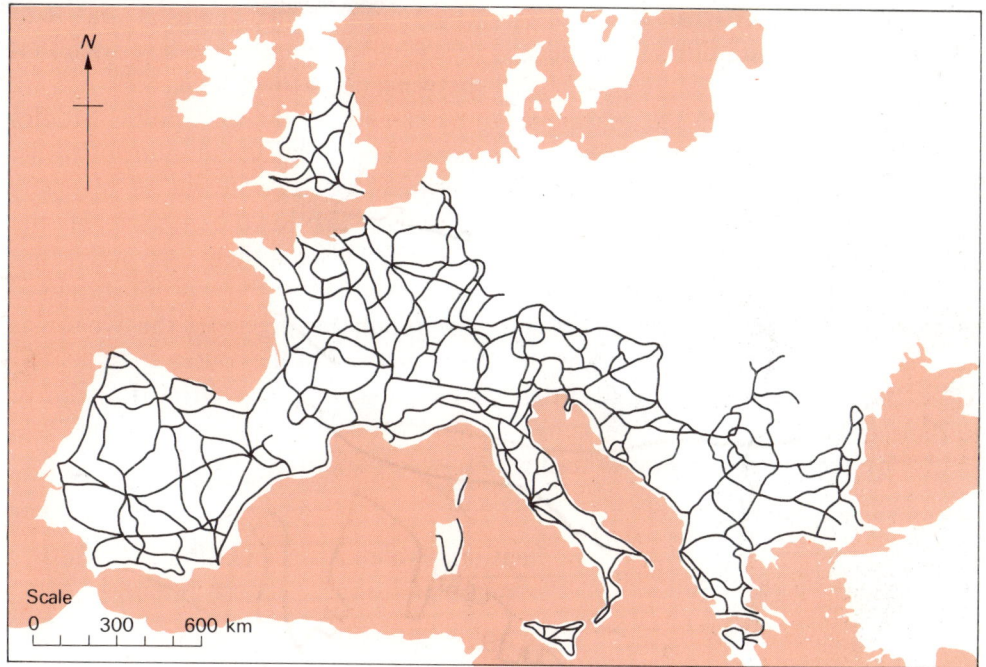

Fig. 8.2 The main post roads in Europe, 1850

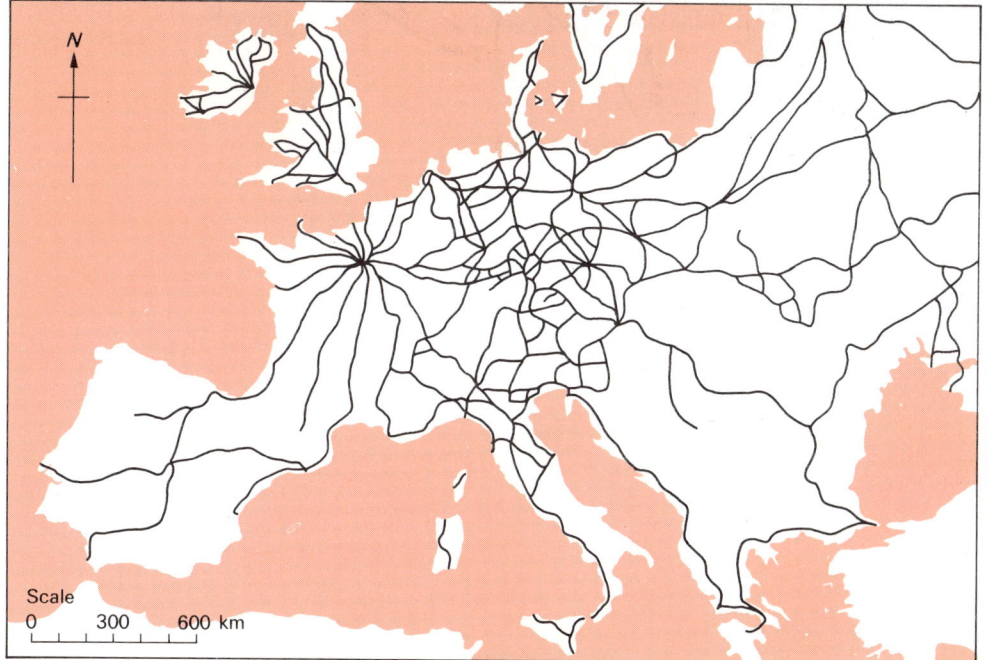

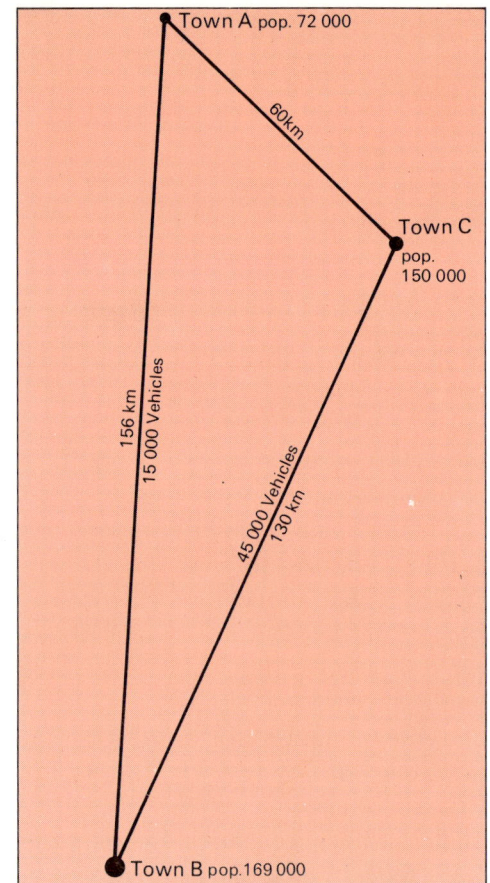

Fig. 8.3 A simple route network between three towns

Town A pop. 72 000

60km

Town C pop. 150 000

156 km
15 000 Vehicles

45 000 Vehicles
130 km

Town B pop.169 000

A traffic flow model

As a result of traffic studies it has been found that:

(i) The further towns are apart, the less traffic passes between them.

(ii) The larger the towns are the larger is the volume of traffic travelling between them.

These two very simple points allow us to build up a model of traffic flow and to relate or compare this flow of traffic between various towns in order to plan an efficient road network. We shall consider the relative flow of traffic (F_{AB}) between two towns A and B to allow us to compare the flow with that between other towns (Fig. 8.3).

Let us take the first point. Studies have shown that the amount of traffic between any two towns is inversely proportional to the square of the distance between them; secondly, that the amount of traffic is proportional to the population of each of the two towns at either end of the route.

We can therefore write the relative flow of traffic F_{AB} between the two towns A and B as follows:

$$F_{AB} = \frac{\text{population of town A} \times \text{population of town B}}{\text{square of distance between A and B}}$$

$$= \frac{PA \times PB}{AB^2}$$

where AB is the distance in metres between town A and town B,
PA is the population of town A,
PB is the population of town B.

If we apply this to Fig. 8.3:

$$F_{AB} = \frac{72\,000 \times 169\,000}{156\,000 \times 156\,000}$$

$$= \frac{1}{2}$$

Similarly, taking towns B and C:

$$F_{BC} = \frac{PB \times PC}{BC^2}$$

$$= \frac{169\,000 \times 150\,000}{130\,000 \times 130\,000}$$

$$= \frac{3}{2}$$

From these calculations we can see that the relative flow of traffic between towns B and C (F_{BC}) is three times that between towns A and B (F_{AB}).

If we knew the actual volume of traffic between town A and town B was 15 000 vehicles per day we could predict that there would be three times as much—45 000 vehicles per day—between town B and town C.

*3 How many vehicles travel between town A and town C?

By using the model we can predict the relative flow between towns, and if we know the actual volume of traffic between any two towns then the actual volume of traffic between these two and a third can be predicted.

*4 List the uses you can think of for this model when planning the position and traffic network for a new town.

Planning a road network

*5 You are an adviser to the Government of Eurovia and you are required to suggest the layout of the country's main road network. You are, however, limited by the amount of money available. Eventually all the towns will need to be connected but at present you can afford only:

(i) One stretch of motorway linking one pair of towns only, and

(ii) 1000 km of ordinary main roads.

(a) On a copy of Fig. 8.4 draw in your proposed roads. Building through mountains increases the cost; for each mountain range you go through, 100 km of ordinary road must be sacrificed.

(b) Mark on your map the motorway and main road routes you have selected.

(c) Explain the reasoning behind the network you have created stating carefully what your priorities have been.

(d) Mark in a different colour where you would locate your next 1000 km of road and give your reasons.

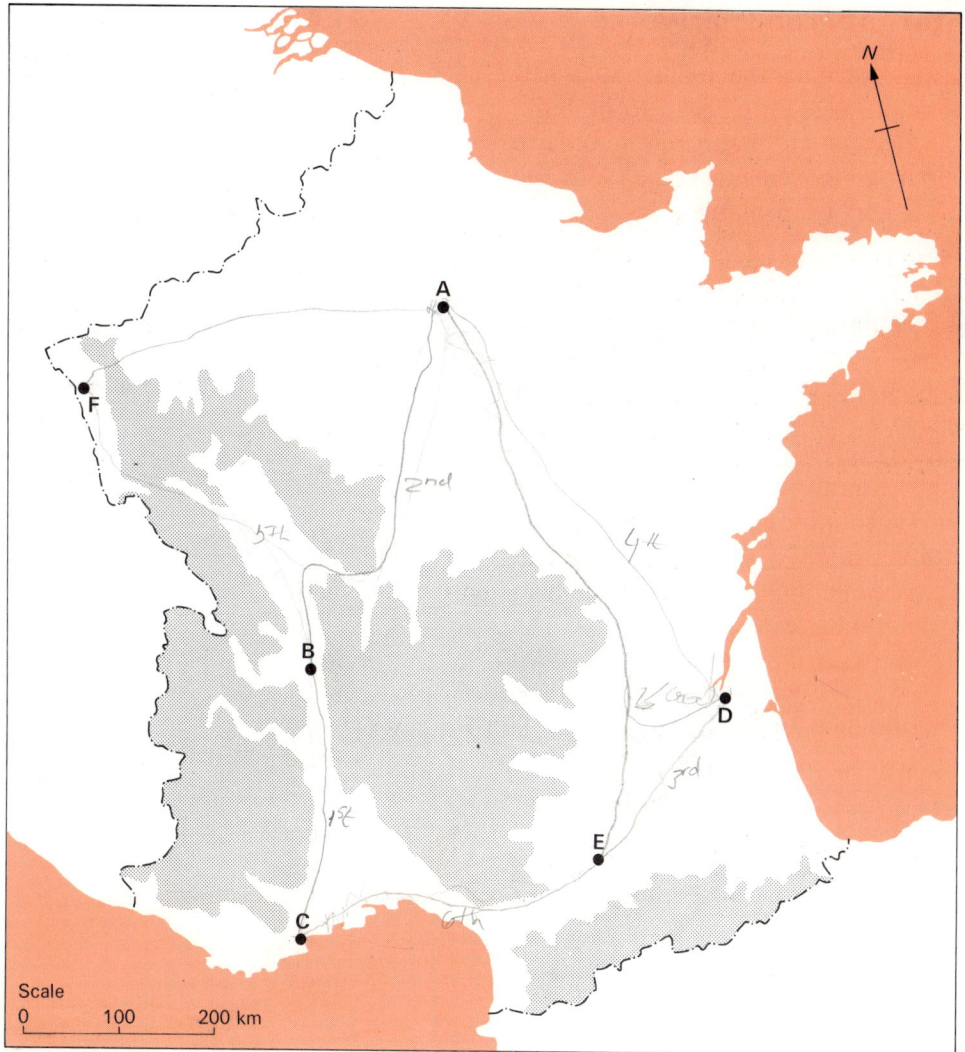

Scale

0   100   200 km

Key

Size of population

Town A 5·0 million
     B 2·5 million
     C 2·0 million
     D 500 000
     E 250 000
     F 300 000

[ ] Land over 300 metres

Fig. 8.4 Eurovia—before the development of a transport network

Inter-city road networks

It was not until the 1930s that a network of fast roads began to be built. The German autobahnen were built to help troop movements in the 1930s and 1940s and were planned to focus on Berlin.

Elsewhere in Europe the growth of motorways has been irregular, and for a long time the over-all pattern of the motorway network was hard to find. Fig. 8.5 shows Europe's motorway network in 1964. Apart from Germany the first motorways were single routes simply connecting one town or city with another. As these routes grew in number it became sensible to plan them on a national scale.

Now with increased European co-operation between countries, an international network of motorways is being planned and built to join and integrate the national networks. The E-Route scheme proposed 75 000 km of fast international highways to give Europe an integrated road system. So far less than half the present E-Route network is up to the original standards proposed (Fig. 8.7).

6   (a) Study Fig. 8.7 and decide which countries have only individual motorway sections, which have a national network, and which countries are joined by international motorway links.
(b) If you were to plan Europe's motorway system, where would you build motorways in order to make the network truly international?

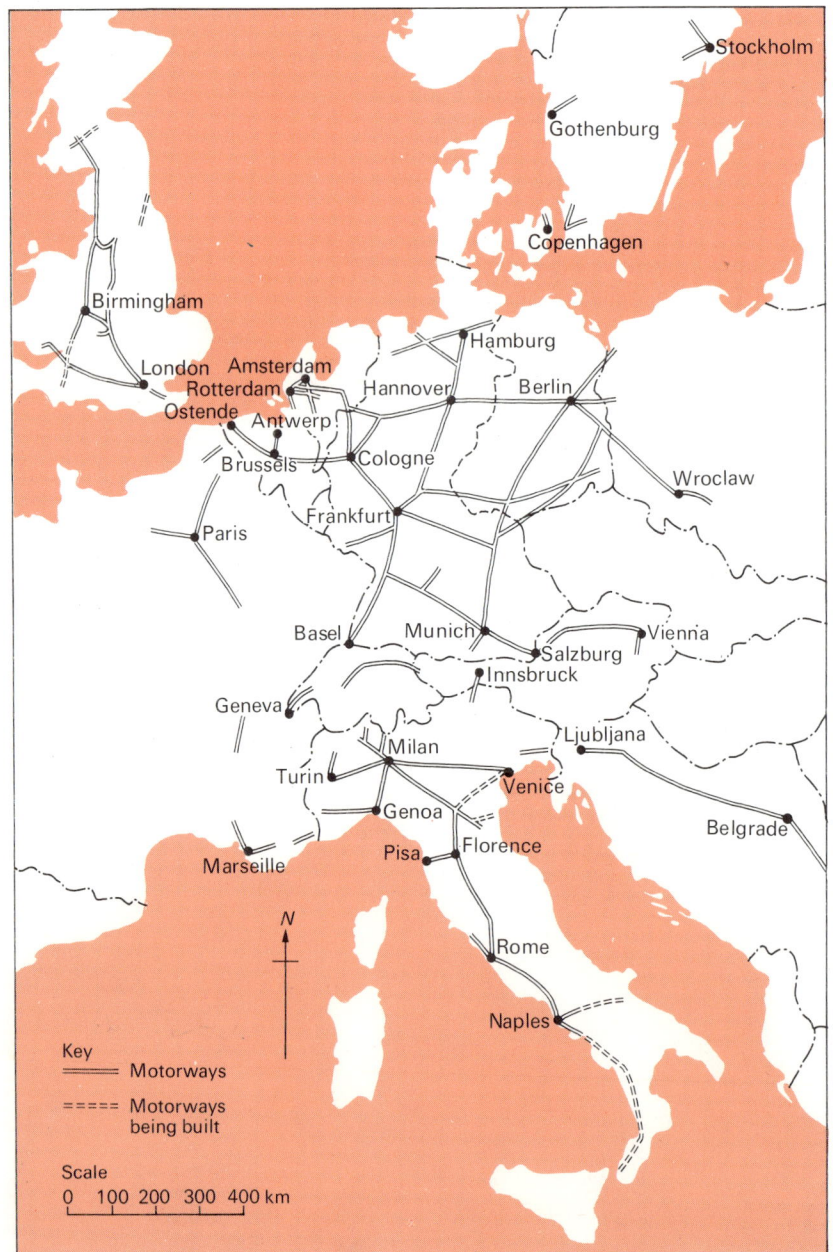

Fig. 8.5 Motorway development in Europe in the 1960s

Fig. 8.6 Inter-city traffic on a German autobahn

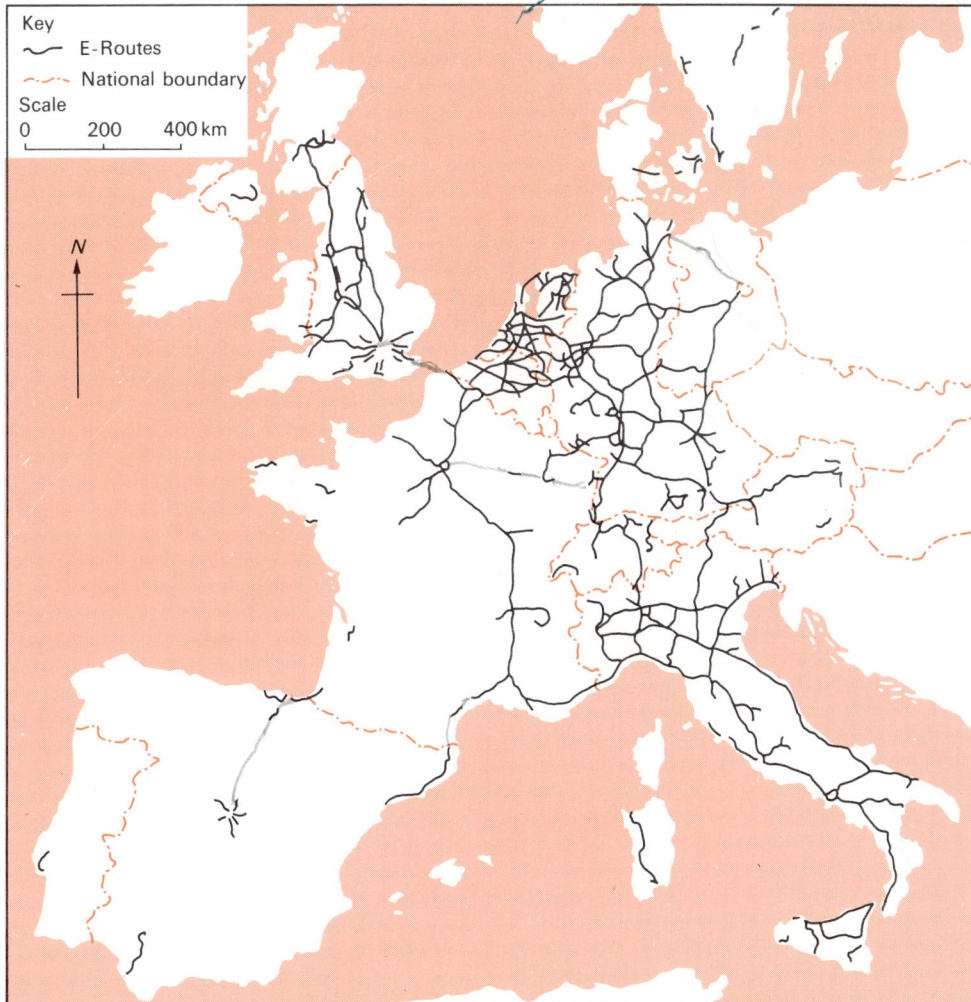

Fig. 8.7 E-Routes in the 1970s

Growth of railways

Most of Western Europe's railway network was built in the second half of the last century. At this time there was no other means of transport to compete with the railways in conveying people and goods, quickly and safely. Canal transport was slow, the motor car was just being developed while aeroplanes and hovercraft had not even been invented. As railways were so popular, lines were laid in preference to roads. The position of raw materials for industry, such as coal, greatly influenced the siting of the early railway routes and these lines played a large part in helping industry to expand. In fact 80 per cent of railway traffic is still in the form of freight for industry. Industry depended on coal, iron, and steel; it is not surprising, therefore, that railways developed to link coalfields with iron and steel centres. You have read in Chapter 6 how the development of railway lines helped the exploitation of iron-ore mining in Sweden.

In the nineteenth century most railways were planned as single routes. For example, the first public railway was the individual line running from Stockton to Darlington in England, which opened in 1826 to help industry transport heavy goods. It was not until later that railways became planned as a system. In continental Europe the first

Fig. 8.8 The opening of an early German railway (from a contemporary engraving)

railways were built around 1836 as individual lines running in and around the three cities of Amsterdam, Lyon, and Prague. By 1840, all the major cities in England were connected by railway, and by 1846 it was possible to travel by rail from Paris to south-west France, Switzerland, and Hamburg. Ten years later, railways had reached Spain, Italy, Hungary, and the city of Gdansk, lying then on the western boundary of Poland. The railway line from St. Petersburg (now called Leningrad) had reached Moscow. By 1876 there were railways in what is now Yugoslavia and lines were being constructed on a vast scale throughout Russia. Many of the European railway lines were built to the design of British engineers with the help of British 'navvies' or labourers.

7   (a) On an outline map of Europe, mark and label the cities and countries mentioned in the last paragraph.
     (b) Draw different coloured lines to show the limits reached by the railway builders in:

(i) 1826	(iv) 1846
(ii) 1836	(v) 1856
(iii) 1840	(vi) 1876

Fig. 8.9 A vehicle being unloaded from a 'piggy back' train

Planning German railways

In 1950 German railways carried seven out of every ten tonnes of goods carried, but now their share has fallen to a mere 40 per cent, as waterways, roads, and pipelines have taken over much of the railways' role. This competition has forced the railways to use modern methods to move goods and unusual ways to attract traffic. Although by 1970 over half the trains that ran were electric, there were still 1500 steam engines being used mainly in remote rural areas. Now all of these have been withdrawn from service, and many of the remote lines are being closed down. Many of the people who work on the railways are not being replaced when they retire or change their job.

The European Economic Community transport policy does not allow subsidies unless these are for lines running through areas of high unemployment.

8   In the following exercise you are to decide what should be done for the railways. Except for six members of the class who take roles 2 to 7, all the other members of the class should be members of the Board, and take role 1.

Role 1: You are members of the Board of the Federal German Railways, and are deciding what the future of the railways should be. Listen to the points of view put forward by the six speakers and then decide which of their suggestions you will adopt, to make your railways efficient and profitable.

Role 2: You are a politician representing an area close to the border with East Germany. Your area faces great difficulties because much of its transport network was designed to focus on Berlin which is now of course in the middle of East Germany. This has resulted in your area not being attractive to industry. You must tell the Board that despite the E.E.C. not favouring subsidies, transport in your area needs one!

Fig. 8.10 Containers are now the standard form of freight carried by rail

Role 3: You are the leader of a German Railwaymen's Trade Union. You see the need for a modern efficient railway but you have the interest of your 400 000 members at heart. You are determined that as few of your members as possible should lose their jobs. You take the point of view that for social reasons it is best that instead of being made redundant, and losing their jobs, people who leave the railway or retire should not be replaced—a policy of 'natural wastage'.

Role 4: You are the traffic manager of the Federal Railways and want to increase the use of the railways by both freight and passenger traffic. You want the track modernized for high-speed trains, container trains, freightliners, and also 'piggy back' trains carrying loaded lorries on flat trucks at just less than the cost of a normal rail journey. You want to close down all the remote rural lines and concentrate on the kind of job the railway does best, carrying goods traffic between 100 and 300 km, and passengers between 50 and 800 km, and commuter traffic.

Role 5: You are an E.E.C. Commissioner. You take the point of view that every country should concentrate on the economic activity it is best at, and so you are against any subsidy. Indeed you must point out that subsidies are illegal in the E.E.C. unless they are to help railway routes to run through areas requiring regional development in order to attract industry.

Role 6: You are the manager of a lorry firm. You are against the railways being subsidized, because they are in competition with your firm, and a subsidy might lead to the railways taking away your customers by providing a cheaper quicker service. You would be in favour of 'piggy back' trains carrying your lorries at the same price as the fuel you would use on the journey, especially since your lorries would wear out less rapidly.

Role 7: You are a politician representing an urban area. Traffic congestion is a big problem on the streets of your town. You feel that underground railways or underground tramways are the answer in your town.

At the end of the statements there should be a discussion, and a vote should be taken by all members of the Board on each of the speakers' proposals:

(a) Is the main purpose of your railway to provide a service to those in need, or to make a profit?

(b) Should railways near the border of Germany receive a subsidy?

(c) Should there be any redundancies, or should a natural wastage policy be introduced to cut down the size of the labour force?

(d) Should the railways be electrified and made suitable for high-speed, container, or 'piggy back' trains?

(e) Should you try to compete with lorry firms or co-operate with them? Can you do both?

(f) Should any of your lines be subsidized, such as those close to the border, or in areas needing economic development?

(g) Should you build underground commuter railways and tramways and gain the income provided by commuter traffic?

*9 After the vote has been taken you should write a report saying what your decisions were and why you took them.

*10 Try to find out which of the policies described have actually been carried out by the Federal Railways.

Railways today

Railways are especially useful for long-distance journeys for both passengers and goods. For passenger traffic, railways have found that they are best equipped for journeys of between 50 and 800 km. For goods traffic they can compete successfully with other forms of transport over distances between 100 and 300 km.

*11 Which of the following forms of transport do you think is best suited for passenger and goods journeys over the distances shown in Fig. 8.11: road, rail, waterways, air, pipeline? Fill in a copy of the table.

The trouble with national railways is that their networks are often so small that relatively few journeys inside the country are long enough to be profitable. This has led to a tradition of co-operation growing up between Europe's national railways in both passenger and goods traffic. For passenger traffic travelling from city to city, railways have an advantage since they can run fast and comfortable services to and from the centre of each city.

12 Fig. 8.12 gives a list of the Trans-European express services. On an outline map of Europe mark and name these cities, and join them up with railway lines.

Fig. 8.11 Table for Exercise 11

	0–50 km	50–100 km	100–300 km	300–800 km	over 800 km
Passengers	Road Rail	Road RAIL	Rail (Road)	Rail (Air)	Air
Goods	Road Water	Road (rail)	Rail (Road) P.P	Rail (Air) P.P.	Air Pipeline

Fig. 8.12 Trans-European express services

Route	Name of train
Amsterdam–Munich	Rembrandt
Amsterdam–Zurich	Edelweiss
Avignon–Milan	Ligure
Basle–Milan	Gottardo
Bremen–Milan	Roland
Bremen–Vienna	Prince Eugen
Brussels–Hanover	Diamant
Frankfurt–Amsterdam	van Beethoven
Geneva–Barcelona	Catalan-Talgo
Geneva–Milan	Lemano
Hamburg–Klagenfurt	Blauer Enzian
Hamburg–Zurich	Helvetia
Hook of Holland–Geneva	Rheingold
Munich–Milan	Mediolanum
Munich–Zurich	Bavaria
Nuremberg–Brussels	Saphir
Paris–Amsterdam	L'Etoile du Nord
Paris–Bordeaux	Aquitaine
Paris–Brussels	Brabant
Paris–Dusseldorf	Paris-Ruhr
Paris–Frankfurt	Goethe
Paris–Hamburg	Parsifal
Paris–Milan	Le Cisalpin
Paris–Nice	Le Mistral
Paris–Strasbourg	Stanislas
Paris–Toulouse	Le Capitole
Paris–Zurich	L'Arbalete
Zurich–Milan	Ticino

Waterways

The information in your table in answer to Exercise 11 tells us a great deal about the fall in goods traffic on Britain's inland waterways. Very few British canals are long enough to come into their own. Most British canals were built in the eighteenth and nineteenth centuries to link places which were important in those days. These places are less important today. Compared to European canals ours are very narrow and only very small, specialized narrow boats can use them. Their future would seem to be as pleasure facilities, and waterway holidays are increasingly popular.

Most European waterways are rivers whose courses have been straightened and deepened to form canals. Fig. 7.9 (page 96) shows many of these, and what size of barges they carry. The canals are man-made waterways whose routes often run between drainage basins. Often the land between the drainage basins is hilly, and it is expensive and difficult to build wide canals there. These canals suffer from the same disadvantages as British ones.

Fig. 8.13 Possible airport sites around a capital
city in the 1920s

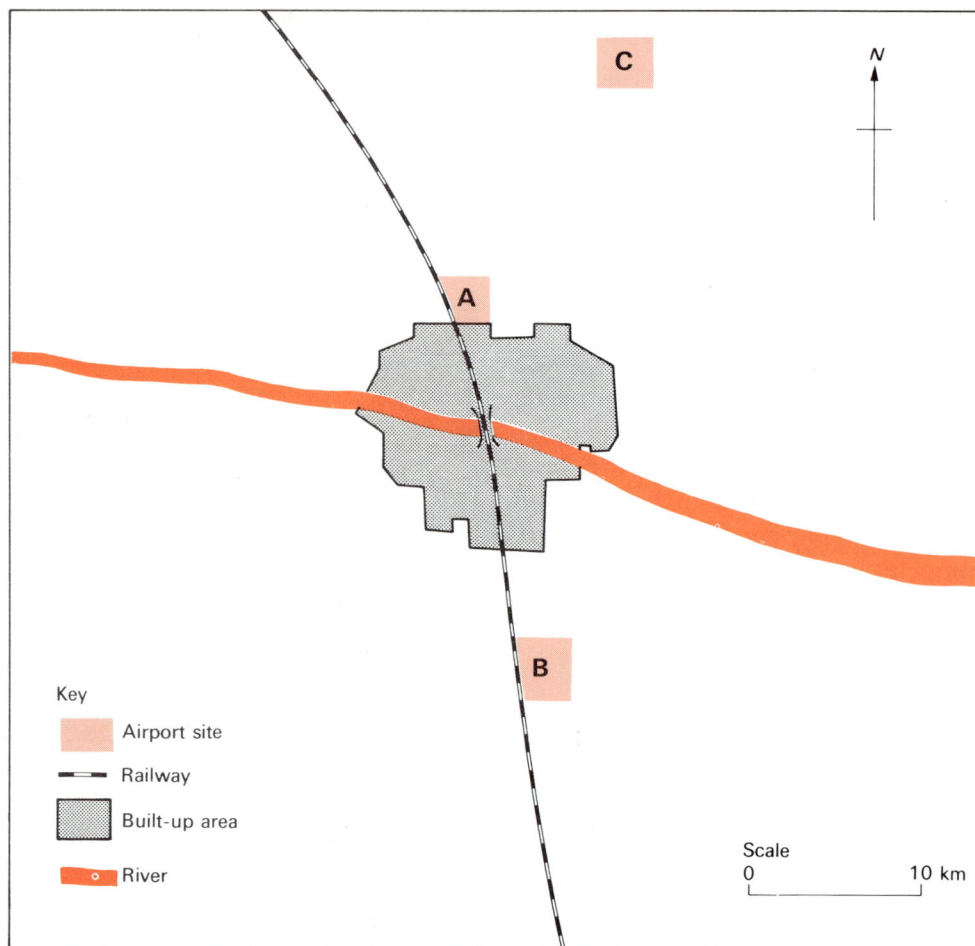

Fig. 8.13 Possible airport sites around a capital city in the 1920s

Key
Airport site
Railway
Built-up area
River
Scale
0   10 km

Siting an airport

Fig. 8.13 shows a large capital city in the 1920s. The city council has decided on three possible sites on well-drained flat land for building an airport. When making a choice of site for an airport, remember:

(a) Land prices are higher nearer the city.

(b) Most passengers wish to travel to and from the centre of the city, particularly politicians, businessmen, and tourists.

(c) An airport needs large areas of well-drained flat land.

The class should divide up into:
Airlines—four different ones.*
Passengers—tourists from abroad.*
      —businessmen.
      —politicians.*
Industries—Electronics firms.
      —Hotels (Splendid, Gigantic, Enormous, Grotesque).
      —Light engineering firms.
      —Catering firms.
Airport workers.

13   *Decision 1—1920*
Which site on Fig. 8.13 should be chosen: A, B, or C? The class should discuss this before voting.

14   *Decision 2*
Each of the groups above, except those marked with a *, should choose a site on the map to suit their needs, close to the airport or close to the city.

By 1940 the city has grown rapidly in all directions and its built-up area now surrounds site A. The airport has obviously been very successful and many firms have chosen to locate around it. Passenger traffic is growing and there is now need to cater for more and bigger aircraft.

15   *Decision 3—1940*
Should the present airport be expanded, or should one of the other two sites be chosen for a new airport?

The problem facing most airports is that although their original site was out in the country, they attract industries, and soon become surrounded by buildings which make it difficult for the airport to grow any further. Fig. 5.4 (page 60) shows how Paris has developed a series of airport sites, each bigger and further away from the centre of the city. But the city has up till now always grown out to surround the airport site.

Fig. 8.14 shows part of the reason for this. Airports provide a great deal of employment, and the people working at the airport will not want to have too long a journey to work.

16   (a) Study Fig. 8.14 and make a list of the different types of employment shown on the map of Schiphol Airport, Amsterdam.
(b) How do you suppose airport workers travel to and from their work place?

17   Which airline belongs to which country?
(a) Sabena   (i) West Germany
(b) KLM   (ii) Switzerland
(c) Swissair   (iii) Italy
(d) Alitalia   (iv) Netherlands
(e) Lufthansa   (v) Belgium

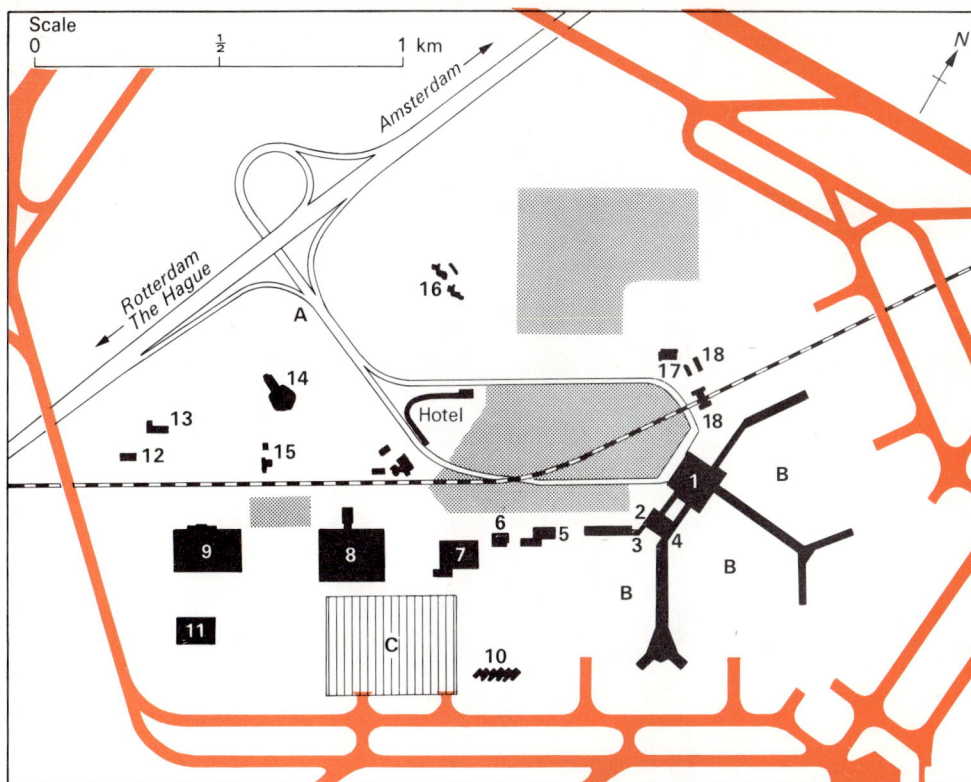

Fig. 8.14 Plan of the traffic area at Schiphol airport

Scale
0   ½   1 km

Amsterdam

Rotterdam
The Hague

A

Hotel

16

18
17

18

1

B

2
3   4

B

6
5

B

7

9

8

C

10

11

12

13

14

15

Key

▬ Runway		**A**	Main entrance
— Motorway		**B**	Traffic apron
▪▪▪ Railway		**C**	Freight apron
▨ Car park			

Main buildings
1   Terminal building
2   Airport Authority building
3   Air Traffic Control tower
4   Crew centre
5,6,7 Airline buildings
8   Freight terminal
9   Public bonded warehouse
10 Offices and workshops of oil companies
11 Freight building
12 Workshops
13 Police and fire services
14 National Aeronautical Museum
15,16 Service stations
17 Bus station
18 Technical services, Airport Authority

Fig. 8.15 Schiphol airport, Amsterdam

18 Fig. 8.16 shows the major airports of
part of Western Europe.
(a) Which countries' main airports
are not in the main industrial areas?
(b) Which country's main airport is
not that of its capital city?

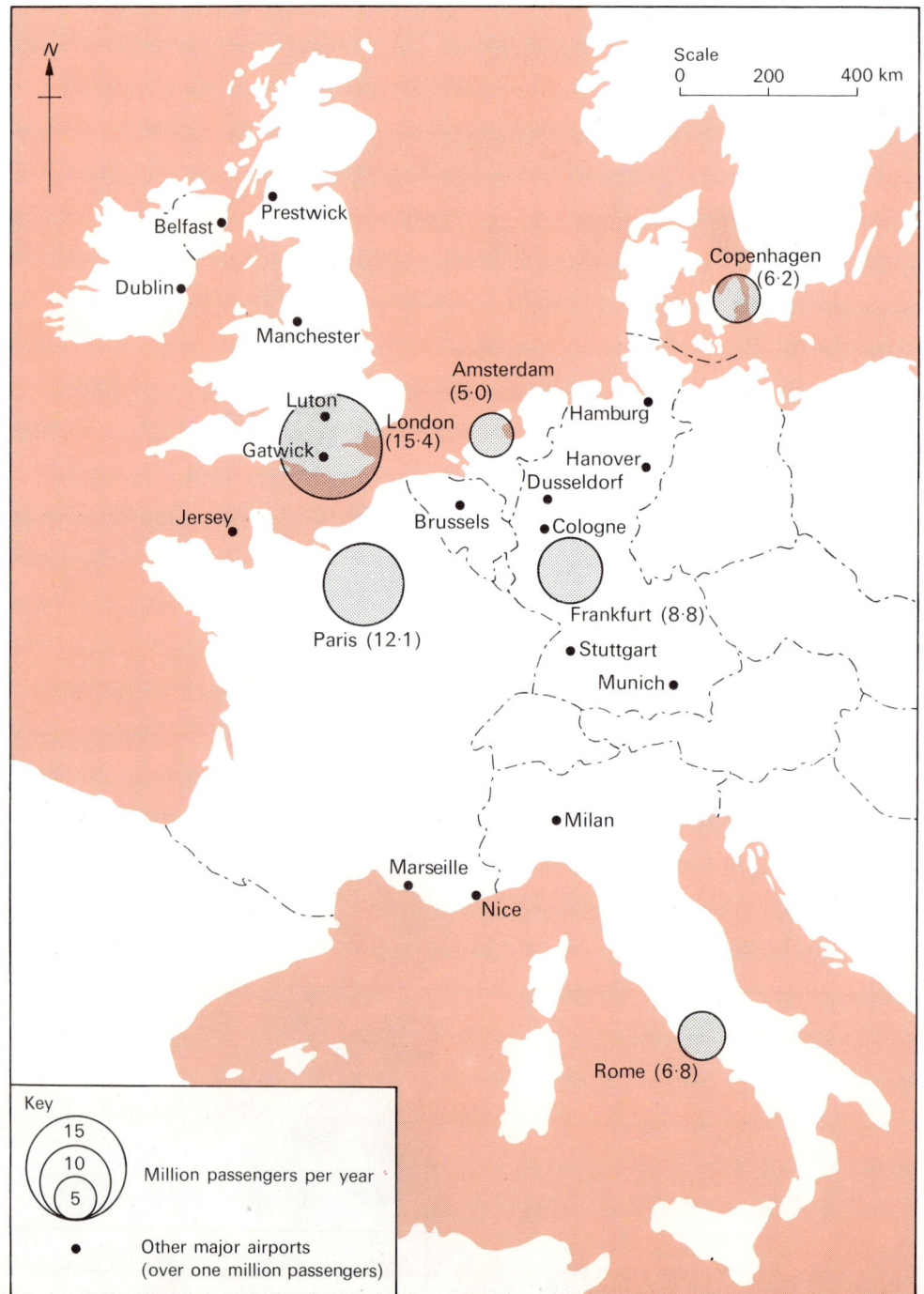

Fig. 8.16 Major airports in part of Western Europe

Patterns of pipelines

Since 1960 pipelines carrying oil and its products have spread across Europe. They are cheaper to run and safer than road, rail, or water transport for carrying oil. They can be buried so that they are invisible. Pipelines are expensive to build and, if the pattern of demand changes, it is much more difficult to divert the oil to a new destination. Ideally then a steady demand for a large volume of a single liquid is necessary.

Early pipelines connected ports with local refineries, and then with large cities inland. Later pipelines were longer and crossed national boundaries. The pipeline from Marseille in France goes through to Karlsruhe in Germany. The refineries at Ingolstadt are supplied from Trieste as shown in Fig. 8.17 and oil is now pumped from Ingolstadt to Karlsruhe.

19 Look at Fig. 8.17 and write down which European countries have:
(a) Local pipelines?
(b) International links?

*20 On an outline map of Europe draw arrows to show the pattern of direction of oil flow.

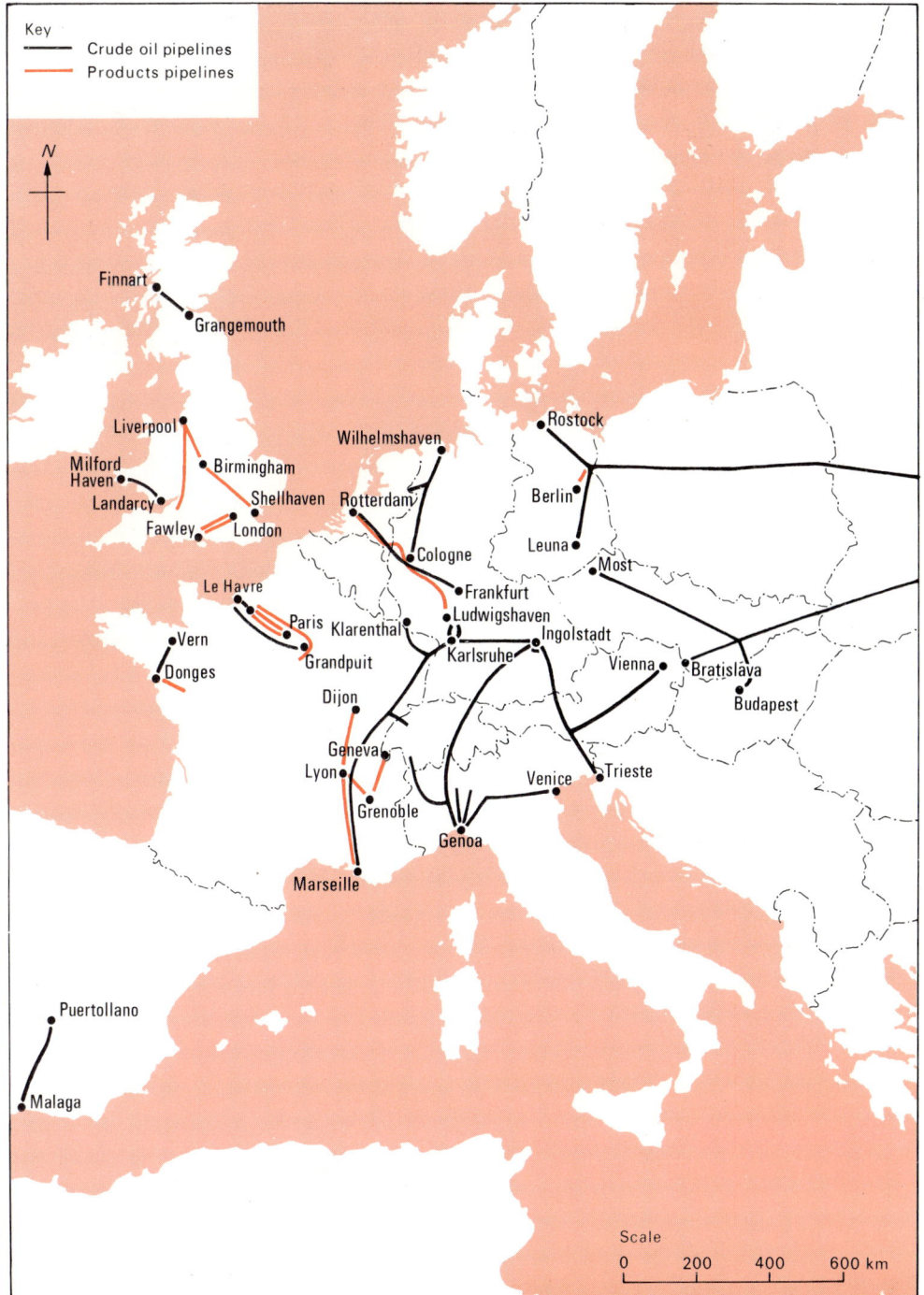

Fig. 8.17 Major oil pipelines in Europe

Fig. 8.18 Cost of transport

Distance	Cost by train per unit	Cost by lorry per unit
Up to 100 km	15p	10p
100–500 km	20p	15p
500–750 km	22p	25p
750–1000 km	25p	35p
Over 1000 km	28p	45p

Workback

21 What are the advantages and disadvantages of road and rail transport for each of the following journeys:
(a) A family holiday to the seaside 400 km away?
(b) A commuter to work in the City of Paris living in the suburbs?
(c) A Fiat car being transported from Turin to Paris?
(d) Coal from the Ruhr in Germany being sent to the IJmuiden steelworks in the Netherlands?

22 What reasons can you think of for railways having lost money in recent years?

23 What main changes are taking place on European railways as a result of competition from roads?

24 What factors influenced the location of a country's railway lines?

*25 'Today perhaps the only proper descendants of the nineteenth-century navvies are those who make the motorways, but the scale of building is different, so much smaller that ... Brunel or any of the railway engineers, would have been astonished that such roads should be built in little pieces here and there, and take so long ...' Terry Coleman *The Railway Navvies* (Hutchinson, 1965).
(a) Do you consider that this comparison is a fair one?
(b) Is the scale of building 'so much smaller'?

(c) From your comparison of the network in 1964 and today, do you consider that the motorway network has taken longer to build than the railway network, which took over 100 years?

*26 (a) On an outline map of Western Europe mark and name the following major railway and commercial centres: Stockholm, Copenhagen, Hamburg, Cologne, Amsterdam, Brussels, Strasbourg, Zürich, Paris, Lyon, and Marseille. Draw a scale on your map.

A marketing firm sends the same quantity of electrical parts to each of these cities but the cost of transport varies as shown in Fig. 8.18 with increased distance travelled.
(b) Choose a headquarters in one of these cities and write a few lines supporting your choice. Mark the HQ on the map.
(c) From your HQ draw straight line links to all remaining cities.
(d) Mark in blue those journeys where it would be more economical to use the freightliner rail services and in red those where road transport is the cheaper.
(e) One thousand units per day have to be taken from HQ to each of the cities. Calculate the total transport costs for one day for your firm. Which member of the class has the lowest total?

Summary

This chapter has examined some of the features of the different ways of transporting goods and people in Europe today. Each form of transport was developed at a different time, and has its own problems today. More and more the countries of Europe are trying to plan the growth of transport on an international scale, to make the route networks more efficient.

9 Pulling Europe together

In Chapter 1 thirty-four countries were identified within Europe. None of them is very large but some have exerted a powerful influence in the world and have commanded great empires in the past. Today those empires have disappeared and there has been a movement towards co-operation.

Following the Second World War the U.S.A. exerted its influence on Western Europe's economic recovery. In the East, Russia saw to it that her satellite countries adopted communist systems of government. Countries such as Sweden and Switzerland wished to remain neutral while Yugoslavia adopted her own brand of socialism. The political motive for co-operation between the non-communist countries of Western Europe was very strong. Nevertheless it was not easy to achieve this when each country had its own languages, traditions and ways of life.

Economic blocs

In 1948 Belgium, the Netherlands, and Luxembourg decided to work together to encourage trade between themselves by reducing customs duty on imports. They were small countries made poor by the Second World War and were competing for trade against very much larger ones. They felt that by getting together they could become prosperous more quickly.

The customs union between the three countries was called Benelux. Its success encouraged three other countries of Europe to join it. They were France, West Germany, and Italy, who together with the three Benelux countries signed the Treaty of Rome in 1957. They promised to work together to reduce customs barriers and to co-operate economically with the eventual aim of uniting politically. This union called itself the European Economic Community (E.E.C.) or Common Market.

In 1959 another economic bloc was established. Austria, Norway, Portugal, Denmark, and the United Kingdom formed the European Free Trade Association (E.F.T.A.). Sweden, Switzerland and Iceland joined later and Finland became an associate. This group worked for its countries to trade freely but they had no intention of combining their politics.

The United Kingdom was at first reluctant to join the E.E.C. because of her links with the Commonwealth, but over the years trade with Europe increased and in 1973 the U.K., Denmark and the Irish Republic became members. (The U.K. and Denmark left E.F.T.A. at this time.)

1 (a) On a copy of Fig. 1.1 (page 10) shade in dark green the three countries which were the original Benelux members; put them in the key.
(b) Shade in medium green the three countries who joined with Benelux in 1957 to form the E.E.C; put them in the key.
(c) Shade in light green the three countries that joined the E.E.C. in 1973; put them in the key.
(d) Head these three groups in your key as the E.E.C.
(e) Shade in the E.F.T.A. countries in a different colour and add these to your key.
(f) Other important countries (such as East Germany, Poland, Hungary, Czechoslovakia, Bulgaria, and Rumania) are linked to the U.S.S.R. for trade and defence and are known as COMECON countries. Shade these countries in red on your map; put them in the key.
(g) List those countries which have not joined any of these organizations.

The E.E.C. nine and E.F.T.A. seven have now agreed to trade between themselves in industrial goods.

Concentrations of industry

The Ruhr in Germany is associated with coal and steel production, Toulouse in France with aircraft, and Milan and Turin in Italy with Fiat cars. But there are many other industries in all these centres of production. It is rare for an industry to be as dominant or important in its area as it may appear at first sight. To find out how far our impressions are correct we need to be able to measure the size and importance of each industry and compare them with other industries in the area.

One of the ways of doing this is to look at the proportion of people employed in various industries from the primary, secondary, and tertiary sectors. Fig. 9.1 lists the percentages of people employed in selected occupations in the eleven regions of Italy which are shown on Fig. 9.2. In the Milan area (Region 2), 51 per cent of the labour force are employed in

Fig. 9.1 Percentage distribution of selected industries in Italy

Region	Agriculture	Manufacturing	Other services
1	5	35	10
2	3	51	8
3	5	27	15
4	6	20	13
5	8	30	6
6	8	30	12
7	35	15	8
8	10	20	10
9	32	12	10
10	32	14	8
11	32	16	8
National average	16	24	10

manufacturing, whereas, as can be seen from the national average at the foot of the column, only 24 per cent are employed in manufacturing in the country as a whole. The greater the percentage employed in manufacturing in a certain area compared with the percentage for the whole country, the more it can be said that manufacturing is localized or concentrated there. By dividing the local value by the national value a **location quotient (L.Q.)** is obtained as follows:

$$\frac{\text{local percentage in manufacturing}}{\text{national percentage in manufacturing}}$$

In this case $\frac{51}{24}$ = L.Q. 2·1

If an L.Q. value is greater than 1·0 then that industry is said to have a greater concentration than average and if less than 1·0 then that industry has a lower than average concentration in that region.

2   (a) On a copy of Fig. 9.2 shade in red the regions with an L.Q. greater than 1·0 for agriculture and leave blank those areas with an L.Q. of 1·0 or less.

L.Q. = $\frac{\text{regional percentage in agriculture}}{\text{national percentage in agriculture}}$

(b) Shade in blue the regions with an L.Q. greater than 1·0 for manufacturing.

(c) Using the information now contained on your map how far is it true to say that the greatest concentrations of manufacturing industry are to be found in northern Italy and the largest concentrations of agricultural industry in the south?

Fig. 9.2 The regions of Italy

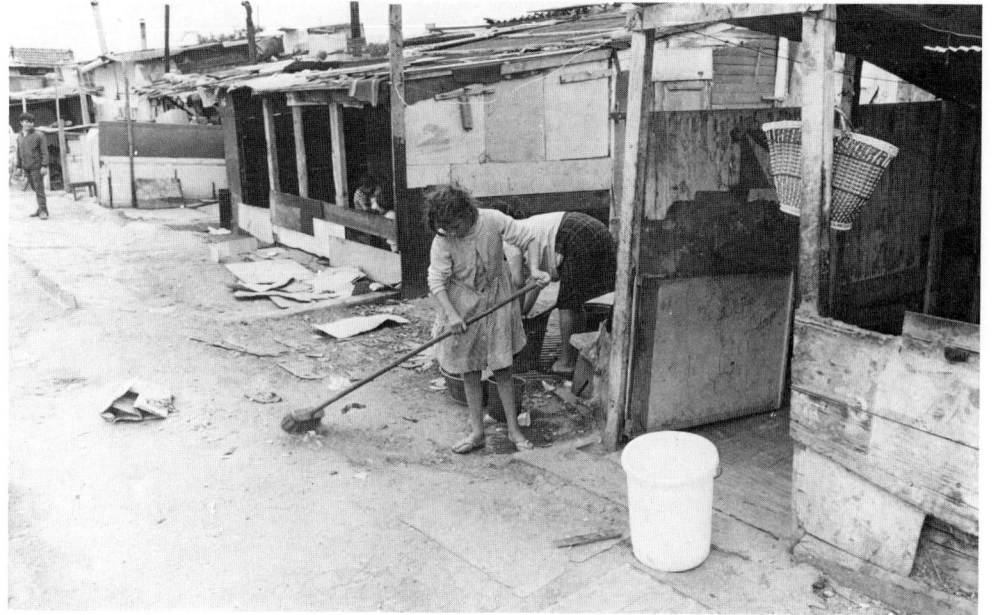

Fig. 9.3 Immigrant workers in prosperous industrial Germany

Fig. 9.4 The *bidonville* slums near Paris housed migrant workers and their families in the 1960s. Many have now been cleared

Jobs attract workers

These concentrations of industry in certain parts of Italy are very important to the Italian people because wages vary greatly between industries. The better-paid jobs are often found in manufacturing and if these industries are concentrated heavily in one part of the country then it encourages movements or **migrations** of people to these areas. This often breaks up communities and families and makes the poor areas they have left even poorer. Since 1945, over 2 000 000 Italians have moved to those regions which have the greatest concentrations of manufacturing industry.

3　Mark with arrows on your L.Q. map the direction in which you predict these workers will have moved.

The third column in Fig. 9.1 shows how employment in 'other services' varies. Since every town needs, for example, teachers or doctors, the L.Q. is more often close to 1·0 and this is true for most tertiary industry in urban areas; but even so the higher values are in those regions with above average manufacturing or secondary employment. A successful group of industries will attract more service industry than a declining group of industries and in every European country service industries are becoming more important.

The migration of people you have been predicting in Exercise 3 is not confined just to Italy; it is also happening between countries. In 1970 alone, France received 300 000 immigrants. Spanish workers are employed in large numbers in the steelworks of the Netherlands; many Italians work in German and Swiss industrial towns. In fact, almost one-third of the workers in Switzerland have migrated there from other European countries. A study of Fig. 9.5 will show why this is so.

Fig. 9.5 The distribution of wealth across Europe

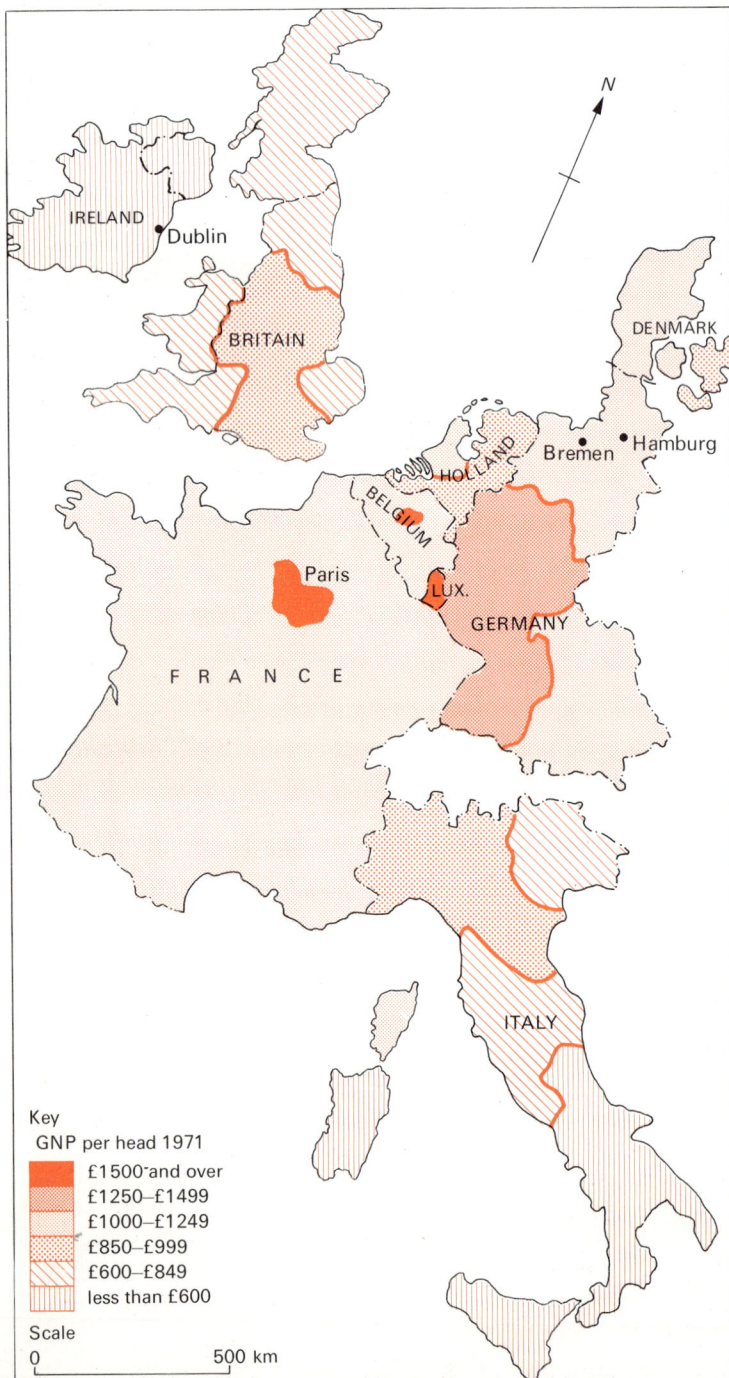

Fig. 9.6 Population changes in the Common Market

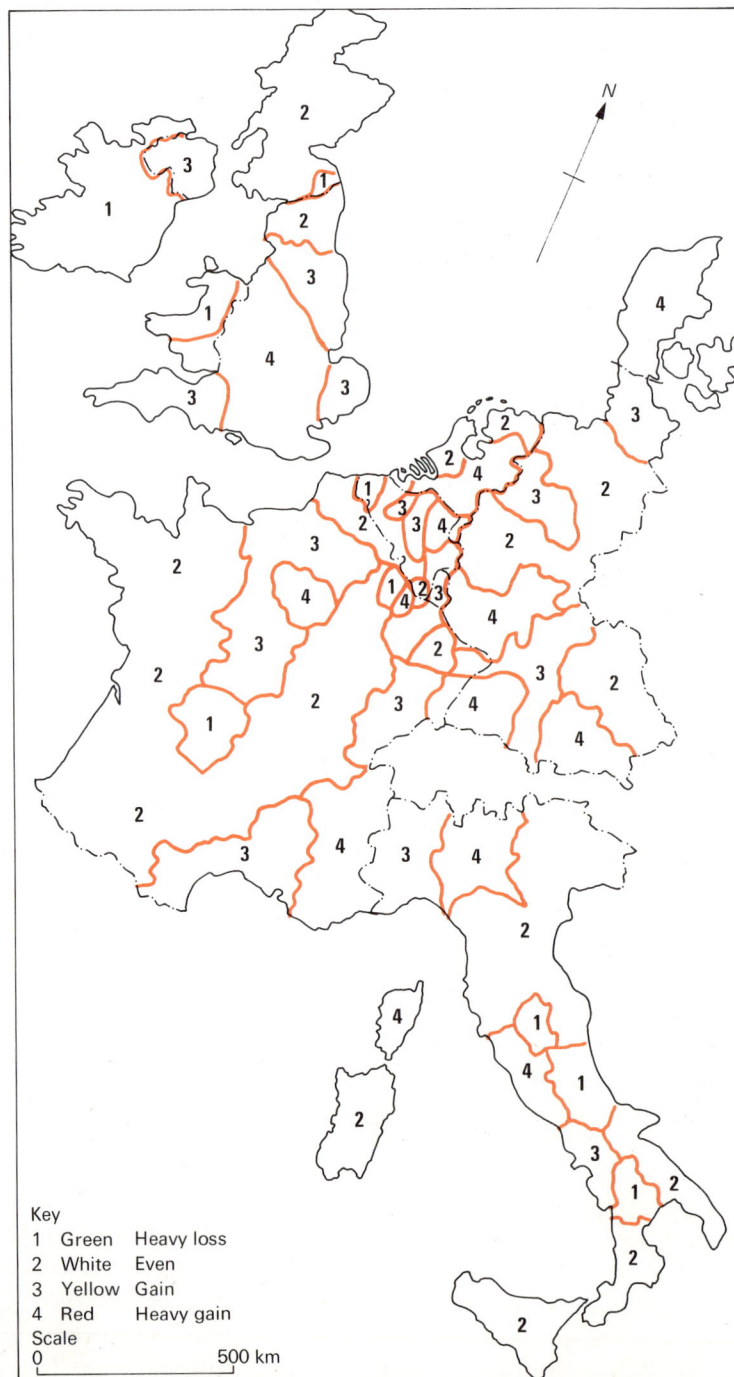

Key
GNP per head 1971

- £1500 and over
- £1250–£1499
- £1000–£1249
- £850–£999
- £600–£849
- less than £600

Scale
0   500 km

Key
1 Green   Heavy loss
2 White   Even
3 Yellow   Gain
4 Red   Heavy gain

Scale
0   500 km

4 (a) Fig. 9.5 is a wealth map of Western Europe. Trace the coastline of Fig. 9.5 and then draw a line to enclose all those parts where average wealth is more than £1250 per person per year.

(b) Using the information shown in Fig. 9.5, shade in red on your tracing the areas *to* which you might expect people to move and in green those areas *from* which you would expect people to migrate. Title your map 'European migration'.

(c) On a copy of Fig. 9.6 shade in the numbered areas according to the colour scheme shown in the key.

(d) How does this map compare with your predictions of European migration?

(e) Add to your European migration map the names of the areas which are suffering from heavy losses. Use an atlas to help you.

Thus employment and higher wages have attracted millions of immigrants, many of them permanently. In Germany and Switzerland their dependent families have not been welcome and the male workers were very much isolated in their own groups. In France the workers' families were allowed entry but the *bidonvilles* or shanty towns caused scandal in the late 1960s (Fig. 9.4). In much of Europe there has been a particular labour shortage for unpleasant and unskilled jobs; these are the ones that migrant workers often fill.

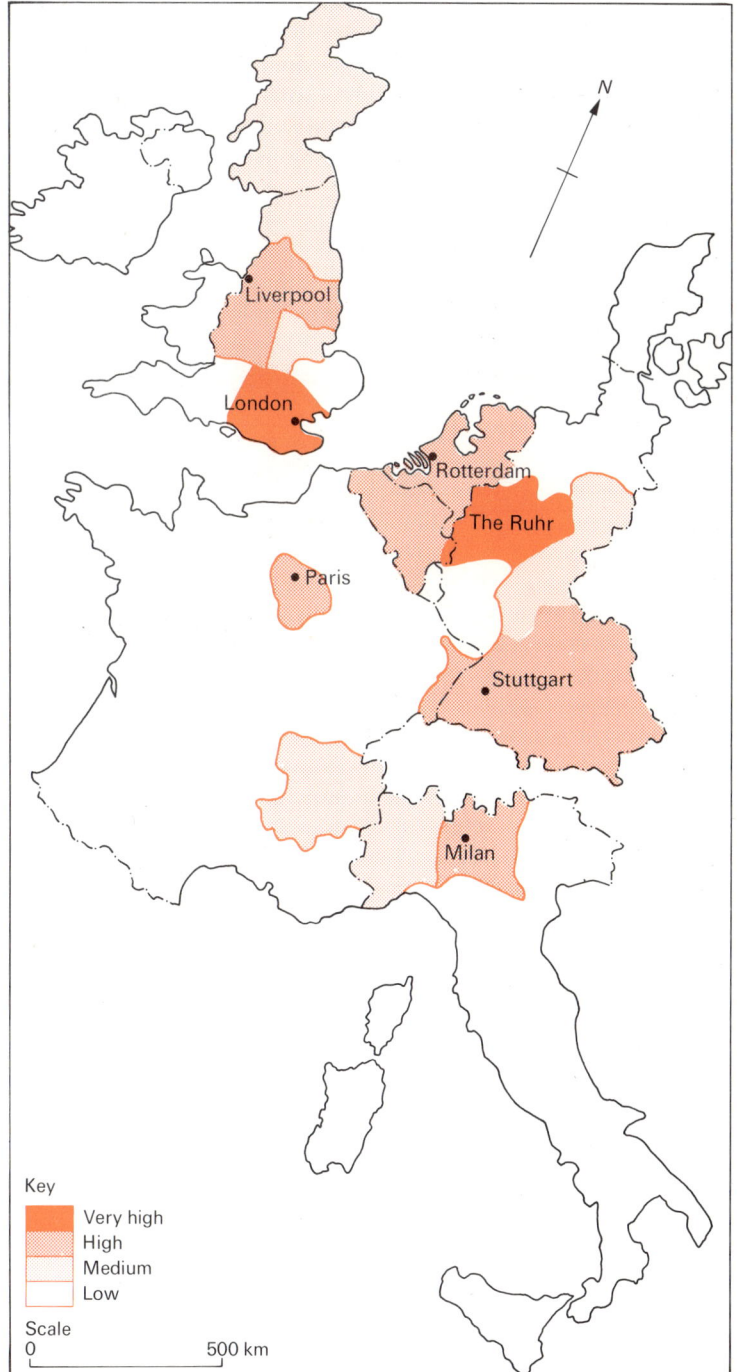

Fig. 9.7 Industrial employment in the Common Market

Key

▨	Very high
	High
	Medium
	Low

Scale
0   500 km

Fig. 9.9 Core and periphery

(a) Core

More wealth

More population

More industry

(b) Periphery

Less wealth

Less population

Less industry

Core and periphery

Industry naturally tends to locate where it can operate profitably. Many things influence whether a particular location will be profitable or not. Each firm will obviously have to consider its costs very carefully before deciding on a location for a factory site. It is hardly surprising that firms in the same type of industry find that one particular area offers the best combination for their needs (Fig. 9.8). This explains concentrations of industry appearing in certain regions (Fig. 9.7).

The areas with greatest concentration of industry are to be found in a belt stretching from Liverpool through London, then into Belgium and the Netherlands, and along the River Rhine through Germany. There are also separate pockets of industrial concentration around Paris in France, as well as around Milan and Turin in northern Italy.

A comparison of the three maps in Figs. 9.5, 9.6, and 9.7 shows that people have moved in large numbers to where industry is most heavily concentrated and provides better-paid jobs. This in turn has increased the prospects of wealth and attracted more people who form a larger market for other products, goods, and services. Such a region may be called a **core area**. In other areas the lack of wealth has encouraged people to move away and not enough industry finds it profitable to operate in these areas. Such areas left on the outer fringe of the prosperous parts are often known as the **periphery** (Fig. 9.9).

Fig. 9.8 Location needs for industry

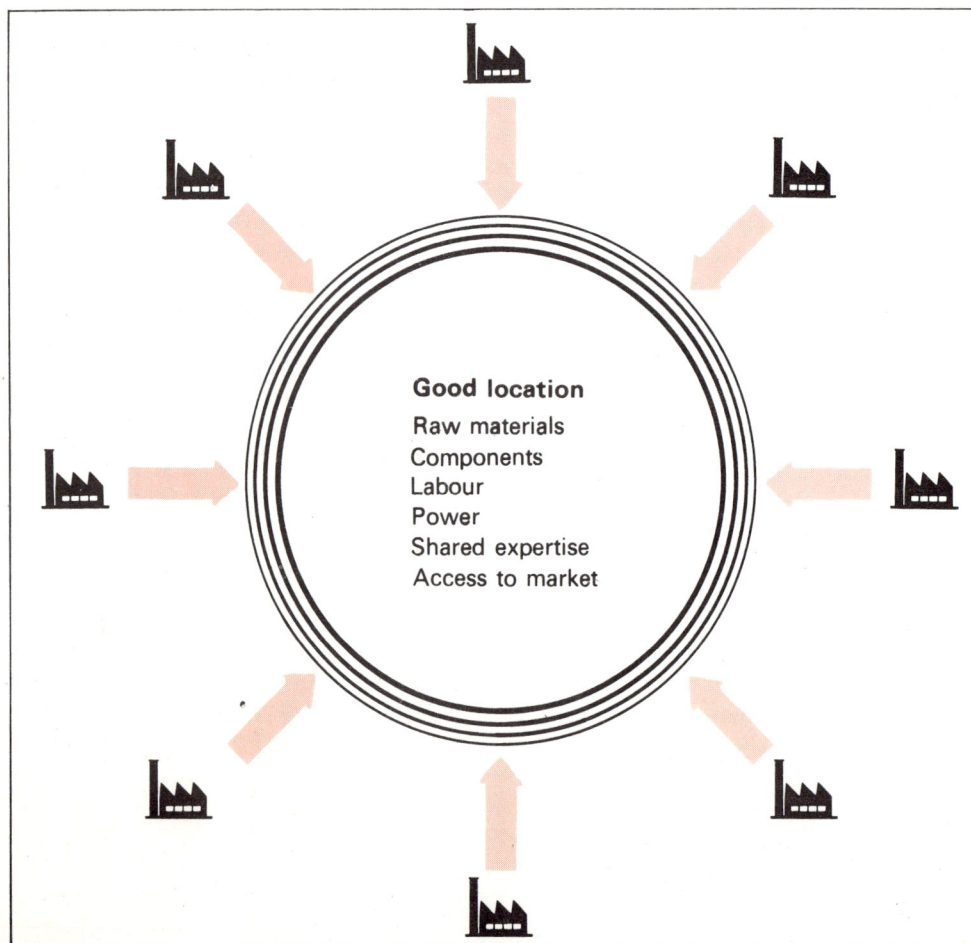

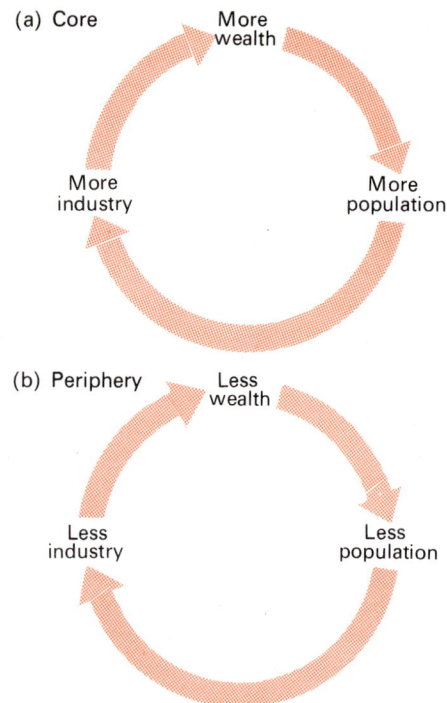

Good location
Raw materials
Components
Labour
Power
Shared expertise
Access to market

5   On a blank outline map of Europe and using the information in Figs. 9.5, 9.6, and 9.7 to help you, mark those areas which you think form:
(a) The core.
(b) The periphery.
(c) Mark and name five cities in your core areas.

Regional planning

Where there are great variations in wealth within a country, governments are trying to even out the differences. We have already seen in Chapter 6 (page 87) how they try to influence the location of industry. These policies try to direct industry into the periphery. This is only part of the planning problem, other things may need to be done within the peripheral areas themselves.

Let us look at Italy again. Although over 30 per cent of Italy's population lives in the South, it creates less than 20 per cent of the country's wealth. Much of the land is hilly with poor, thin soil. Good farmland is scarce and many farmers are poor. They grow olives and wheat, and rear sheep on the hilly pastures. There were many big estates which were often very badly run. There were few other jobs than farming since industries did not want to move away from the North to an area with few roads, poor drains, slum houses, and polluted water. So, since 1945, over 2 000 000 farmers have moved to work in the cities of the North; those who stay are often old and are some of the poorest farmers in Europe.

6   Look at Fig. 9.10.
     (a) How many farms are under 10 hectares in size?
     (b) What percentage of the total number of farms is this?
     (c) What percentage of the total farm area do they form?

Italy's government has tried to help the people here and to increase the amount of food produced. The big estates have often been broken into smaller farms owned by the farmers who used to work for the big landlords. Since 1950, 400 000 hectares have been given to 100 000 families. The new farmers were taught more modern farming methods. They were helped to grow new types of crops. The land reform areas are shown in Fig. 9.11.

7   (a) Use your atlas to name the main reform areas.
     (b) How many areas are:
         (i) Near the coast?
         (ii) In the mountains?
         (iii) Near major cities like Rome, Milan, and Venice?

The government has tried to encourage new industry to locate in the South. A big steelworks at Taranto was supposed to help this. Yet farming still employs two-thirds of the workers and many people are still leaving. Worse still, during the recent decline in industry, many people have lost their jobs in the North and have come back to the South often bitter and angry to face unemployment here too.

Large-scale help for the poorer parts of Europe is no longer just given by individual countries to their own regions. The Common Market has funds to which all the countries contribute which can be made available for helping areas in the Community which have problems. Southern Italy and Southern France are just two areas where financial help in farm reorganization is coming from the Common Market.

Fig. 9.10 Farm sizes and holdings in Italy in 1961

Size of holding	Number of holdings in 000's	Percentage of total number of farm holdings	Percentage of total farm area
1–10	3845	89	35
11–30 ha	333	8	20
31–60 ha	73	2	9·5
Over 60 ha	49	1	35·5
		100	100·0

Fig. 9.11 Land reform regions of Italy

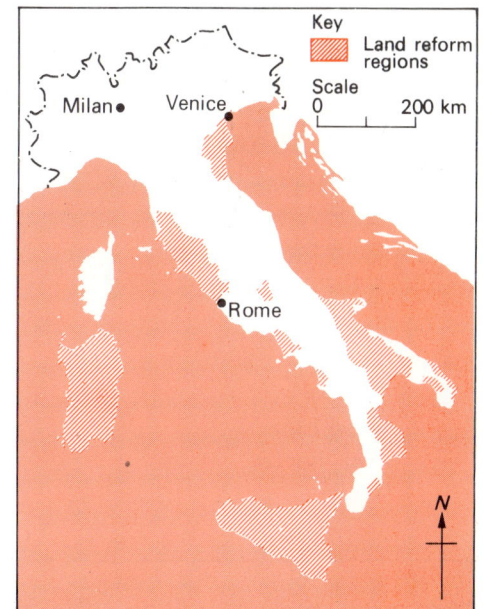

The Common Market and farming

About 10 million people within the Common Market earn their living from farming. Farming is dependent on the weather so its output varies from one year to the next. This makes it very difficult to control food prices.

8 Divide the class into ten groups. Each group is one farming family with 12 hectares of land which will be used to produce dairy produce, wheat, and barley.

First 5 years

(a) Throw a die for the number of hectares you will use for dairying. Throw the die again for the number of hectares of wheat. Any hectares remaining of your twelve will be used for barley. You now have your farm land-use pattern for the first year. Fill this in on a copy of Fig. 9.12.

(b) Toss a coin to see whether you will make a profit (heads) or a loss (tails) due to large quantities of imports flooding the market. Add 'P' or 'L' to the table.

(c) Add up the total hectares of dairying for the whole class and fill in the table. Add up the hectares of wheat and barley in the same way. Read off from the profit or loss graph (Figs. 9.13 and 9.14) how much you will receive for each hectare. Fill this in on your table.

(d) Work out how much your farm made in the first year? Divide the total profit or loss by 12 to find out what you made per hectare. You need to make an average profit of £20 per hectare to make a living.

(e) Repeat this process until you have been farming for five years. Fill in

Fig. 9.12 Accounts table for the first 10 years of the Common Market game

	Land use on your farm	Profit or loss	Land use on all farms	Price per hectare	Your farm profit	Your farm loss
Year 1	Hectares of dairying		Hectares of dairying	Dairying	Dairying	Dairying
	Hectares of wheat		Hectares of wheat	Wheat	Wheat	Wheat
	Hectares of barley		Hectares of barley	Barley	Barley	Barley
				Total		
Year 2	Hectares of dairying		Hectares of dairying	Dairying	Dairying	Dairying
	Hectares of wheat		Hectares of wheat	Wheat	Wheat	Wheat
	Hectares of barley		Hectares of barley	Barley	Barley	Barley
				Total		

Fig. 9.13 Profit graph

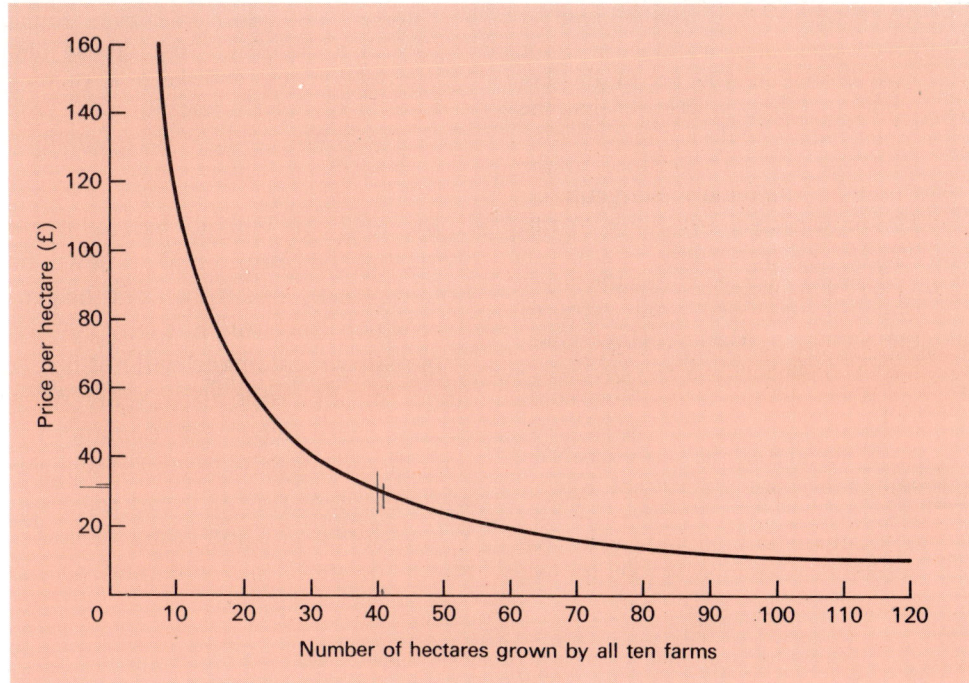

Fig. 9.14 Loss graph

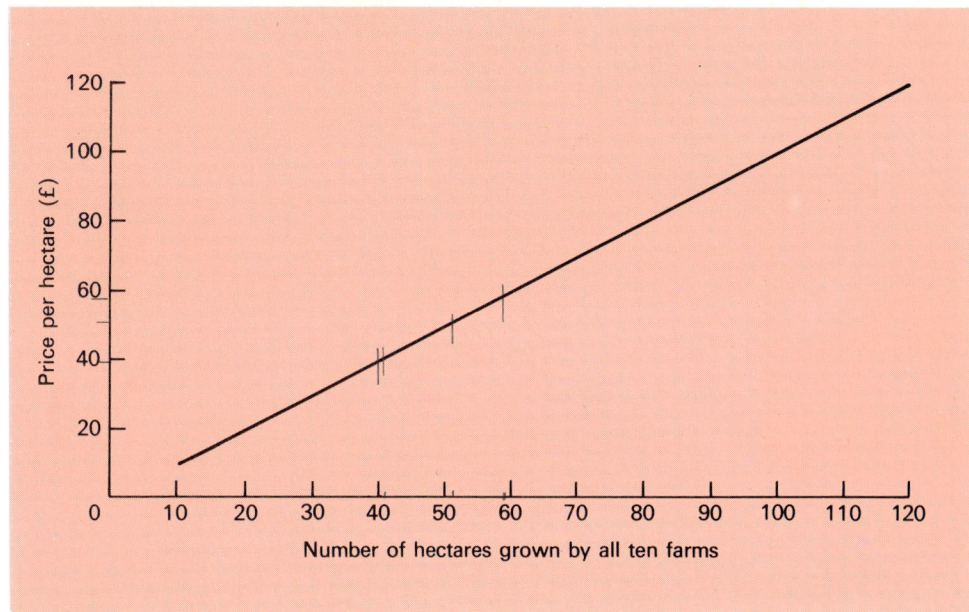

your figures on the accounts table as you play.

(f)(i) Which crops made you the most profit and why?

(ii) Which crops were the least successful?

(iii) Which combination of crops was most successful and why?

9 *Second 5 years*

(a) You now have a free choice as to how many of your 12 hectares you use for each crop. Otherwise the conditions are the same as before. You must still toss the coin each year to see whether you are making a profit or a loss. Fill in another copy of Fig. 9.12.

(b) Are you being any more successful now that you have a free choice of crops?

10 *Third 5 years*

Your country has now joined the Common Market. The Common Market has a Common Agricultural Policy which aims to help farming by preventing farmers from making heavy losses.

(a) Choose through class discussion a target price per hectare that you would like to achieve for each crop. Fill this in on a copy of Fig. 9.15.

(b) Go back to your farm and choose your land-use pattern for the year. Find out how much of each crop everyone has grown, and work out from the *profit graph* (Fig. 9.13) what you would get for each hectare. Fill in your table.

(c) Your teacher will now throw the die to see whether the economy of the Common Market is doing well or not. The higher the number thrown, the more of your produce people will want, and the more they will be prepared to pay for it. Multiply your prices per hectare by the number thrown on the die. Fill in your table.

(d) Does the price you would now get per hectare reach the target price for each crop that you set at the beginning? If the price is lower than the target price, you do not make a loss. You just sell your produce to the Common Market at the target price. How much have you made in this way?

If the price is higher than the target price, do not sell your crop to the Common Market. How much have you made in this way?

(e) When all the farms have completed their calculations find out how many hectares of each crop has been sold to the Common Market. Keep a note of this.

(f) Continue farming until you have been in the Common Market for five years. You must start each round with a discussion to establish new target prices, and keep a running total of the amounts of each crop which are held by the Common Market.

By now you will all be making a living and the Common Market will be holding stocks, or surpluses of the produce which you could not sell.

In reality the demand will not be the same for all crops in a year. As a country gets richer the demand for more luxurious food like meat will rise while the demand for bread may fall. When things are not going well, demand for meat may fall, and people will eat more bread. So the Common Market will build up surpluses of different goods at different times and butter or beef 'mountains' or wine 'lakes' will be created.

Of course if you are a very efficient farmer on good land who can produce a large amount from each hectare at a low cost, you can make more than others under this system. But if you are a poorer farmer working difficult land you can still survive.

11 What do *you* think should be done with the surplus food held by the Common Market as butter mountains or wine lakes?

Fig. 9.15 Accounts table for the third 5 years of the Common Market game

	Target price per hectare	Land use on your farm	Land use on all farms	Profit per hectare	Profit x die	Your farm profit	Your farm profit from sales to Common Market
Year 1	Dairying	Hectares of dairying	Hectares of dairying	Dairying		Dairying	Dairying
	Wheat	Hectares of wheat	Hectares of wheat	Wheat		Wheat	Wheat
	Barley	Hectares of barley	Hectares of barley	Barley		Barley	Barley
					Total		

All the Common Market countries put money into the Common Agricultural Policy funds according to their wealth. This money is not only used to buy crops at the target prices. The C.A.P. also provides money to help make farms more efficient as we have seen in southern Italy and France, and to retrain farmers who wish to leave the land in the poorer areas and take jobs in industry.

Summary

'European' patterns are real ones compared with thirty years ago. We can cross frontiers more freely, trade freely, help ailing industries, and receive aid for our own problem areas. However, Europe is still far from self-sufficent. We are still dependent on the rest of the world, particularly the developing world for many of our foods and raw materials. It is to that area that we shall turn in Book 3.

Workback

12 Study Fig. 9.16.
(a) Which country would you prefer to work in?
(b) Which country would you prefer to live in?
(c) Write a paragraph to explain the reasons behind your choices.

13 Do you consider that you live in a core or peripheral area:
(a) In Europe?
(b) In your own country?

14 Discuss whether you think a government is wise in encouraging firms to move into peripheral areas. Should they not perhaps concentrate on their core areas to increase their nation's wealth?

Fig. 9.16 Table for Exercise 12

Country	Average weekly hours of work	Average hourly earnings in Eurodollars	Motor cars per 1000 population	TV sets per 1000 population	Telephones per 1000 population
Belgium	36·9	5·50	259	252	272
Denmark	—	5·30	248	308	428
France	42·5	4·10	288	235	236
West Germany	40·7	5·20	280	305	302
Irish Republic	—	—	164	178	127
Italy	41·4	3·40	257	213	246
Luxembourg	40·8	5·20	357	257	397
Netherlands	40·8	5·70	257	259	344
United Kingdom	42·4	2·70	251	315	366

Climatic data

Latitude and longitude	Station	Altitude in metres	Average monthly temperature °C											
			J	F	M	A	M	J	J	A	S	O	N	D
67° N 14° E	Bodo	20	−3	−2	−1	2	6	10	14	12	10	5	2	0
66° N 24° E	Haparanda	2	−11	−11	−8	−2	4	12	15	12	8	2	−5	−10
63° N 10° E	Trondheim	20	−3	−3	0	4	8	12	14	14	10	5	1	−2
60° N 5° E	Bergen	40	2	2	3	6	9	12	14	14	11	7	4	3
60° N 18° E	Uppsala	1	−4	−5	−3	3	9	14	17	16	10	5	0	−4
55° N 12° E	Copenhagen	27	0	0	2	5	10	15	17	18	15	10	6	3
51° N 0° E	London	46	4	5	6	8	13	15	17	17	14	10	7	5
51° N 4° E	Brussels	50	4	3	6	9	13	17	18	18	15	10	6	3
48° N 2° E	Paris	130	4	4	7	10	14	17	19	18	16	12	7	4
47° N 8° E	Zürich	500	4	2	9	10	15	16	15	17	14	10	4	0
45° N 12° E	Venice	0	−2	0	4	10	15	19	20	19	16	10	4	−1
43° N 5° E	Marseille	80	7	8	10	13	16	20	22	21	19	15	11	8
40° N 3° W	Madrid	667	5	7	9	12	17	21	25	25	20	14	8	4
39° N 9° W	Lisbon	95	10	12	13	14	17	19	22	22	20	17	14	11
42° N 12° E	Rome	46	7	8	10	14	18	22	24	24	20	17	12	8
41° N 14° E	Naples	15	8	9	11	14	17	21	24	24	22	18	14	10

Station	Average monthly rainfall (mm)												Average annual rainfall
	J	F	M	A	M	J	J	A	S	O	N	D	
Bodo	90	80	101	73	55	70	50	123	127	169	102	90	1130
Haparanda	24	27	19	37	22	39	44	64	69	59	49	45	498
Trondheim	109	76	86	63	60	48	71	86	112	127	99	86	1023
Bergen	158	146	131	196	84	126	113	160	270	237	201	204	2026
Uppsala	40	27	24	35	35	50	51	74	53	44	59	47	539
Copenhagen	46	38	28	32	43	57	55	69	63	45	57	46	579
London	53	41	38	37	47	43	51	57	41	52	57	50	567
Brussels	60	46	46	43	58	66	74	74	66	71	61	61	726
Paris	51	50	34	40	62	49	49	82	50	43	56	51	617
Zürich	73	60	57	62	83	108	105	115	83	39	101	60	946
Venice	37	48	61	78	65	69	52	69	59	77	94	61	770
Marseille	56	32	45	38	49	11	5	41	50	76	52	55	510
Madrid	30	34	40	61	42	23	16	14	39	45	38	42	424
Lisbon	100	82	95	60	44	13	8	3	42	46	72	98	663
Rome	71	66	33	40	41	22	7	15	45	93	102	75	610
Naples	116	85	73	62	44	31	19	32	64	107	147	135	915

Index